BRIDGE
ACROSS
JORDAN

(revised edition)

BRIDGE ACROSS JORDAN

(revised edition)

by Amelia Boynton Robinson
Schiller Institute, Inc.
Washington, D.C.
1991

©1991 Schiller Institute
ISBN: 0-9621095-4-1
Library of Congress Catalog Number 90-62730

Front cover photo: Hawkins Studio, Tuskegee, Alabama
Back cover photo: Philip Ulanowsky, Leesburg, Virginia

On July 21, 1990, Amelia Boynton Robinson was awarded the
Martin Luther King, Jr. Foundation Medal of Freedom by the
New York State Martin Luther King, Jr. Foundation, for
"courage, conviction and outstanding services to state
and nation during the turbulent decade of the 1960s." The
awards ceremony was held in Selma, Alabama.

The Schiller Institute wishes to thank Lewis du Pont Smith for his
generous contribution toward publication of this book.

Book design: Efthalia DeGroot

Project editors: Marianna Wertz, Christina Huth
Composition: World Composition Services, Inc., Sterling, Virginia

Please direct all inquiries to the publisher:
Schiller Institute
P.O. Box 66082
Washington, D.C. 20035-6082   SIB 91-002

The roots of the Selma right to vote movement, which politically enfranchised the African-American people and advanced the cause of freedom and justice for all people, can be traced back to the seed planted by Amelia Boynton, when she began her voter registration work in 1929. Let me thank Amelia for allowing me to receive the freedom fruit from the tree she was wise and loving enough to plant.

— Rev. James Bevel
former director for Nonviolent Direct Action, SCLC
former director of the Right to Vote Movement, Selma

I cannot remember when I didn't know Amelia Boynton Robinson. A remarkable, strong-willed, college-trained black woman who led a dedicated and dangerous civil rights struggle in Selma, Alabama many years before Martin Luther King, Jr. King once told me Mrs. Robinson was a reason he came to Selma. She continued the struggle after King and the organizations left. Her faith, courage, intelligence and devotion are extraordinary and the manner in which she used them say so much about the real America. This powerful book about her life should be required reading in the White House, the Congress and every school and college in America. The nation owes Amelia Boynton Robinson much.

—J.L. Chestnut, Jr.
author, *Black in Selma*

Over the past two decades, Amelia Boynton Robinson has inspired me with her humble simplicity and the complex manner in which she tells her story of the movement.

—Edith M. Savage
Member of the Board
Martin Luther King, Jr. Center for Nonviolent Social Change

CONTENTS

Editor's Preface

Man is created free, and is free,
Though he be born in chains.
— Friedrich Schiller

This second edition of *Bridge Across Jordan* incorporates the major part of the first edition's text, published by Carlton Press in 1979, leaving out only the foreword, introduction, and last two chapters. The book was originally conceived as the story of the struggle for civil rights in Selma, Alabama, and was written at a time when the national civil rights struggle, whose most famous leader was Dr. Martin Luther King, Jr., was still very much current history.

In 1991, essentially one generation later, the story must be told again, but from today's standpoint. Our nation and our world are very different than they were when Amelia Platts was growing up in the old South. Today the struggle for freedom is international: Peaceful revolutions against tyranny, modeled on the nonviolent principles practiced by the movement of Dr. King, have transformed the face of Europe in the past two years; even Communist China is being rocked by the power of man's unquenchable thirst for freedom.

Amelia Platts Boynton Robinson requested that the Schiller Institute publish an updated version of her book to bridge the gap between the Selma struggle led by Dr. King, and

the international fight for freedom today, led by Lyndon
LaRouche. She has herself played an important leading role
in making that bridge palpable to the participants in the
struggle today, as she amply documents here. Her recent
trip to eastern and western Germany for the Schiller Institute,
recounted in the closing chapters of this book, opened a
living dialogue between Germany's revolutionaries and
those who fought with Dr. King.

Editing this second edition has brought me countless
happy hours in association with Amelia Robinson, who
must be counted among the true pearls of our nation. As I
told her once during a stay here, I felt as though I were
caring for a precious artifact in our national archive, in
working with her. She is truly a living heroine and the
embodiment of what Dr. King identified as *agapē*—the
Christian notion of love. No one who has come into contact
with her, who has read her words about the struggles she
and her loved ones have undertaken, can fail to be moved.

Marianna Wertz
Vice President, Schiller Institute
Leesburg, Virginia
January 15, 1991

No Man Is an Island

They drew a circle and left us out,
Heretic rebel, a thing to flout,
But Love and I had a way to win,
We drew a circle, and took them in.

Knowing that it is everybody's business to be justly treated by law, I think it is my and everybody's business to fight injustice regardless of race, for no man is an island. That is why I first wrote *Bridge Across Jordan* in 1979 and that is why I am releasing an updated version in 1991.

As Martin Luther King, Jr. crisscrossed the world, bringing love to all peoples in the name of *agapē,* he was jailed, scorned, and even feared by many people of all races, until people began to understand the true meaning of his doctrine: Love thy neighbor, for no man is an island, no man stands alone. For preaching the truth, he was killed.

Today, a revolution for freedom is sweeping much of the world, while in America, despite the successes of the Civil Rights Act, there remain millions of people hungry, jobless, sleeping on the street, unable to attend school; there remain segregation and discrimination in the homes, schools, churches, and communities. In these changing times, we are out of step with reality and we are losing our sanity. We think we are so fortified, that we fail to seek the good judgment of Americans who might give advice, which might turn this country around and rebuild it, so it can be respected again.

I have found such Americans in the organizations associated with Lyndon LaRouche, the political leader and economist, who today is serving a fifteen-year prison sentence
because of his political views. I am a board member of the
Schiller Institute, which was founded in 1984 by Helga Zepp-
LaRouche, wife of Lyndon LaRouche and a leader in her
own right in Germany. The Schiller Institute's goal is to
achieve freedom for all nations of the world—"that all men
might be brothers"—as Friedrich Schiller, the great German
Poet of Freedom, for whom the Schiller Institute is named,
stated in his famous *Ode to Joy*.

I joined the Schiller Institute because I found it to be
continuing the civil rights struggle, in the footsteps, as it
were, of Martin Luther King. As a board member who has
worked with Schiller Institute since its inception, I have
found this organization more able to carry out the program
of Dr. Martin Luther King in the economic area than any
other that I know. The organization may not be the most
popular, but this is because it is continuing the struggle for
civil rights throughout the world, fighting drugs, corruption,
injustice, and discrimination. It was just such fighting
against corruption and challenging the highest political
officials for which Dr. King gave his life. The Schiller Institute has picked up the broken pieces of Dr. King's dream.

Today, as it was during Dr. King's life, members of the
Schiller Institute, and of other organizations associated with
Lyndon LaRouche, are being persecuted and thrown in
prison, as LaRouche himself was, because they have dared
to preach the truth about this country and the evil into which
it has fallen. Knowing this, I know that this is my fight, too.

What other way can one carry out Martin's movement,
than to fight against and expose discrimination, illegal
drugs, corruption, and injustice?

Martin Luther King, Jr. on *Agapē*

Dr. King gave the world the concept of *agapē* as a political
principle. The following is from his essay, "Six Principles
in the Philosophy of Non-Violence," written in 1958: "In

speaking of love at this point, we are not referring to some sentimental and affectionate emotion. It would be nonsense to urge men to love their oppressors in an affectionate sense. Love in this connection means understanding, redemptive good will. Here the Greek language comes to our aid. There are three words for love in the Greek New Testament. First, there is *eros*. In platonic philosophy *eros* meant the yearning of the soul for the realm of the divine. It has come now to mean a sort of aesthetic or romantic love. Second is *philia*, which means intimate affection between personal friends. *Philia* denotes a sort of reciprocal love; the person loves because he is loved. When we speak of loving those who oppose us, we refer to neither *eros* nor *philia;* we speak of a love which is expressed in the Greek word *agapē. Agapē* means understanding, redeeming good will for all men. It is an overflowing love which is purely spontaneous, unmotivated, groundless, and creative. It is not set in motion by any quality or function of its object. It is love of God operating in the human heart."

Charity, Love, *Agapē*

> *Charity suffereth long and is kind: charity envieth not; charity vaunteth not itself, is not puffed up, doth not behave itself unseemly, seeketh not her own, is not easily provoked, thinketh no evil; rejoiceth not in iniquity but rejoiceth in the truth; beareth all things, believeth all things, hopeth all things; endureth all things.*
>
> —I Corinthians 13:4

This Bible verse I dedicate to a living human being, Lyndon LaRouche, Jr., who to me and millions of others is the epitome of *agapē.* Though imprisoned, he gives rather than takes, he loves rather than hates those who falsely accuse him of trumped-up political charges, unjustly in the name of justice, because of his attempt to rid this country and the world of its most degrading evil, drugs, by exposing the huge popular institutions through which its millions, even billions of dollars flow.

I compare the trials and crosses, which my husband Samuel William Boynton and I had to bear, to Lyndon LaRouche's punishment for trying to save the world from collapse, which will surely happen if injustice and hate are not stamped out.

Lyndon LaRouche has been given fifteen years in prison for, among other things, having exposed banks engaged in laundering drug money and drug-trafficking. Naturally, the news media gave the public another reason. And what about a young woman, Rochelle Ascher, who was given 86 years in prison for not having had a surety bond while raising campaign funds for Mr. LaRouche? I know, because I was at the trial. And what about Michael Billington, who received 77 years for the same offense; and Donald Phau, who received 35 years; and Anita Gallagher, who received 46 years, and her husband Paul, 41 years; and Larry Hecht, who received 40 years; and the six others railroaded into prison with LaRouche and sentenced to three to five years; and the many yet to be tried, whom the government intends to send to prison?

It is time for American citizens to hit the streets again for justice! Injustice has no respect of person or color. Unfortunately, it was disregarded for more than 200 years, when it was aimed at African-Americans, but, like cancer, which starts in a certain place in the body, it eventually destroys the entire body, for it has no respect of organs. This cancer of injustice has no respect of race. Mr. LaRouche and most of his prison companions are white. The cancer of injustice is aimed to destroy the Constitution and democracy, while setting up a secret government dictatorship. We Americans, through decent and true leadership, have given the world a taste of democracy. Let us practice what America preaches while our country still has time.

Tear Down the Walls of Hate

It is most interesting to see how America has sold the democratic way of life to the communist countries and how, because their citizens were seeking freedom and became restless, the *material* walls came tumbling down. But these are not the most meaningful walls. Until the mental walls in our inner selves are replaced by *agapē,* the tumble of the material walls will only be a sham.

You can tear the walls down in Germany and free those people, but I think we'd better think about how much we have to tear down here and how much we have to build up. We have to tear down the walls of warring with ourselves and with our own people here. Tear down the walls of wanting; people here are starving and have nowhere to turn. We should tear down those walls, and build up within ourselves a world without war and without discrimination.

African-Americans have dealt justly with America in making hundreds of thousands of contributions in all fields, which we have given to help make America great. And what do we get for it? The shortest month in the year to discover ourselves! The Voter Registration Board once opened for only two days per month and only four hours each day, before the right to vote expired and Congress spent more time and money to extend it. That's wrong!

We are Americans and are entitled to *all* of the rights and privileges of all citizens.

If we walk in human dignity and integrity; if we have love for everybody, realizing that we are all children of God, whether we are on this side of the ocean or the other side, we are our brother's keeper; if we realize that kindness can turn away the greatest wrath; if we have compassion for those who are not as fortunate as we are, we will be able to defeat the devil, to say to him, as Christ said when he was tempted by him, "Get thee behind me, Satan."

Millions of dollars and thousands of manhours were recently used to save two whales that might have finally freed themselves. America was in sympathy with the mammals. Just across the waters, hundreds of African babies were dying hourly of starvation at the same time. America turned its back and blocked it out of its mind. That's America today.

When we ignore evil, poverty, and injustice around us

and do nothing about it, we become an accomplice to it. This is the way many of us felt during the struggle in the civil rights movement and afterward. Thousands of dollars were spent and much time given in training people for various jobs—jobs that never existed.

We cannot help but look back at the distance from whence we as African-Americans have come, at the Bull Conners, Jim Clarks, George Wallaces, and at all of the injustices and evil we endured from slavery until 1965. But the battle has just begun. We look back only to measure our success.

This is why I have decided to reprint *Bridge Across Jordan:* Lest people forget the evil and injustice we faced, and we be condemned to repeat our errors as a nation. I also hope that, especially with the contributions of Lyndon LaRouche and his associates in this updated version, I can help point the way to a solution to the problems which continue to plague and threaten mankind as a whole today.

Amelia Platts Boynton Robinson
January 15, 1991

In the Garden of Gethsemane

A prophet is not without honor, save in his own country. —Matthew 13:57

Those of us who find ourselves in Gethsemane—a Gethsemane where we are told that we must take a role of leadership with our eye on Christ on the Cross—often experience something which, unfortunately, most people do not. We tend to look at things from a different standpoint.

Before trying to situate how I see the recent period, and the period immediately before us, I should try to communicate what my viewpoint is, a viewpoint which I know is shared in some degree of very close approximation by everyone who has gone to Gethsemane with the view of the Cross in his eyes, saying, "He did it, I am now being told that I must, too, walk in His way."

What I suggest often, in trying to explain this to a person who has not experienced it, is to say: "Imagine a time 50 years after you're dead. Imagine in that moment, 50 years ahead, that you can become conscious and look back at the entirety of your mortal life, from its beginning to its ending. And, rather than seeing that mortal life as a succession of experiences, you see it as a unity. Imagine facing the question respecting that mortal life, asking, "Was that life necessary in the total scheme of the universe and the existence of mankind, was it necessary that I be born in order to lead that life, the sum total of that number of years between birth and death? Did I do something, or did my living represent something, which was positively beneficial to present generations, and implicitly to future generations after me? If so, then I should have walked through that life with joy, knowing that every moment was precious to all mankind, because what I was doing by living was something that was needed by all mankind, something beneficial to all mankind."

If I am wise, then 50 years after my death, in looking back at my mortal life, I know that from the beginning with my birth, to the end with my death, that my truest self-interest was the preservation and enhancement of that which made my having lived important to those around me and those who came after me.

That is the beginning, I think, of true wisdom; that is the beginning of the Passion, which sometimes enables each of us when called to walk through our own peculiar kind of Gethsemane. It is from this standpoint, that the mind of an individual such as our own, can efficiently comprehend history in the large.

A second point, which I often raise, I think is essential to understand the few simple observations I have to make here. It is that, in human reason, in the power, for example, to effect a valid, fundamental scientific discovery, which overturns, in large degree, previous scientific opinion, we see a fundamental distinction between man and all beasts. This power of creative reason, typified by the power to make a valid, fundamental scientific discovery, and also the power to transmit and to receive such a discovery, is that which sets man apart from and above the beasts.

The emotion associated with that kind of human activity, whether in physical science, in the development of creative works or performance of creative works of classical culture, or simply in the caring for a child to nurture that quality of potential for discovery in the child, is true love. Creative activity is human activity, and the emotion associated with that kind of activity, is true love.

We start from that and say that society must be based on these considerations, that every human being, being apart from and above the animals, has the right·and the obligation to live an important life. Every human being has the right to do something, such that if one looked back 50 years after the death of that person at his or her whole mortal life, one could have said, that life was necessary to all humanity. At the same time, one could distinguish some use of this creative power of reasoning as the activity which made that life important, simply, sometimes, the development of that creative power.

We have, in the entirety of the approximately 2,500 years of Western European history, which includes the history of the Americas, two conflicting views of mankind. One view shares more or less the standpoint I've just identified: We view the human individual as bearing the divine spark of potential for reason, as a sacred life; a spark of reason which must be developed by society, nurtured by society, given opportunity for fruitful expression by society; a quality of activity whose good works must be adopted by society, protected by society, and preserved by society, for the benefit of present and future generations. That is the republic, the republic as conceived by Solon's constitution of Athens—a notion of republic, which, in our time, is made nobler by the Christian understanding, which transforms and elevates the contributions of Solon and Socrates after him.

On the other side, there is the conception of Sparta, a privileged oligarchy, brutalizing the Helots, the slaves, the so-called lower classes. That, too is a model society, not a republic, but an oligarchy.

The struggle between these two views of mankind is epitomized by the struggle between President and General George Washington, on the one side, and King George III on the other. George Washington was a soldier and statesman of the republic, not a perfect one, but a good one. On the opposite side was poor King George III, the puppet of the evil Earl of Shelbourne, and the epitome of oligarchism, the heritage of Sparta. The tradition of King George III, which deems that some men must be kept slaves, is an oligarchical view, which *hates* the idea of the equality of the individual in respect to the individual human being's possession of that divine spark, the individual human being's right to the development of that spark, the nurture of its activity, and the defense and perpetuation of its good works.

Such is the conflict. In our time, the great American Republic, by virtue of the cultivation of ignorance and concern with smallness of mind, and neglect of the importance of what comes after us in the living of our mortal lives, has been so undermined, degraded, and corrupted, that we as a nation no longer are the nation we were conceived to be, but instead have become a nation brain-drained in front of our television sets, thinking with greater passion about mere spectator sports or mere television soap-opera than we do about urgent events in real life. We are a nation seeking gratification in drugs, in sordid forms of sexual activity, in other sordid entertainments, in that kind of pleasure-seeking, which echoes the words *Sodom and Gomorrah.*

And so, oligarchism, that which George III of England represented back in the eighteenth century, has taken over and rules the land which was once George Washington's.

What this leads to is this. Today, there is a great revolution around the world against tyranny in all forms. So far, this revolution has manifested itself within the communist sector against communist tyrannies. But it is coming here, too. Wherever the divine spark of reason is being crushed by oligarchical regimes, with all their cruelties, the divine spark of reason within human beings inspires them to arise, to throw off the tyranny—not out of anger and rage against tyranny, but because the divine spark of reason in each person *must be affirmed.* We seek not merely to be free from oligarchy; we seek to be free from oligarchy, because not to do so would be to betray the divine spark of reason in ourselves and in others.

The secret of great revolutions, of great civil rights movements, as Dr. King's example illustrates, is this capacity,

which the Greek New Testament called *agapē*, which
Latin called *caritas*, which the King James version of the
Bible calls *charity*, which we otherwise know as *love*.
Whenever this power of love, this recognition of that
divine spark, setting us above the beasts, prevails, wherever people can approximate that view of the sum total
of their lives, as if from 50 years after their deaths,
whenever movements arise which, out of love, produce
people who are willing, not fruitlessly, but for a purpose,
to *lay down their lives*, so that their lives might have
greater meaning, for this purpose—there you have the
great revolutions of history.

If we were to project events on the basis of what is taught
in the schools about revolutions and other struggles of the
past, then the human race at present were doomed. If we
say that people struggle against this and that oppression,
and so forth, and out of rage or whatnot, overthrow their
cruel oppressor, we should lose; the human race would
lose. However, if we touch the force of *love*, the spark of
divine reason, we unleash a force, a creative force, a divine
force, which is greater than any adversary, and we win.

Those revolutions, which are based upon the appeal to
this divine spark of reason within the individual, prevailed.
Those which worked otherwise produced abominations, or
simply failed.

Yes, we must struggle against injustice. But it is not
enough to struggle out of anger. We must struggle out of
love. And that we learn best, who have had to walk as
leaders of one degree or another, through our own Gethsemane, with the image of the Cross before us.

That is the best I can say. I might say it better, but what
I try to say with these poor words, is the best I can say
summarily, on the subject of current history. I believe, that
the great upsurge of humanity, implicit in the optimism I
express, is now in progress. I am persuaded that we shall
win, provided that each of us can find in ourselves, that
which makes us the right arm of the Creator, a man, a

woman of providence, within the limits of our own capacities and opportunities.

> *Lyndon H. LaRouche, Jr.*
> *Dictated from prison*
> *Rochester, Minnesota*
> *January 17, 1990*

A Beautiful Soul

If some day in the not too distant future the true history of the United States. were to be written, then the name of Amelia Boynton Robinson should take a prominent place therein. When the memory shall have vanished of all the mediocre and corrupt politicians, who in their time were so much played up by the media when America found itself in decline, then Amelia will be known and loved by future generations. It will be said of her that she was one of those extraordinary individuals who saved the honor of the United States, by fearless resistance to the tyranny that was trampling on human rights.

Amelia Boynton Robinson was not only a close collaborator of Dr. Martin Luther King and herself one of the leading lights of the civil rights movement, but also, in spite of having reached nearly four score years, continues to be a leader in the international freedom movement. Her trailblazing interventions into the revolutionary process in the German Democratic Republic at the beginning of 1990 clarified in a wonderful way the coherence between the American civil rights movement and the peaceful revolutions in Eastern Europe. The fact that this grand old lady of Dr. King's movement was able to go to a country and help people who were in a difficult psychological situation shake off the communist dictatorship, shows that mankind's love of freedom and the battle for inalienable rights corresponds to the universal nature of man, regardless of differences between nations or generations.

It is an incredible boon to know Amelia. Everyone who gets to know her soon discovers that she is a person who is particularly blessed. For me, although I have had the good fortune in my life hitherto to meet a great number of good and exceptional people, she belongs to that handful of *pearls* whose mere acquaintance enriches one's own life. Amelia's generosity of heart is so clearly to be seen that she inspires her fellow man to wish, as if it were the most natural thing in the world, to become a better person.

In the same manner, no matter what the concrete situation might be, Amelia always commands a seemingly boundless capacity for taking the sufferings of others into her own heart, and making the concerns of others her own. Indeed, I believe that she is constitutionally incapable of seeing an injustice without instantly feeling the need to do something to set it right. I think that Amelia is what Friedrich Schiller called a "beautiful soul."

For Schiller, who was called "the poet of freedom," and who throughout his life was very much inspired by the lofty ideals of the American Revolution, the "beautiful soul" was the highest standard of beauty of character. He understood thereby those people who can always blindly trust their feelings, because these would never contradict their reason. A beautiful soul is that man or woman for whom reason and feeling, necessity and freedom, coincide. For Schiller, this is the goal of the formation of one's own character, which can be reached if one will educate his or her emotions to that height which is reason's own.

Whether one lives thus is shown never so clearly as in old age. While lesser people in their later years become moody or ungenerous of feeling, Amelia is a perfect example of a human being who has maintained her integrity throughout her entire life. Such individuals are in riper years more beautiful than a young person can possibly be. In a conversation Amelia once told me something which clearly reflected the principle by which she lived: "I am so thankful to God," she stated, "for the experience I had over the years, which is quite something. I tell the young people, stay clean, even if you are only a kid. If you do anything wrong, it comes back to you when you try to rise up and be somebody. Make sure that you are prepared in yourself as you go along, so that if any opportunities present themselves, you'll be able to step into that spot."

When in the spring of 1990, during about a six-week period after the peaceful revolution in East Germany, Amelia took part in the process that was leading to the reunification of Germany, she once again had found such a "spot," for she could tell the people of what was then still the GDR, precisely those things important to them. Admittedly, the peaceful revolution in Eastern Europe marks a more dramatic strategic branching point than that presented by the civil rights movement of the 1960s, but ultimately what was at stake in both was the same question of human rights.

The changes in Eastern Europe signify the coinciding end of two epochs. On the one hand, they signify the end of post-1917 Bolshevik dictatorship, and with that the death of communism as an ideology. But at the same time these changes signify the end of the division of Europe by the post-war order, and the failure of the attempt of the two superpowers to cement their dominion over other peoples through the imposition of new Yalta accords. A great number of factors contributed to this mighty uprising. The two most important, however, were undoubtedly on the one hand the incapacity of the Soviet economy, in the long run, to sustain a continuing armaments program at the expense of the civilian sector, and with that the standard of living of the population; and on the other hand, the positive effect of the Polish pope, John Paul II, upon the capacity of peoples to resist.

Admittedly, again and again, manifestations of the peoples of the East's desire for freedom did occur, such as the

1953 uprising in the GDR, the 1956 Polish and Hungarian uprisings, the Prague Spring of 1968, and the strikes in Gdansk in 1970. But these uprisings were always brutally beaten down by the communists, without the West's ever having mobilized effective support for the freedom fighters. Pope John Paul II, the pope from Poland, on the contrary, gave the oppressed peoples new hope, above all naturally in Poland itself and in the Baltic, from there as echo effect in the satellite states of Eastern Europe, and finally in Ukraine. All of them, however, had one thing in common, namely the faith that there is an authority higher than even the worst dictatorship, and that it is precisely this higher power, which gives mankind its inalienable dignity.

In the early GDR, it was first the priests and the artists for whom, because of their calling, the idea of inner freedom meant the most. From them first stemmed the resistance, and it would take eleven years before the prayers for peace in the churches and the Christmas demonstrations became those powerful ones which finally brought about collapse of the regime. The representatives of the church quite consciously chose the theme of the right to travel abroad, to put themselves at the head of the movement. Very soon, the stream of refugees became a flood, and thousands of people, mostly young families with their small children, sought by way of the consulates in Prague, Budapest, and Warsaw to escape the ugly reality beneath the communist castles in the air.

And fear was ever present, for the memory was fresh of the words of Erich Honecker's then-crown prince, Egon Krenz, who had roundly supported the bloody massacre in Tiananmen Square on June 4, 1989. Precisely this fear was felt on October 9 in Leipzig, when Honecker, still with pomp, had the 40th anniversary of socialism in the GDR celebrated, which turned out, however, to be the celebration of its downfall. The military and the police stood at the ready, the order to shoot had been given, and, but for a hair's-breadth, it would have been a new Tiananmen Square massacre of the demonstrators, had not its organizers made superhuman efforts to preserve the peaceful character of the demonstration, and not to provide even the slightest excuse for provocations.

Only four weeks later, on that memorable 9th of November, 1989, the Berlin Wall was opened. Never will those scenes be forgotten, as people from East and West fell into each other's arms and wept tears of joy. The Ninth Symphony of Beethoven, the wonderful composition of the "Ode to Joy" of Friedrich Schiller, was the work which was spontaneously chosen by people as just that which gave their ideals their best expression. A highly dramatic period followed: After only a few weeks, the successor regime to Honecker's, that of Egon Krenz, was dissolved, and the weathervane government of Modrow followed. There was one lesson, however, the peaceful revolution did have to learn in the succeeding weeks, namely that the old communist party apparatus would immediately launch a counterattack, as soon as the intensity of the demonstrations decreased.

When Amelia addressed the most diverse meetings and groups in March 1990, there still reigned a great insecurity; whether the reunification of Germany would proceed was still palpably uncertain, and even a reversal of direction was possible. The fact that Amelia Boynton Robinson intervened just then as representative of the American civil rights movement, gave people a decisive courage and strength. For even if behind the Iron Curtain, people's knowledge about the U.S.A. was not very extensive, still Martin Luther King was for them a highly regarded figure. Again and again, Amelia was asked what her battles had looked like, and above all, how she understood the principle of nonviolence.

"I made the comparison," Amelia related, "between our struggle in America and how they struggled for their freedom. And even if they were behind the Iron Curtain, I knew what they needed, because of the fact that we suffered the same thing down in the South. We have to keep fighting to free people, regardless of where they are, in Europe or anywhere else." Untiringly, she insisted to people how important it is never to give up the battle, no matter how difficult it may be at any given time. And this grand old lady was proud and happy when she got as a present—a small plastic cross mounted on a fragment of the Berlin Wall.

Amelia Boynton Robinson is today one of the leading members of the Schiller Institute's international movement. "Since this is today the organization fighting for freedom, this is the organization I should belong to," she declared to her listeners time and again about the continuity of the American civil rights movement and the Schiller Institute movement. "Dr. King would be so proud to know that his death was not in vain, that the struggle is carried on," she repeatedly emphasized.

It is indeed no coincidence that today the leading representatives of Dr. King's movement work together with the Schiller Institute. For what binds the two together at the highest level is the unshakeable dedication to the battle for inalienable rights of all the peoples of this planet. And precisely as Dr. King referred back to that document in American history, which serves as a most noble foundation for civil rights, namely the Declaration of Independence, just so that document belongs to the founding principles of the Schiller Institute's international movement. It is this image of man, that conceives the individual in the image of God, that places human dignity upon the highest possible basis, which lends the movement, then and now, its strength.

Amelia is a wonderful woman, and I know that she draws her enormous spiritual strength from her deep faith. "Plans cannot be made without God," she would often say. "We must trust in God, and if we have faith, then we will also have the certainty that we can break the chains of hatred, which hold so many of us captive, and then the good, which should exist in this world, can also be made to do so in reality. If then from this faith we draw the certainty that we *must* win, then miracles will happen."

There is still infinitely much to say about Amelia. But here I should like to bring out only that element which for me is the most important. I have known Amelia since 1984, and have admired her as a person whom I should like to emulate in old age. But it was above all a few long discussions in the spring of 1990, and our joint political battle, at a time which by all human reckoning could be the beginning of a new Golden Age, which bound us together. We felt a great spiritual kinship, and so we mutually adopted each other, she me as her daughter, and I her as my mother. We both feel an immense gratitude that we have found each other.

Helga Zepp-LaRouche
Founder and Chairman,
Schiller Institute
November 1990
Wiesbaden, Germany

PART I

Growing Up
In the Old South

*Cast down your bucket
where you are.*
—Dr. Booker T. Washington

CHAPTER 1

My Family

*Love is the chain whereby to bind a child to
his parents.*   —Abraham Lincoln

I was born in 1911 and reared in Savannah, Georgia, in a
family of mixed heritage, like most Americans—African,
Indian, and German on both sides. As I grew to be a young
adult, the principle of "doing unto others as you would have
them do unto you," and the religious training we received
in our little church, Church of God, made an impression
upon me, which prepared me for whatever the future held
for me.

Now I am neither a tot nor a young adult, but a seasoned,
experienced woman, having climbed through many thorns,
thistles, and rough and rugged mountains of life. Despite
many adversities, I am still here, endowed by our Creator
with more than a reasonable portion of health, strength,
and presence of mind. I believe that, surely, God means for
me to work toward spreading his message of truth and
justice.

If I were to die and could come back to this earth in a
family of my own choosing, I would choose to come back
into the same family, with the same parents, sisters and
brothers, and live in the same communities. Why? Because
I value the forceful impression of morality which my parents
made upon our characters, molding men and women who

made great contributions to America, though they may be unsung heroes. I am very proud of every member of our family.

For my parents, their children came first. Among the ten children they had, the oldest ones were old enough to be the parents of the younger ones. Our names were Wilhelmina Eugenia (named for my father's mother), Alvarena (who died in infancy), Elizabeth, Harold, Eloise (who died at age nine), Anna, Amelia, Geneva, Audrey, and George.

The home training given to us by our parents was responsible for the Platts family of 3203 Burroughs Street, Savannah, Georgia shining like a beacon light in the community and wherever we were known. We felt that we had to be leaders, because this is what the community expected. I felt that, just as the two-story house my father built towered above the neat, one-story houses, so were we to demonstrate our home training.

Our house was always filled with children, not only from the community, but those whom my parents took into our home, to give them the opportunity to attend school, or the children of adults who were evicted or had nowhere to go.

The following is a partial list of businesses and professions which members of my family have held:

- chairman, teachers' executive board
- executive, personnel department, U.S. Air Force base
- Headstart nursery school owner and director
- Sunship shipyard blueprint interpreter
- manufacturer of hair preparation
- music composer
- band leader
- singer
- teacher
- dentist
- home economist
- doctor
- professional athlete
- professional story-teller
- bridal caterer

- minister
- realtor
- fashion designer
- model
- dressmaker (seamstress)
- contractor
- beautician/cosmetologist
- inventor
- speech communicator
- registered nurse
- insurance agent
- professional photographer
- air traffic control supervisor
- airlines representative
- plumber
- draftsman
- regional secretary supervisor
- poet
- author/lecturer
- post office department supervisor
- botanist
- attorney
- artist
- embassy diplomat
- psycho-physicist (an original title)
- director of university psychiatry department
- deep-sea diver
- armed forces member
- stockbroker

CHAPTER 2

My Parents and Grandparents

Train up a child in the way he should go,
and when he is old, he will not depart
from it. —Proverbs 22:6

My father, George Platts, was born in 1866, just after the end of the Civil War. He was one of the most gentle, refined, and cultured men I have ever known. He was born in Fairfax County, in Brunson, South Carolina. Because of the distance from Savannah, Georgia, I was an adult before I visited his native home. The other children were luckier. My father took all of them there. However, we were visited often by many of his cousins, aunts, and uncles.

He was born three weeks after his father's death, the youngest of six children. Most of his education came at his mother's knee, yet he turned out to be a great mathematician. As a half-breed (Indian/African), his mother refused to depend upon either race alone to rear her children, because she wanted her family to be close-knit and her children to be independent.

My mother had a large picture of my father's mother, whom I never met, hanging in our living room. My grandmother appeared in this picture not to have any hair. I said, "Mama, Grandmother didn't have any hair!" Mother said, "Her hair was very long and she wore it back, with one long braid down her back. She was a half-breed and she married your grandfather John Platts (the original German was Platz and some in the family also spell it Platt), who died three weeks before your father was born." He came from a very quiet, dignified family, who owned a big farm. My father's mother was a Johnson before her marriage to my grandfather Platts.

My father received only three years of formal education, walking five miles a day to a shabby building called a school, taking a dinner bucket with him, because often he would leave before daylight and return after dark. When he would have us study our lessons around the dining room table, he would tell us about the blue-back speller and the McGuffey's Reader he used.

Having a wholesale and retail wood yard, my father had to go to South Carolina often to buy trees five and ten acres at a time. He hired men to cut down the trees and cord the wood, and then the real processing began. After the trees were felled and cut into cord wood, mules were hired with a dozen men taking the wood to the river and loading it on a barge. The barge took it to Savannah, where it was loaded in freight train boxcars or freight cars and brought within two or three blocks of the wood yard. From there, the men helping to run the wood yard (my father had one truck and two mules to help the workers), took the wood from the train and systematically stacked it in such a way that it was at times several feet deep and eight or more feet high.

We had the only telephone in the community and, because of the power saw and the amount of electricity to be used, Papa had to run a special power line at least two blocks, just for the business. Our house was put on an independent line, with a quarter meter.

In 1918, my father's pains from rheumatism became more severe and he and Mother thought a different climate would be best for his illness. A few years later, he and my older brother began to gather material for a cross-country trip, seeking a dry climate. There was no stone left unturned to make the trip the most comfortable possible. They took with them a large tent and a new Ford touring car, with all of the comforts of a then-modern camper. It was a very successful trip and they returned two years later, much wiser, with the information and the knowledge gathered over those two years. In those days, there was little travel from the extreme east to the extreme west of the continent.

A story which, I feel, best typifies the love my father engendered in his children, through his morality and his love, concerns my brother George. One day a friend of Papa's came to him, saying, "Mr. Platts, I think a lot of you and your family and hate to see one of your children break the record you and your family have established. Your son George (then about ten years old) was smoking, and I know you do not approve of that." Papa agreed, thanked him and, as soon as he had left, called George and told him what his friend said. George declared that he did not smoke and the man was wrong. Papa said this man would not lie, and proceeded to give George a lecture and a whipping.

A few days afterward, the same man was talking with my father when a fellow the size of my brother was seen walking on the other side of the street smoking. The man cried out, "There he is Mr. Platts." Papa said, "That's not my son. My son is in the house." My father was the type of man who humbled himself to the extent that he went to his son, saying "Son, I have done you a terrible wrong and I ask your forgiveness." George said our father stood ten feet tall in his estimation.

Since my father's trip West gave him no satisfaction as to a new location to move our family, he and Mother took a trip to Philadelphia, and that is where the family settled in 1926, when I was already at Tuskegee Institute. My father's health was continuously deteriorating when he was in his fifties, a few years after the family established residence in Philadelphia. The three-story, six-apartment house we purchased needed a lot of work done on it and Papa and his two sons kept it in the best of condition. Since many people were coming north, my mother and father had gone into the real estate business, which proved very successful.

As the day began on a hot day in July 1934, Papa said to my brother George, "Don't tarry, son. We must finish that

porch today. This is the last day I am going to work on it."
During the early part of the day, a friend stopped to chat
with him and in the religious conversation, he said, "I'm
ready any time God calls me. I'm just waiting for the summons to come." George said he didn't think anything of his
comments, as Papa turned to him, saying, "Don't tarry, my
son, we must finish this job before dark." The job was
finished. Later that evening, my father, in the middle of a
quiet conversation with our family, slumped over in his
chair and passed quietly away.

My mother, Anna Eliza Hicks Platts, was born in 1874 in
Beaufort, South Carolina, the third child to Anthony and
Eliza Eikerenkoetter Hicks, who were the parents of five
children. One child died in infancy, and the only son died
a young man. A daughter married Josiah Beck, a businessman from the North, and a second daughter, Ella Victoria,
married a cabinet-maker living in Jacksonville, Florida.

When I was young, Mama took me to Ridgeland, South
Carolina to see her mother and father. That section was still
inhabited by some of my grandmother's Cherokee tribe
family, many of whom spoke only Cherokee. My grand-
father, Anthony Hicks, was called Brother Anthony. When
Aunt Patsy saw me, she said, "Uh, him luke lak By-Antinie."
Everybody agreed and knew what she meant, which was,
"Ah, she looks just like Brother Anthony," my grandfather.
To this day, most of my family of the older generation call
me Ban-Tinnie.

Grandfather Anthony died when I was about three years
old, but I remember his tall, slender frame as he made an
addition to his two-story house. He was kind and jolly and,
unlike Grandmother, would play with us.

When many Africans came to this country, they came as
free men, as did my great-grandfather, whose African name
was Bart, and who took the name Bart Hicks. He was a
professional builder in Africa, who somehow made it to
Liverpool, England, where he used his skills, and then
moved to America, where he had relatives who were slaves
in South Carolina, where he settled. He brought with him

to America a white indentured servant, to serve as camouflage if he were accosted by those who were looking for free
blacks to enslave them.

Take a trip to Beaufort, South Carolina and stroll down the
riverfront. You will find blocks of strong, towering buildings,
over 125 years old, built by my great-grandfather, who
brought with him from Africa the art of building. Bart was
the architect, contractor, and builder. You may rest assured
that the laborers were black, too.

There was much work to do in those days, and few people
were skilled enough to do it. My great-grandfather was a
wheelwright, a blacksmith, a cabinet-maker, as well as a
builder. He and his son Anthony and others working with
them built brick warehouses, which still stand on the waterfront of Beaufort and are still in use.

After landing in Richmond, Virginia from Liverpool, Bart
met a half-breed woman, Margaret Johnson. Because she
was expecting, he left her with her parents and went to
Ridgeland and Beaufort (both in the same county) to start
his building work. After the baby was a few months old,
Great-Grandmother Margaret got on a horse with her baby
boy, Anthony, and, after days of riding, reached Ridgeland,
South Carolina.

My great-grandmother on the other side was a Cherokee
Indian, Starry Eye, the daughter of Chief Running Water. At
age four, running through the woods behind her mother,
she was kidnapped by Jean de Ribault, a French Huguenot.
Being separated from her own race, she met and married a
German duke, Josiah Eikerenkoetter. There still remains in
the family a Rev. Josiah (Joe) Eikerenkoetter, and Rev.
Frederick (Freddie or Ike) Eikerenkoetter, an evangelist and
one of the better-known persons of that family. My grandmother Eliza Eikerenkoetter, daughter of Starry Eye and
Duke Josiah Eikerenkoetter, married Anthony Hicks, the
son of Bart Hicks.

Anthony Hicks, my grandfather, had a half-brother who
was a slave and bought his freedom, whose name was
Robert (Hicks) Smalls. Robert Smalls became one of the

first African-American members of the U.S. Congress, elected during Reconstruction.

Born in South Carolina, Robert Smalls was fascinated with boats and was allowed to work on some of them. Self-taught, he and his daughter learned how to read and write, as well as the way to maneuver the Rebels' gunboat, *The Planter.* During the Civil War, he was able to get eight other people of color to enter the gunboat and, with his family, left the Beaufort dock and landed in Charleston, South Carolina, where they turned the boat over to the Yankees. This story was told me by my mother, who was close to the Smalls family.

My sister, Ann Platts Cole, who is a poet and author, wrote the following poem in honor of our mother on a Mother's Day following her death:

To Mother, wherever, my dear, you are,
You are our leader, our guide and our star,
You loved us, you helped us when things went astray,
You prayed with us, stayed with us hours of the day,
And oh, just to think of those growing up years,
When you heeded our cries and dried all of our tears.
Although we rebelled and dissented, we find
The wisdom you tried to ingrain in our mind.
And, Mother dear, dear Mother there is naught left to say,
Except that you're worthy of this special day.

I clearly remember going about with mother in her horse and buggy in the city of Savannah in 1921, when I was ten years old. My induction into politics was knocking on doors and ringing doorbells, giving women the proper information, taking them to the registration board and/or taking them to the polls to cast their votes.

From the earliest time I can remember, I tried to follow in my mother's footsteps. She was firm but always had a reason. She believed in whipping but not beating. She gave the adults of the community the right to chastise or whip us if they caught us doing anything wrong. I'm sure all of this helped to keep us straight, until it became a habit to strive to do right.

Our parents never told us to strive for any particular type of business or profession, but to be an example for others, behave ourselves and do the best we could in school. Daily there was some type of caution, an example of someone who fell because he did wrong, or a conversation, which would drift where a Bible verse would be used.

Mother was very wise in getting her point over. There were many mottoes, such as "Keep your eyes on the objective, not on the difficulties"; "If you make a better mousetrap, the world will beat a path to your door"; "Hitch your wagon to a star"; "The sky is the limit"; "There is always room at the top," and many, many more. She instilled in us the ability never to hate, but turn hate into love; for if you hate, the hater is destroying himself and the hated still goes on about his business.

When I was small, I remember Mama having several odd jobs, though her principal profession was always dressmaking and tailoring. She would bring in the house pictures of all sizes, old and faded, and return them bright and shiny. I wondered what she was doing. She was earning money by painting gold picture frames. Another time she had a little school at the house and still another time she made an attempt to make toilet articles. All of these were done at home, so she could be with her children.

The Prophecy

God helps them that help themselves.
—Ben Franklin

One day in 1921, a man arrived at our house wearing an old suit, which had been worn until it was green. This was not so unusual, as many people who were hungry or looking for a place to stay often stopped by our house, and nothing about it made me think he was different. As he came up the front steps, I was on the porch. He asked, "Is your mother home?" I said, "Yes, sir," and proceeded to find Mama. As she came down, the man introduced himself, saying he traveled by foot from California. Mama asked him to have a seat in the swing on the porch. I left them to do some chores.

Later at the dinner table, Mama related her conversation with the stranger. She said that the old man had told her, "Your house will be divided. The husband will leave and the children will be scattered throughout the country, and you will be alone. But don't be disturbed. You, too, will leave and, not long afterward, you will all be back together again, but it will not be here in Savannah." Mother asked him how he got here. This was his story.

"I am a prophet. God uses me as his messenger. One night, a big, bright light appeared at the foot of my bed. A voice as clear as ever said, 'I have a message I want you to take to my children.' I asked God, 'Where am I supposed to go?' and God said, 'I will guide you all the way, for you are going east. When you get there, I will let you know the city and guide you to the house. When you open your mouth, I will tell you what to say.' "

Mama said to herself, "This man is a con man, who wants something to eat. He doesn't know what he is talking about." She asked him if he wanted something to eat and a place for the night. He wanted a drink of water and a sandwich, which he took, and then left.

Later, as mentioned above, my father and brother left to seek a more healthful living place in the West. My sister Geneva went to live with our aunt in Jacksonville, Florida. My oldest sister Wilhelmina, who lived in Detroit, went to Philadelphia. My sister Elizabeth, who lived in South Carolina, also made her home in Philadelphia, and my brother George went to visit her. Sister Audrey was sent to my father's sister for the summer, in Brunson, South Carolina. Ann went to Howard University to study, and I went to Tuskegee. Nobody was left home but Mother.

While I was studying in Tuskegee, my father wrote Mother, asking her to meet him in Tuskegee on his way back from the West, where he had traveled and worked in California, Louisiana, Texas, New Mexico, and Arizona. It had been nearly three years since I had seen either of them. It was a grand meeting for the four of us—Papa and Harold returning from the West, Mama coming from further east, and me. They then returned to Savannah, but not for a long time. Harold went to Palm Beach, Mama to Philadelphia, and I continued my studies at Tuskegee.

My father's health did not improve, so they sold their various properties in Savannah and, with the proceeds, Mama went back to Philadelphia and invested the money in an apartment complex with six houses. Finally, some years later, all of us got together again. Mother never looked at the incident as a coincidence, but as an act of God, warning the family and preparing us for the situation.

When my father passed in 1934, there were about four

houses of the six rented out, but before my mother retired from the real estate business, she had as many as 27 apartment houses. She gave each of her children a three-story brick building before she retired. That was the peak of the business. She had done real estate on the side in Savannah and took it up full time in Philadelphia when my father died.

At the end of her life, Mother said that she was tired of living, but she remained very active. She worked in the church, was secretary of the Philadelphia Negro Chamber of Commerce, director of a community choir, and gave of herself wherever she could.

The morning she died, in June 1965, she said she was going away. She ate a better breakfast than she had recently eaten and laid down. When the doctor and the minister went into her room, she smiled and waved goodbye. She was 92 years old and had lived a full, fruitful life. What a beautiful life to live and a wonderful way to die! She lived and died a queen.

CHAPTER 4

My Sisters and Brothers

The destiny of the colored American ...
is the destiny of America.
— Frederick Douglass

I remember my oldest sister Wilhelmina as another mother. We all respected her as our second mother. Wilhelmina had no children herself from any of her marriages, but she dearly loved children. In the late 1930s in Philadelphia, Wilhelmina took her neighbors' children as her own, especially when they were babies. Training and loving them as she did, other people asked her to take care of their children, too. Within a few years, she had so many children that she opened a day care center, either the first or among the first in the city, and hung out her shingle, "Aunt Willie's Day Care Center." Many of the children were in the third generation of being cared for by "Aunt Willie."

In her spare time, Wilhelmina and Audrey, our baby sister, developed a powdered barbeque sauce, the first of its kind.

Wilhelmina gave up the day care center several months before she died in 1972, though she continued to be concerned for the moral, physical and educational background of the children she had to give up.

Elizabeth was the third child of my parents' marriage, the second, Alvarena, having died in infancy. Like all of our parents' children, she had so much caring and sharing to give. Though she and her husband had five of the most wonderful girls (no boys), they also kept a houseful of other children. Their lives were touched, often in the most minute way, by little seeds of kindness, love, and respect, which were scattered in their hearts, took root and grew. One could never be at their home visiting for more than a couple of hours without seeing other children among their own. My older son, even though an adult, often speaks of the warmth and love he received as a lad while visiting the Smith family.

As a younger sister, I adored Elizabeth, which made me follow her every chance I had. I have several very poignant memories of our childhood together.

Elizabeth and her husband lived in Ridgeland, South Carolina, then in Charleston, and later in Philadelphia. Being an industrious couple and having children, they managed to keep their heads above the poverty level during the Depression.

Later, there was a clothing industry at home, using the basement as the factory and renting other sewing machines, placing them in homes where people wanted to stay with their families. Hundreds of thousands of garments were returned to the factory each month, while hundreds of people had the opportunity to make money. Many of the youth, including all of her children, nieces and nephews, as well as students needing a job were welcomed to come, be trained, and work to make money for themselves.

This business was in operation for more than 30 years. Today, as a result, many of the children and grandchildren are government employees, stylists, models, and clothing specialists.

There could be no more affectionate brother than my brother Harold, our parents' first-born son. He was much older than the younger son, so he was my father's shadow. He was witty, full of fun, smart, and tender-hearted. The latter quality was taken from both my mother and father.

The first job I have ever known my brother to hold was at a candy shop, and of all the other jobs he had in his life, candy was always his first love.

In the *Philadelphia Daily News* of October 31, 1988 (Hallowe'en), there is an illustrated story on my brother, titled "The Sweet Life of a Candy Man . . . Movie Actor, Carpenter, Boat Builder and Innovator," by Ron Avery, staff writer. It is a loving account of Harold's multi-faceted life, including his bit part in the silent film *Son of Zorro,* while he and my father were in California. He had a candy-making business in Philadelphia for 58 years, and was the inventor, in 1919, of candy apples. Since his death in May 1989, his only living son, Donald, has taken over the business. He was the father of two sons, one of whom preceded him in death.

Eloise, the fifth child, died at age nine. It was hard for my parents to take the death of my sister Eloise at such a young age. From birth, she was not a healthy child. My mother did not believe in medicines. My grandmother could always supply us with medicines from herbs. That and a dose of castor oil each spring kept us generally in good health.

My father told my mother one day that he was going to take Eloise to the doctor. Mother said, "George, she is doing fine. I don't think she needs to go to the doctor." After a discussion, she was taken to the doctor, who gave her some medicine to be taken three times a day. Mama complained that Eloise seemed to get sallow and pale. She said, "I hope the doctor knows what he's doing." Within a couple of weeks, Eloise died and the doctor said he was sorry, the medicine was just too strong for her system.

I was three years old when she died and I remember how she was stretched on a couch at Grandmother's house, while people were gathered in the living room. Though the room was dark, I tiptoed across the hall, pulled the veil back, kissed her and returned to the living room, saying, "Eloise is gone to Heaven. I saw her."

My sister Ann was my pal, my best friend, and often we said we were twins. We were known as Fritz and Hans, or the Katzenjammer Kids. She made the suggestions and I did the leg work. We protected each other in our little schemes, which otherwise might have brought punishment or scolding.

She made such an impression because of her elocution, her poise, and ladylike elegance, that the entire community suggested that their girls emulate her. She spent much time reading books and learning to play music. We were often asked to be on school and church programs and in many cases we were almost the entire program ourselves.

Mother was superintendent of our Sunday school and several times president of one or another of the Parent Teachers Associations for our schools, and she was always busy writing skits and short plays, or pantomime programs, which drew large and appreciative audiences. Ann inherited these qualities from my mother more than I.

Ann attended Georgia State College (now Savannah State University) and was so popular that I refused to continue attending the same school, which I believe was a relief to her. After graduation, she attended Howard University, then married and became the mother of two children, both of whom have contributed greatly to society.

For more than 25 years, Ann was chief of 200 secretaries of the Eastern Air Force Base District. All records of inductions and retirements came through her office for that region.

My sister Geneva was younger than I and the most witty member of the family. She was a beautician, who showed interest in her profession at an early age. More than that, she was a professional makeup artist. It was fascinating to see her make an ordinary-looking person into a pretty person.

Having aligned herself with style professionals, she often was invited to be the makeup artist for professional characters in New York, and later in Philadelphia. She had no children of her own.

Crippling arthritis during much of her life, similar to my father's, compelled her to close her business and caused her death in 1977.

I asked my mother to give me our baby brother George, because he was just like a live doll. He and our father (for whom he was named) became "my father, my friend." While Papa lived, my little brother George tried to be just like him and my two brothers formed a team to do the repairs on the accumulated real estate holdings. George did the interior and my brother Harold did the exterior.

Curiosity caused George to take odd jobs while growing up. He worked with undertakers, cosmetic factories, bakers, and others, but continued to take courses in architectural drawing, which landed him a job at the Sunship Shipyard in Pennsylvania as a first-class draftsman. He often told me of the large steel beams carried by cranes, which had to be placed precisely on the lines of the blueprints, as he supervised the operation.

At the same time, George had a small factory in his basement, where he made a type of hair preparation which made the hair grow, and which was approved by the National Cosmetology Association. He was recently forced into retirement from an active life by health problems. He is the father of four girls.

As our baby sister, Audrey could have been spoiled and dependent, but being an offspring of my mother and father, she too made a contribution in the family's history.

At the tender age of about ten, she developed rheumatic fever. I'm sure my aunt, with whom she spent several months during her childhood, didn't know how to deal with it and perhaps my father's rheumatic genes made a contribution to her condition.

When the family moved to Philadelphia and became united again, Audrey finished school, became a nurse, married, and had two children. She and her husband built a home in the country in New Jersey. She passed away in 1959.

CHAPTER 5

Memories of
My Childhood

Our acts our angels are, or good or ill,
Our fatal shadows that walk by us still.
—John Fletcher

Before I was born, my family lived on Maple Street in Savannah and their home was destroyed by fire. The family escaped injury and moved to a neighborhood on the outskirts of the city known as Dutchtown, where I was born on August 18, 1911. We moved back into Savannah six months later.

My father moved us to a small island outside Savannah, known as Isle of Hope. The street car ran to within a block of the house, which made it possible for the older children to go to school and for Papa to go to work as a carpenter-contractor in larger institutions, among them Cuyler Street School and what was then the Georgia State Building, where he did the carpentry for the interior.

Living at Isle of Hope, a summer resort, was a heaven for me, for this was the first place I could get into anything, right or wrong. The house had about six rooms and a large front porch. In the back, there was a duplex with at least two rooms on each side. On the east side of the house was a park (actually just a couple of lots), where beautiful cedar trees were growing with several benches under them. In the back was the boat and river.

I don't believe we were any different from other kids. We

thought it was Papa's job to leave home in the morning, go where there were many trees, and shake them all day. As the fruit (money) fell to the ground, he would pick it up, and stuff his pockets, leaving one pocket free to shake a candy tree and fill it.

Of course, that was a child's fantasy, but what was not a fantasy was the way my father kept his family well fed. He never believed in paper-bag shopping. On the first of each month, a dray (a big wagon) and later a truck from the Alexander Wholesale Grocery Company would unload staple groceries, such as 100 pounds of flour, 100 pounds of rice, and a half dozen other staples, with grosses of other commodities, into the storage room. Though islanders came by the house selling seafood at least three times per week, salt and canned seafood were among the groceries. The city cold storage always kept the carcass of a cow, of which Papa often brought home large pieces.

I was always known as a daring child, getting into mischief more than others. I learned, however, that being daring can be fruitful, profitable, brave and/or foolish. It has saved many lives, accomplished many aims, and brought forth many inventions, but if wisdom is not used, it can end up in disaster.

I recall one summer morning when I was ten years old. My sister Ann and I were in our room. My father used the L-shaped room opposite ours as an office, before he built one. We were just relaxing, when she said she smelled smoke. The two of us scampered downstairs, opening doors, closets and cabinets, expecting to find fire somewhere. We returned to our room. Still smelling smoke, we examined every room except Papa's office, which was locked. However, entering our room again and looking at the window opposite ours, I found the smoke filling the room.

We began to scream. Ann ran to the telephone and alarmed the community. I could not sit and wait for the fire truck, so I opened our window, held onto the sash, stretched my long legs to Papa's window and pushed his window up with the help of my other hand. I then jumped or crawled from one window to the other in a room full of smoke. Our neighbor, Mrs. McCollough, took an axe and opened the door to let me out, while other neighbors brought water, because the blaze had begun to spread. When the fire department reached 3203 Burroughs Street, the fire was out.

I was given a five-dollar gold piece for my bravery. Looking back on this episode, there could have been an explosion in the house, which would have killed me. Daring but unwise.

CHAPTER 6

Tuskegee Institute

No race can prosper till it learns that there
is as much dignity in tilling a field as in
writing a poem.
　　—Dr. Booker T. Washington, *Up from Slavery*

It was a coincidence, but I feel that it was meant to be, that I was asked to recite a poem during a program at the A.M.E. church in Savannah. We were members of the Church of God, but we were asked to take part in programs in many churches of different denominations.

The poem I recited was "When Melinda Sings," by Paul Lawrence Dunbar. Not realizing I had made any impression in the recitation or singing, I was surprised when I was told a couple wanted to see me. The couple, Mr. and Mrs. E.J. Bruce, was elderly, living in Savannah, but were former instructors of Tuskegee Institute.

Each time I had the chance, I visited the home of Mr. and Mrs. Bruce, because they had a small room with everything relating to Dr. Booker T. Washington, Dr. George Washington Carver, Tuskegee Institute, and others connected with the founding of the school.

Of course, I was very impressed and decided that this was the school I wanted to attend. Mother gave me every negative reason why I would not like to attend. The food was bad, I'd have to walk miles from the dormitory to the last room, and I would have to work in a field. I asked her if there were any girls at the school and, when she said yes,

I said, "If they can eat slop, work in the field, and walk a mile to school, I can learn to, too." As my father and older brother were touring out West, Mother communicated with him and I was permitted to enter Tuskegee the following fall.

Reaching Tuskegee, I was fascinated by the beautiful buildings, the young men and women, who exhibited their executive ability by keeping the students mindful of the rules and regulations, and the cleanliness of the campus. The Tuskegee campus, with its buildings built by students, who were asked for their input in its design, and the restriction of students to the campus, was different than what I was used to at my former school, Georgia State College (now Savannah State). But, being a member of a sheltered family, the confinement and restriction to the campus were nothing new to me.

Just on a biographical note—In addition to graduating from Tuskegee (Institute) University, I took courses at the following universities: Tennessee State, Virginia State, and Temple University. I also spent two years at Georgia State Industrial College, from which I transferred to Tuskegee.

Tuskegee University, founded by Dr. Booker T. Washington, is a key institution in the history of African-Americans, as well as in my personal life.

The following statement, taken from Tuskegee University's Statement of Institutional Mission and Purpose, gives an idea of the importance of the institution: "Tuskegee University is a national, independent, and non-profit institution of higher learning that has a special and unique relationship with the State of Alabama. With distinctive strengths in the sciences, engineering and other professions, the University's basic mission is to provide educational programs of exceptional quality which promote the development of liberally prepared and professionally oriented people.

"The University is rooted in a history of successfully educating black Americans to understand themselves against the background of their total heritage and the promise of their individual and collective future. A primary mission has been to prepare them to play effective professional and leadership roles in society and to become productive citizens in the national and world community. Tuskegee University continues to be dedicated to these broad aims.

"Over the past century, various social and historical changes have transformed this institution into a comprehensive multicultural place of learning whose primary purpose is to develop leadership, knowledge, and service for a global society. Committed deeply to academic excellence, the University admits highly talented students and challenges them to reach the highest possible levels of intellectual and moral development. The University also believes strongly in equality of opportunity and recognizes that exquisite talent is often hidden in students whose finest development requires unusual educational, personal and financial reinforcement. The University actively invites a diversity of talented students, staff, and faculty from all racial, religious and ethnic backgrounds to participate in this educational enterprise."

CHAPTER 7

Dr. Booker T. Washington

You can't hold a man down without staying down with him.
     —Dr. Booker T. Washington, *Up from Slavery*

I possess first editions of the two autobiographies of Booker T. Washington, the founder of Tuskegee Institute, which I protect with pride. The first is: *Booker T. Washington's Own Story of His Life*, copyright 1901, by Booker T. Washington. The other is *Up From Slavery*, copyright 1900-1901. This volume is dedicated to his wife, Margaret James Washington, and his brother, John H. Washington. The many experiences of slaves, recounted in these books, were confirmed by the horror stories I heard as an agent in Dallas County, Alabama, 70 years afterward.

Dr. Washington writes in his autobiography that he had been asked many years before to write about his life, but he didn't think that he had done enough in the world to warrant an autobiography. That in itself betrays a mind of greatness and humility, qualities which I'm sure touched many lives.

In his autobiography, Dr. Washington gives very revealing information on his own background. He describes his slave master, who would send him on horseback, when he was merely a baby, to the mill, with corn to be ground into meal. Often the corn or meal would fall off the horse, taking him with it, and for hours he would wait for someone to pass and put him back on the creature. Although his mother was the cook in a wealthy household, she could not feed her children from the kitchen, which forced her to get whatever she could from elsewhere to feed her children. She customarily prayed at night with them for freedom. When Booker was given a new shirt, his brother had to wear it first, in order to remove the sharp stickers woven into the shirt, which was made of refuse flax. Dr. Washington had no clothes to speak of before he was six years old.

Dr. Washington's mother was the noblest embodiment of womanhood. Though illiterate, her lessons in virtue, thrift, and honesty were embedded in him. She inspired him to hope for and expect a better life. Consequently, when Booker saw a black man reading a newspaper, he became determined to learn to read. Although he was unable to go to school, he studied the labels on salt barrels, and with a book his mother bought for him, taught himself to read.

After the Civil War, Dr. Washington, his mother, and his brothers were free. In 1865, the family moved to West Virginia. By this time, Booker's mother had re-married, and persuaded her husband, Booker's stepfather, to permit him to attend public school for half a day. Now that he was free, Booker could choose his own name, which he did—Booker T. Washington.

One Sunday morning, an old man saw him playing marbles and chastised him for not being in Sunday school. Although he had never heard of a Sunday school, he put his marbles aside, followed the old man, and became a regular student at the Sunday school. He remained as an adult, became a teacher and, finally, the superintendent.

Booker also worked in a coal mine in West Virginia, where he heard the miners talking about a school for black boys and girls and immediately decided to go. The name of the school was Hampton Institute, which was located in Hampton, Virginia, near Norfolk in the southeast corner of the state. But when Booker started out from near Charleston, West Virginia for Hampton Institute, he did not know where it was located. His mother and brother got a few things together and he started on foot, traveling part of the way by rail, part by stagecoach, and part by foot, sleeping under boardwalks. Arriving in Richmond, still hungry and dirty, he saw ships in the distance. He was given work, enough to buy food.

Once he had earned enough to continue the journey, Booker again set out. When he arrived at Hampton Institute and applied for admission, the principal, Ms. Mackie, asked him to clean a large room. Booker had had previous experience in cleaning for a Mrs. Ruffner in West Virginia, who had made him clean perfectly. This prior experience caused him to do his task in such a way that Ms. Mackie could find no dust remaining as she ran her white handkerchief over the furniture. He was admitted, despite having no money for tuition, and this served him as an important lesson throughout his life.

After graduation from Hampton, Booker returned to West Virginia and taught for three years, all the while recruiting students to attend Hampton, including his brother John and half brother James. Later, all were employees of Tuskegee Institute.

Booker furthered his studies by attending Wayland Seminary. He also worked politically to have the capital of West Virginia moved to Charleston. He began to study law, until he realized that his ability to contribute to the improvement of Americans, black and white, would be constricted in that profession. Booker wanted to reach out to as many people as he could, and knew that law would limit him in doing so.

While at the end of the second year of teaching at Hampton in 1881, General Armstrong, founder and president of Hampton, was asked to send a teacher to the little town of Tuskegee, Alabama, someone to organize and become the principal of a normal school to be started in that town. He asked Dr. Washington to accept the job, which he did.

In 1881, Tuskegee was barely on the map. Dr. Washington finally reached Tuskegee in the middle of June 1881. The school doors had not yet opened, but $2,000 had already been appropriated by the Alabama legislature and a board (all white members) had been appointed to control the expenditure. Despite these preparations, Tuskegee had no building, no grounds, and no equipment necessary to start a school. Nonetheless, on July 4, 1881, a school was opened in an old church and a tumbledown shanty.

On the first day, there were 30 students, mainly those who had been teaching in the public schools in that vicinity. Although other students enrolled, they could not financially afford to remain for the nine-month school term. Dr. Washington therefore planned to create industries to employ students, so that they could earn at least a part of their board.

When student enrollment increased, Tuskegee purchased 100 acres of land with the help of a $500 bank loan. In Dr. Washington's lifetime, a total of 2,500 acres was acquired. Among the teachers who were recruited to teach agriculture, business, and science, was Dr. George Washington Carver. Word of this black educational institute spread throughout the country, and many interested people contributed to assist in building the school. Still standing today and in use on the campus are buildings which were built by students from scratch, starting with bricks and including everything that could be made or manufactured by students.

Those under the tutelage of Dr. Washington digested so much food of knowledge that they were filled with instruction and wisdom that changed most of their lives for the better. One of the mottoes taught at Tuskegee, which heavily influenced Dr. Martin Luther King and his movement, was "Cast down your bucket where you are, in making friends of all races by whom we are surrounded." Many have interpreted this to mean that one should not run from his land of birth looking elsewhere for something better, just dig a little deeper.

In fact, this motto was the central feature of Dr. Washington's famous address to the Atlanta Industrial Exposition in 1895, the first time a black man had addressed a large

gathering of white leaders in the South, and which made
him an overnight celebrity around the world. I will quote
from that speech, reproduced in *Up from Slavery:* "A ship
lost at sea for many days suddenly sighted a friendly vessel.
From the mast of the unfortunate vessel was seen a signal,
'Water, water; we die of thirst!' The answer from the friendly
vessel at once came back, 'Cast down your bucket where
you are.' A second . . . third and fourth signal for water was
answered, 'Cast down your bucket where you are.' The
captain of the distressed vessel, at last heeding the injunction, cast down his bucket, and it came up full of fresh,
sparkling water from the mouth of the Amazon River. To
those of my race who depend on bettering their condition
in a foreign land or who underestimate the importance of
cultivating friendly relations with the Southern white man,
who is their next-door neighbour, I would say: 'Cast down
your bucket where you are'—cast it down in making friends
in every manly way of the people of all races by whom we
are surrounded."

In his lifetime, Dr. Washington addressed many organizations and congregations (sometimes six or eight meetings
in 24 hours). He addressed all audiences which invited him,
of all colors. But such a heavy non-stop schedule was too
much for him. His unceasing activity is thought to have led
to his early death.

CHAPTER 8

Dr. George Washington Carver

The truth shall make you free.
　　　　　　　—John 8:32

One could never fully appreciate Dr. George Washington Carver, one of Tuskegee's most renowned professors, unless one had had the opportunity to know him personally. In walking and talking with him as we did, we would see the light of hope for the world and feel the closeness of communication with God. His life stood out as one of forgetting self and wanting to give service, particularly to the poor.

As a pre-teenager, before I ever heard the name Tuskegee or Dr. Carver, our next door neighbor asked my mother to let me visit Georgia State (the black college on Thunderbolt Island) near Savannah with her. Mother readily agreed. As we approached the auditorium, I heard a fine, shrill voice, and I could not decide if it was a man or a woman. I tried to giggle, but there was no one to giggle with me. As we approached our seats near the front, seeing the speaker at the podium only added to my desire to giggle, but the atmosphere was so electrified with his presence that it rubbed off on me and I calmed down enough to hear Dr. Carver talk.

Dr. Carver was explaining the many uses of the peanut. But first, he told the story of his closeness with God and their conversation, which he later repeated in Selma at our farmers' conference and which shall never be erased from my mind.

His story was as follows: Before becoming a teenager in Diamond Grove, Missouri, after a refreshing spring rain, he strolled into a field beyond the plantation house to breathe God's refreshing air. It was a pleasant, warm evening, the field was partly surrounded by woods, the sun was making its way toward the West, the vegetation was glistening from the rain and a beautiful rainbow spanned the skies. He felt as near to God as he ever had. He gave a great sigh, saying, "Dear God, please make me wise to the wonders of this beautiful world's yields of the earth." God said, "If I make you wise to everything, you will be as wise as I, but name one or two things." And he said, "Dear God, make me wise to the peanut and the sweet potato," and He did.

I can never forget that story, and the second time I heard him tell it, 30 years later, it had an even greater impact on me.

Dr. George Washington Carver means more personally to my family than anyone will ever know. I was a student of home economics at Tuskegee, and Dr. Carver was our guest instructor at least four times during my senior year. My husband Bill Boynton was a regular student under his supervision, and made use of the training given him in crop rotation and growing cover crops that put nitrogen in the soil, before planting the permanent crop.

When Bill and I married and our son was born, we asked Dr. Carver to be his godfather. He kindly accepted, and at birth sent Bill a check for $5; at age one, he sent $1, at age two, $2, etc., until he was four years old. I still have the $2 check in Dr. Carver's own handwriting. When Bill was five, his godfather, Dr. Carver, died.

En route to Dr. Carver's funeral at Tuskegee, which was held on January 5, 1943, my son Bruce Carver (as usual) asked me to tell him a story. I started with the usual "once upon a time"—telling him of the baby traded for a horse, how that baby grew up to question the workings of the

universe, how he began to teach himself, how he conversed
with God in the field, and finally, added that he was the man
who had visited our house after speaking at our farmers'
conference.

"Who was that?" I asked. Bruce Carver looked puzzled.
Thinking he would remember a different incident, I said,
"You remember the medicine I told you I mixed for you (Dr.
Carver suggested red onions and sugar, a teaspoonful every
four hours), and you said you didn't like it. Who was that?"
He thought a while and said, "I know, that was Jesus Christ."
Of course I set the record straight.

CHAPTER 9

Tuskegee's Achievements

*The tortuous road which has led from
Montgomery to Oslo is a road over which
millions of Negroes are traveling to find a
sense of dignity. It will, I am convinced, be
widened into a superhighway of justice.*
—Dr. Martin Luther King, Jr.

Tuskegee has grown from an old shack and church, a
school with 30 students in 1881, to a campus of 2,500
acres and more than 3,000 students today. It is a school that
has as its foundation love, respect, honesty, and Christianity,
to serve as an example to mankind. Cleanliness in mind and
body have been indelibly imprinted on the hearts and minds
of all students entering the great halls of Tuskegee Institute.

A visitor to the George Washington Carver Museum will
find reminiscences of the past that laid the groundwork for
the Extension Department and the 4-H Club, which is so
popular today.

It was Booker T. Washington who personally visited
homes in Macon County in the 1880s, until he got the "Jessup
Wagon," which went from house to house teaching farming,
cleanliness, and housekeeping. Later there was an equipped
truck known as the Movable School, which had a nurse,
home economics, and farm agents. The three stages of the
traveling extension department can be seen on display today.

Mr. Thomas M. Campbell of Tuskegee Institute, whom
Booker T. Washington employed to teach better farming
methods to men in the rural areas, is responsible for many
improvements on the farm and a "first" in several fields. He
was the first agricultural extension agent and later became

the federal extension agent, having been appointed by the U.S. Department of Agriculture as director of agriculture for seven lower southern states. He had all African-American extension work under his supervision. During his supervision, the 4-H Club extension service was born on the campus of Tuskegee Institute.

One idea which Booker T. Washington brought with him from Hampton Institute was the necessity of cleanliness of body, which he put in the following terms: the hands, the heart, the education of the head, and hygiene. The four H's (not as it is presently used) was Tuskegee students' symbol long before the 4-H Club became popular. Wouldn't it be appropriate for historians to tell this story, like it is?

Some other Tuskegee "firsts" included the foundation laid for night school in 1881, when the Institute recognized that not all students could attend day school; and extension classes, which were first held at Selma University, in Selma, Alabama, in the early 1940s, when instructors from Tuskegee Institute and Alabama State College in Montgomery traveled to Selma once or twice a week. Much of such progress is due to Booker T. Washington and the Institute's system of outreach, before such a concept ever came into general usage.

To me, it seems very important that we give honor to whom honor is due, particularly in respect to an entire race of people. The African-American family should be able to tell their children the part the African-American people have contributed and are contributing to this great country.

We shall continue to prosper in proportion as each individual improves his usefulness in the community, as each individual makes himself such a pillar in prosperity and character that his community will feel that his contributions, of whatever type, cannot be spared.

Tuskegee Normal and Industrial Institute was and still is a shining example of what African-Americans can do if they can get their fair share and are able to tear down the damnable, ungodly, obstructing mental wall of discrimination and hate. Dr. Washington laid the foundation for what can be done to make this world just.

(Top) Grandmother Eliza Eikerenkoetter Hicks; Mother and father, Anna E. (Hicks) and George G. Platts

The Platts family circa 1917. Amelia Platts is bottom right. Inset: brother George (not yet born when this picture was taken)

Clockwise from top left: Sister Geneva Platts McCullough; Sister Elizabeth Platts Smith; Brother Harold Platts and his wife Rose; Sister Ann with her daughter, Dr. Gloria T. Smith.

*This is the Boynton family in 1942: S.W. Boynton, Amelia Platts Boynton,
sons Bruce and Bill, Jr.*

"He lifted the veil of ignorance from his people and pointed the way to progress through education and industry."

Tuskegee Institute

The late Dr. Carver at work

This statue of Booker T. Washington, founder and President of Tuskegee Institute, stands proudly at the university. The inscription is: "He lifted the veil of ignorance from his people and pointed the way to progress through education and industry."

This letter from Dr. George Washington Carver asks after the Boyntons' son Bruce. Dr. Carver was his godfather.

TUSKEGEE NORMAL AND INDUSTRIAL INSTITUTE

FOR THE TRAINING OF COLORED YOUNG MEN AND WOMEN

TUSKEGEE INSTITUTE, ALABAMA

In Memory of

MR. S.W. BOYNTON

Known to the Bills and Daughters As

MR. & MRS. CIVIL LIBERTIES

For the past several years, this couple has been responsible for The Civil Liberties Program in the State Association, District and Local Groups because of their Team Work.

The State Association Program which is held on Mondays at 3:00 P. M., has been one of the outstanding Features of the Association.

"The Tuskegee Story" will be featured in color by this Department at the Elks Club Monday. The Public is invited.

MR. & MRS. S. W. BOYNTON

1945 Memorial to S.W. Boynton by the Alabama State Elks Lodge. They were known as Mr. and Mrs. Civil Liberties in Selma.

THE S. W. BOYNTON JUSTICE AWARD

Prior to the admission of Black lawyers to the legal profession in the State of Alabama, lay persons were struggling for a fair and just society. It was the struggle of these lay persons that eventually enabled Black lawyers to be able to practice law in significant numbers in the State of Alabama.

Mr. Samuel W. Boynton was one of those lay persons who, during times of harsh discrimination, served as a lay advocate in the Black community. More significantly, Mr. Boynton, a Selma resident, not only laid the historical foundation for the Voting Rights Act, but also invited the first Black lawyers into the Blackbelt to pursue civil rights cases.

Mr. Samuel Boynton, the father of Selma Attorney Bruce Boynton, died on May 13, 1963. It has been told that the first successful mass meeting in Selma immediately evolved as the result of his death, and as a tribute to Samuel Boynton's lifelong commitment to uplifting the quality of life for blacks in the Selma area. In honor of the late Samuel W. Boynton, and other known and unknown trailblazers for justice, the Alabama Lawyers Association presents the Lay Justice Award to celebrate the bond between the lay and the legal communities.

The S.W. Boynton Justice Award was established by the Alabama Lawyers Association in memory of S.W. Boynton's work to bring civil liberties and justice to Alabama's African-American population. This is their description of the award.

This is the kind of rural poverty the Boyntons encountered in their work in Selma and the surrounding counties.

PART II

Working Under Feudalism

When we ignore evil, poverty, and injustice around us and do nothing about it, we become an accomplice to it.

CHAPTER 1

After Tuskegee:
People Loving People

I believe that unarmed truth and unconditional love will have the final word in reality.
—Dr. Martin Luther King, Jr.

After graduating from Tuskegee, I went back to Savannah to the Extension Department at Georgia State College and filed an application for extension work with the U.S. Department of Agriculture. Instead, I was sent to St. Mary's, Georgia, to teach in a Rosenwald school.

Since this was my first job, I didn't think about the salary of $50 per month but I was fascinated with the big seventh and eighth grades I had to teach. To me, one teacher teaching two classes was unheard of, but I managed.

Each school morning, at least four of the girls would come to the place where I was boarding and accompany me to the school, about two blocks away. This was truly a rural school, but after having seen the schools in Alabama, where one-teacher schools had as many as 105 students, and that teacher made $25 per month, my school with eight teachers and so many classrooms didn't seem bad by comparison.

My school, Camden County Training School, was located on the St. Mary's River across the river from Fernandine, Florida. There were seven other teachers, all except one being from the same family, which was related to the owners

47

of the pretty little island. There was no type of athletics, no recreation, no outlet for the kids.

Immediately, I planned field trips on Saturdays, taught art, and had them raise money for basketball equipment for the campus or playground. My relationship with the students was beautiful, and the cooperation of students and community was unbelievable.

With one exception, the faculty fought the program. After the equipment had been bought and the land cleared away for the basketball and volleyball court, the principal of the school refused to put the baskets up on the playground. The parents of the community completed it. When teachers, principals, and friends from other parts of the state visited the school, the principal was praised because of his foresight in promoting clean sports. Thinking of the struggle my students went through to raise money for the courts, working in the shrimp factories at 4 o'clock in the morning before coming to school, selling candy, and giving fish fries, this praise of the principal angered me very much.

During one of the district teachers' association meetings, with perhaps 200 teachers present, I asked abruptly to speak (off the subject under discussion, of course), and said, "We the students are doing fine and making progress, especially in the manner of good behavior, and the betterment of the school, but we don't get any cooperation from the principal, Mr. Toler Harris, and his teachers." I then sat down, with all eyes upon me.

The following Monday morning, Mr. Harris came into my room and said, "Miss Platts, why did you make that statement Saturday?" I said, "Because it is true and you know it." He said "Miss Platts, you're fired. When you get your check next week, you cannot teach anymore." The students who were in the room began to show how uncontrollable they could be by throwing books, screaming, talking back to the principal, and telling him they were learning for the first time without fear.

To this day, I'm still in communication with two of these

St. Mary's students, with whom I regularly share a warm correspondence and exchange of visits.

Though we were preparing for graduation I left St. Mary's. Since my parents were in Philadelphia, I went there and took courses that summer in my field, home economics, and the following year I taught home economics in a Baptist boarding school, Americus Institute, in Americus, Georgia. From there, I went to Selma, Alabama and became the home demonstration agent of Dallas County, where I remained for nearly fifty years.

CHAPTER 2

Selma in the 1930s

If a man does not make new acquaintances
as he advances through life, he will soon
find himself left alone. A man should keep
his friendship in constant repair.
                                    —Samuel Johnson

On a cool, crisp morning in April 1930, Mr. Dobbs, the state extension agent, and I were on our way to Selma, a place I had never heard of. I was to teach the people of Dallas County, Alabama, of which Selma is the county seat, every phase of home economics. I would walk in the footsteps of a good leader, and I took this as a challenge to excel. A Mrs. Williams, who had the job before me, had resigned to get married; in those days, getting married was the end of extension work for women. Regardless of how good one was, the Extension Department could not see dividing an agent between her work and her husband. I knew marriage would have to wait until later, but this was no real problem, as I was not in love with anyone—only my work.

"It's a very small place," Mr. Dobbs informed me. "When you get there you'll find there isn't room enough to turn around, hardly. The train doesn't stop, it only slows down and there is a large bank of sawdust. When they shout 'Selma!' you jump off." Though Mr. Dobbs was only joking— they shout "Selma" as the first call before the train pulls into the station—I laughed, but believed him. We had boarded the train at Montgomery, and though the distance is just 50 miles, seemingly it took us several hours to reach Selma. As the train slowed down and the conductors called "Selma, Selma, all out for Selma!" I looked at Mr. Dobbs, thinking he would take his little bag and jump off. I was uneasy, because I didn't want to miss it. I did not realize that this was the last stop. Selma was the place where most people came to live when they left the farms. The plantation owners' heirs came as merchants and business people, and the blacks came as teachers, domestics, and all types of laborers.

We were met by the county extension agent, Samuel William Boynton; he took us by car to the place where I would live. I was constantly reminded that this was not Philadelphia (where my parents had gone to live) and neither was it Savannah. The people have to be taught, and you have to be very careful how you act, the county agent said. I was determined to give all my attention to the task and to try to please not only the department but especially the farm people with whom I would work.

This part of the country is called the Black Belt, not, as one might suppose, because of the color of its inhabitants, but because of the rich black soil, noted for its abundant cotton crops.

Next morning I rose bright and early in the large, old-fashioned home of Mr. and Mrs. Dommie Gaines. They were old settlers of Selma and they knew the surroundings, the people, and their attitudes toward outsiders. This was most helpful to me. The white people had adequate public schools and the blacks had only one—Clark, which graduated students from the ninth grade. However, there were several private schools for the blacks, including Knox Academy, a high school run by the Reformed Presbyterian Church; Lutheran Academy and College; Payne University (an African Methodist church school); and Selma University, a Baptist institution. Selma's blacks were proud of this educational center, but illiteracy in this county and those surrounding was as prevalent as in any part of the South.

The first day I went into the county, Bill Boynton gave me

some very good advice. When I talked to the farm people, he said, I had better know what I was talking about, but "always be kind and don't say anything that will make them think your education is so far above theirs that you create a barrier. They may be unlearned, but they are intelligent and can teach you a whole lot you don't know." I had never dealt with rural people before, and I did learn much from them in a short time.

Bill Boynton, whom I married several years later, had a rural background and loved and understood the people. They were eager to get to the meetings, which he tried to make entertaining as well as informative, and they asked Bill many questions that had nothing to do with the farm. Even after he retired, farmers still came to him for information. Being able to help them gave his life meaning. Bill was seldom angry and when he was, it was never because of anything done to him, but because someone had taken advantage of one of his farmers. He encouraged both young and old to continue to educate themselves in the vocation they liked best. There were many ways the state and county programs helped to perpetuate segregation and discrimination in extension work. Bill did not like these methods but he could do little about it. It made his work much harder in helping people to excel.

During the more than 50 years I lived in Selma as an adult, I worked with and touched almost every black family in Dallas County directly. In almost every household, the name Boynton became a household word, because the tenants and farmers depended upon us for guidance.

We were working as home demonstration and county agents employed by the U.S. Department of Agriculture. It was my job to work with the girls through the 4-H Club and the women through the homemakers club. With 52,000 African-Americans in the county, we had no supporting or assistant agent. With the exception of working with the rural blacks, we spent whatever time we could giving lectures, visiting clubs, and giving demonstrations in the city.

There was never a time when the work of black farmers

or 4-H Club members was exhibited jointly with that of the white community. All shows, demonstrations, and fairs took place in the African-American community, visited by blacks, and in most cases, where competitors were working for prizes, the judges were African-Americans from Tuskegee Institute.

There was no such thing as a good road in the black community, let alone paved streets in the black section of Selma. If a black lived on a plantation (most of them did), he had to get to his home the best way he could, unless he lived in the backyard of the owner. You could always tell where the white man's house was located in the country-side, because you simply followed a road, and this always ended at the owner's gate or in his yard. If you wanted to go back to the "quarters," as they were called, you had to leave your car at the road's end and trudge over ditches, gulleys, wagon roads, or unattended fields. Blacks who owned property in the country owned mostly portions away from roads and highways. If the white owner who had property where the road ended didn't want visitors going over his land, they would be stopped. The families behind the plantations would thus be entirely isolated. Some aspects of this situation remain to this day.

We who were county workers always first contacted the white owner, to avoid trouble, but no provision was ever made for our travel in the remote parts of the county. Often we were met by black community leaders and taken to the meeting place by wagon or even by horse or muleback. Little or no transportation, bad roads, and lack of freedom to go whenever and wherever the farm hands wanted to go made the blacks in the rural district "slaves" to the planta-tion owner.

By far the largest number of blacks on farms were share-croppers. Under something very like a feudal system, they were furnished with seed (payment for which was taken out of their profits later) and they also returned half of their yield in payment for the use of the land and a place to stay. The tenant farmer was a cut above the sharecropper. He leased land from the owner and paid rent for it and his lodging.

Booker T. Washington, founder of Tuskegee Institute, had devised a plan to reach as many of the people as possible by putting into operation a school on wheels. At first, the school was a covered wagon, drawn by two horses and equipped with farm implements and some household goods. It traveled in the communities near Tuskegee and was called the Jessup Wagon. Later, this was replaced with a truck, and still later, a trailer equipped with modern implements and home appliances.

Its name became the Movable School. It traveled around giving demonstrations in farming and homemaking in the most remote parts of the state. The health nurse was always quickly surrounded by mothers with babies and the sick.

When Bill and I were part of the program, it was staffed with a farm and home demonstration agent, a health nurse, and a 4-H Club agent. The farm and home demonstration agents invited the Movable School with plow to be part of the demonstrations. We were faculty members of Tuskegee Institute and specifically on the faculty of the Agriculture Department. Our office was on the Tuskegee campus, and all our records, itineraries, and reports were sent to Tuskegee Extension Department.

The Movable School was one of Tuskegee's mammoth projects to teach the uneducated. Its teaching of better farming methods could not help but pay off in greater yields and therefore profit to the plantation owner; nevertheless, we often ran into stiff opposition. The planters and overseers would not allow us to have suitable places to hold the school, and they were even more uncooperative when we asked them to let their tenants attend the one-, two-, or three-day sessions. In most cases, pleading with them to permit the school to come onto their places was in vain, even though we scheduled the school during the time there was less work to be done on the farm.

We once got permission to hold the school on the Sampson farm in the southwest section of the county. Hundreds of people lived on this property, which was owned by a multimillionaire from New York. He came down once or twice a year for the dog trials. The Sampson house itself was occupied by white workers, but nearby, the road gradually faded into the woods, where there were wagon trails and footpaths leading to many rundown shacks occupied by large families. Each Christmas, millionaire Sampson came down and gave his tenants clothes and a few dollars apiece.

We made plans, with the participation of the black county workers, for a session of the Movable School at the Sampson place. When we arrived in our cars and trucks, we were stopped by a white man with a gun. He would not allow us to drive through his property. We backed the trucks and the cars along the highway, then had to carry on foot the equipment and appliances to the remote section, where we would hold the school in one of the little houses. We were exhausted when we got there, and rain had begun to fall.

We set up demonstrations despite many handicaps, one of which was that the house was threatening to collapse from the weight of the large number of people in it. There was no electricity, so we could not use some of the equipment. But in spite of difficulties, the demonstrations were fruitful and were welcomed by the people of the community, who seldom got to any town or went anywhere except to the two stores in Alberta, a tiny village on the road to Selma.

CHAPTER 3

A Feudal Society

*I will let no man drag me down so low as
to make me hate him.*
— Dr. Booker T. Washington

I had read in school that Abraham Lincoln signed the Emancipation Proclamation in 1863. I believed in this until I went to Dallas County, Alabama. There I found that blacks on most of the plantations in the Black Belt were far from free. The reason: Like blacks in many other parts of the nation, they thought, "White is right, and that gives the white man the privilege to lynch, to whip, to segregate, and to exploit."

Most blacks were so convinced of this (unconsciously), that they thought only what they believed the white man wanted them to think. Even if a black man violated the law, as long as he was imposing on another black and if he were a good hand for the white man, his sentence was either light or it was suspended. The city fathers called this "being good to the blacks."

On the large plantations such as we had in Dallas and adjacent counties, there was no such thing as set working hours. The blacks went to the fields early in the morning and worked until it was too dark to see. There were still overseers, who were as inhuman as the Simon Legrees of slavery times. The blacks became either an asset or a liability to the owner when the place was sold. The seller and the buyer always discussed the assets that went with the land and if the tenants were good workers the price went up. If not, the land was sold for only its real estate value. Blacks never got a chance to buy the land; it had become a gentlemen's agreement not to sell them farm land. Only occasionally could a black buy land from a white man, and when he did, the price was almost out of reach.

I have seen landlords as proud of their sharecroppers as they were of their herd of cattle, especially in the days when cotton was king. All the requests for loans, food, clothing, and other necessities had to be made either at the plantation store or directly to the owner, so that he could keep an eye on everyone. There were scheming plantation owners, who watched the growth of the boys and girls, and where there was the least indication of taking a mate, he would encourage it, hoping there would be more farm hands born of the union. He went even further to keep the young couple on his place—adding a room to the already crowded shack of the parents. Cotton hands were needed in large numbers in the 1930s, 1940s, and 1950s.

Many stories of cruel and inhuman treatment of share-croppers were confided to me in those days, and I have no reason to doubt their truth—they were typical and they differed from one another only in specific details. The theme was always exploitation of and contempt (or condescending generosity) for the black.

On some plantations, the owner would discourage the blacks from buying licenses to marry. He would tell them it was a waste of money; he could do the same thing the justice of peace could do. Such fictitious "marrying" made it difficult later to get certain benefits that require proof of marriage.

Because there was government-financed work to be done and the farms became mechanized, the black farmer had to get all his cash from the landlord, and this was almost nothing. If he needed a doctor or his children needed clothing, he would go to the plantation owner, who in turn would call the doctor or the store and tell them he was sending his "boy" with his baby to be treated, or that his "boy's" children needed shoes. Of course the black paid dearly for this type of service—it would all come out of his wages.

I knew a large black farm hand named Jint. His twelve children could not go to school until November because they had to gather crops, and then they could go only if Jint could buy them books and clothing. In March, they had to leave school to plant the crops. Although the owner, Mr. Gibbs, profited from Jint's labor, Jint got nothing but a balance due bill every year. He decided he would leave the plantation, but he had to have money to move, so he bought sugar and began to make illegal whiskey. Mr. Gibbs, his landlord, sold him hundreds of pounds of sugar and knew it was being used for something other than home use. But he bided his time, to turn Jint's pursuits to his own advantage. He was not about to let him, with his big family, leave the plantation—they made up to fifty bales of cotton for him each year. He thought of a scheme to keep him.

Gibbs called the sheriff and told him Jint was drunk from illegal whiskey and Jint was arrested. Right away, Gibbs appeared at the jail and offered to help his sharecropper. At the trial, he was there to hear the judge fine Jint $80. According to the agreement between Gibbs and the judge, the judge reprimanded Jint, Gibbs paid the fine and took Jint back to the plantation to be relegated to harder labor with less pay. For more than a year, Jint did extra work, then took the $80 to Gibbs, who was so surprised that it took him some time to recover. He told Jint that the interest had run the fine up to $250 (which of course he knew Jint didn't have).

After two more years of hard labor on the farm, Jint was able to pay the full amount, which had now increased to $400, and he wanted to leave. Gibbs had to think of another way he could get Jint into trouble. He talked to a neighbor, whose sharecroppers were friendly with Jint's family, and made a deal with him. The neighbor in turn made a deal with one of his blacks. The plan was to invite Jint to a Saturday night party, where they knew he would drink and perhaps clown around. The neighbor's sharecropper would pick a fight with Jint and the officers would again arrest him. The plan worked. Jint was accosted and teased and provoked, and at first he walked away because he didn't want trouble. But when the other black followed him, saying he would kill him, Jint pulled out a knife and cut him with it. Within a few minutes, the officers arrested both of them and charged Jint with assault with intent to murder. Back to court went Jint, thrown on its mercy and that of the landlord.

The judge said, "You are charged with assault with intent to murder. What ails you, Boy? You've been up here before and you just can't keep out of trouble." While he talked to Jint, he was looking at Gibbs and winking. "I'm going to put you where you can stay out of trouble. I'm going to give you seven years at hard labor, and that will keep you for a while."

Jint felt he was doomed for life, but just then Mr. Gibbs whispered to the judge, who now said, "Now, Boy, Mr. Gibbs here says you got a whole pen full of children and you need to be with them. Tell you what I'm going to do. I'm going to suspend your sentence and put you on probation. Do you have any money?" "No, sir," said Jint. "Well," continued the judge, "Your landlord, Mr. Gibbs here, will pay your fine and I will release you to him. Now you go back to the farm and behave yourself. Don't get into any more trouble, and work hard." Jint left the courthouse with his landlord, sentenced along with his family to a punishment far worse than slavery, for it looked now as though he would never get out of debt.

Jint and his family were finally released from this ungodly punishment, but not through the generosity of their master, Gibbs. When the old style of farming (with mules and ploughs) became obsolete, Jint and his family became a liability. The government permitted the owner to put his land in the soil bank, and later Mr. Gibbs died. The old worn-out farm implement, giant Jint, was now a liability, and was set aside without a penny. He left the farm and through the goodness of relatives in one of the Northern ghettoes, he went to make a living for his family. He knew very little about reading and writing and the same is true of his older children, but his younger children still have a chance—a ghetto chance.

On another plantation about fifteen miles from Selma, there was a large number of sharecroppers who never saw the cash that the cotton brought. The owner always called them together after the crops were in and gave each person who was head of his house a good lecture and a few dollars. The owner happened to be a doctor, and any tenant who was ill had to report to him. If the doctor thought the black was ill, he would give him a few pills and send him home to get well over the weekend, and be prepared to start work early Monday morning.

Maria was a small, frail woman I had known since I first came to Selma. She had been ill a long time and had gone to her doctor-landlord for treatment. She had lived on that plantation all her life and she came to me very much frightened. She didn't know what to do and feared for her life, as she had been told she was a liability.

After she was able to talk without sobbing, she said, "I was pickin' cotton and I wasn't able to keep up with the others, when the straw boss come over to fin' out why I so slow. I tole him I was sick and had been to the doctor, but his medicine hadn't he'ped me. The doctor, he operated on me, but the place he cut me never healed. I went back to him so much until he got mad with me and tole me not to come no more. I owed him a big bill and I was too sick to work it out, but I had to go back. At first, he passed by me and wouldn't say nothing. When he was ready to close his office, his nurse came out and tole me I had to go. Next day I went again and he came out to the waiting room and asked me what was wrong. I tole him my side was hurtin' and the place was still bleedin'. Instead of tryin' to do somethin' for me, he tole me to go home and stick a corncob in my side, and he pushed me out of his office and said don't come back."

I was dumbfounded and said he must have been joking.

But Maria said he was not joking and he was angry with her for not being able to produce the amount of cotton she used to. She was once the fastest picker on the plantation— nearly 400 pounds a day.

All this was bad enough, but another great shock was to come. Maria said, "Everybody knows the doctor gave me a botch operation and he won't wait on me. He knows I don't have no money to go to another doctor, and no way to go even if I did. No one else would take me because everyone is scared of that doctor. He tole me to go home and lie down and die, because I wasn't going to live anyway."

Maria said that a few days after the doctor had pushed her out of his office, Tom Brown, who lived on the other end of the plantation, told her that the doctor had offered him $10 if he would take Maria down to the river and drown her.

We were able to do something about Maria. She needed medical attention right away, and we asked churches and individuals to raise money for another operation. We soon had her in the hospital, and after proper care, she recovered.

CHAPTER 4

The Bogue Chitto Community

Every man is the architect of his own
fortune. —Apius Claudius

In the west central part of Dallas County, there is a tract of land, more than 6,000 acres, owned and operated by blacks. Much of this land was inherited from parents, grandparents, and others who acquired it after the days of slavery. Its Indian name, Bogue Chitto (locally pronounced Boga Chitta) means big creek, after a river whose course begins in Mississippi.

Most of the land in this section can grow cotton in abundance if heavily fertilized. It is also dairy land where many grasses can be raised for hay. Now that the price of cotton has fallen to less than $100 a bale (and it costs almost that much to produce it), the people of the community raise only a fraction of their former output. It is all they can do to pay the taxes on the place. They are determined not to sell any of the land, because they look forward to having a township some day and to selling plots for homesteads.

During Reconstruction days, almost every man 21 years of age and over in Bogue Chitto was a registered voter and took pride in voting, because at that time blacks there held political office, even that of deputy sheriff. But in the 1940s, there were fewer than 200 registered black voters in the entire county.

All that remained of a once-thriving community was an old school building, the site of a once-active cotton gin, and what was left of a once-flourishing grocery store. All told, it was the story of a people who retained independence at heart and who had kept their land. The community was hospitable and its warmth seemed to radiate even from the vacant buildings, as surely as from the hearts and homes of its citizens.

The blacks elsewhere called the place "Freetown." At a time when blacks of surrounding communities were so restricted that they could not go off the plantation to town until Saturday, especially when the crops were growing, the Bogue Chitto citizens were free to move about as they willed. They educated their children, but had to send them away to get jobs. They were proud of their ownership, receptive, and willing to follow the guidelines of any program introduced to better the community. The leaders of the community worked to get some type of food distribution project, long before the federal government offered any kind of relief.

After Reconstruction, they had been cheated out of their right to vote. I had that story directly from a white man. I went one day to the office of the statistician of Dallas County to get some information, but I sat nearly an hour listening to this white man, who wanted to talk. The statistician was well acquainted with the local people, and his conversation began and ended with his political activities in that community.

He told me about a sheriff of Dallas County, who had killed blacks "for the heck of it. He killed one in the county and tied him to the running board of his car, and drove through the black section to show what would happen to them if they dared cross his path."

The statistician chortled, "You know, I had charge of all the ballot boxes there until they stopped voting. They were strong voters and we had to do something to keep them niggers from gettin' a lot of offices. So we stuffed ballot boxes and got a little nigger to sneak under the counter and swap boxes we stuffed for the boxes with the real votes. After the voting was over, the little boy brought out the stuffed box, we counted those ballots, and the blacks never knew why they were not re-elected." He gloated over all of this.

I was amazed and too shocked to stop him from talking, so I got the whole story. At last, the conversation turned to my reason for being there, but he was so busy telling me about the past, both personal and in the community, that he brought me the wrong statistics.

Later, I discussed these things with the people in Bogue Chitto. We talked of the wisdom of blacks who bought hundreds of acres of land, the ministers and teachers in the community, the cooperative store and other former enterprises, and the many cunning whites who continued to come to their homes as salesmen, insurance agents, and the like, but the black people had little confidence in them. Like a thorn in their flesh, there were always reminders of the cheating, the swindling, the mistreatment, and the disenfranchising of their forefathers and their relatives. The grandparents of many of the present citizens had been slaves on the ground they now own.

Among my richest experiences in the early 1930s were the visits I had with a woman, who had been brought from Sierra Leone in Africa at the age of twelve, in the 1860s. Aunt Sally remembered many things about her native land. Sometimes she would speak in her mother tongue, which only her daughter and some of her grandchildren understood. Aunt Sally was living in the same hut she was placed in when she was brought to America and Dallas County, Alabama.

One summer afternoon, Aunt Sally asked me to keep her company before the crowd gathered for my monthly club meeting. The yard in which we sat was immaculate. Flowers were painted in circles surrounded by half-buried bottles in geometrical formation. Our seat was a board attached to two old trees.

Aunt Sally lived in a tiny one-room-and-kitchen hut, which stood a few yards from the old picket fence, made perhaps by her husband many decades ago. The hut was dark inside, though the sun shone brightly. There were front and back doors just large enough for an average man to squeeze through, and two windows with shutters half open. One could see the walls of the front room plastered with newspaper to hide the dark boards. I asked Aunt Sally how she got the paper to stick on so neatly. She told me she used flour and water and, to keep the roaches and mice from eating it, she added a bit of blue stone (copper sulfate) to the paste. I remembered that the county agent had told me I could learn a lot from these people.

Aunt Sally predicted, "We are going to have much rain real soon."

"How do you know?" I asked.

She pointed to several patches of clouds. "Yesterday's sunset, last night's moon, and the clouds always tell me what we're going to have." She went on, "You know what the moon bring us? Not what you call a lady all the time. She do lot controlling. Moon come up, big and full, then she get fuller, then she get down. She take all she can from earth's surface and us. Then she turns this way and that way. When you see her ends up, she's full of water and on her back. Soon much rain come, she let it out and keep on 'til she point to the earth. Then her cup is empty and upside down and start picking up more water. The sun help too, picking up much water the moon drop."

Smiling and rocking, she pointed to the cat. "See cat? Look at her eyes. The moon, the water, the sun, all got something to do with cat's eyes. You tell it by the size of cat's eyes. Now they're big, big and round. We always tell when tide is coming in in Africa."

The conversation was so interesting that I secretly wished not to be disturbed, even for a club meeting. I tried to get in as many questions as I could each time I talked to her, for she was the only person I had ever met who came directly from Africa to be sold as a slave. Recovering from her version of the activity of the solar system, I asked, "How did you happen to get here in this section of America?"

"I couldn't help myself," she said. "Africa is my home. White man took it from us. They made animals out of us." Tears began to stream down her face as she spoke of her long years of separation from her native land, her family, and the trials and trouble she had experienced in America. In Africa, she continued, "my father was chief. I lived in clean village; I was much happy. My people weave cloth from grass, bathe in sunshine and river, no fights, no beatings, no killings. We live together like one family. White man bad with bad habits. He telling lies, lies, lies, whipping my husband, tell me to steal.

"Something went wrong in the village, but I didn't know what it was. People walked around shaking their heads, wringing their hands and crying." She spoke of her father in her native tongue. Then she went on in English. She said other tribal chiefs came to their village and there was much talking, everyone seemed sad, and finally the whole village was on fire. She was taken away and believed at the time she was being rescued from the fire.

Her eyes narrowed. "I ran, but they caught me. I fought, but they beat me. I didn't know what they was saying, but it wasn't good. They put me on big ship with many people, some of my own tribe. We stay on boat many weeks, don't know how long, but might be a year. We couldn't walk about boat because chains was on our feet. Baby was born, mother threw him out to the fishes.

"I was sick, oh, so sick, I could die, and I wanted to die. Much people die around me and flies cover their face. White man come down and make black men pick 'em up and throw 'em over in the water. When we got to Virginia we walk around while boat was cleaned out. We had no toilet so it was dirty and the smell was enough to kill you. White men, yes, many white man with whip and stick keep us from going off boat. Boat cleaned out, 'Go back down,' they say. Boat left Virginia with more slaves taking the place of dead ones.

"I change boats, we sail again. More water, more dead ones. All the days was dark on the ship and when we got to Mobile, we got off ship with same chains on our legs. White men and other slaves took us off boat and tied us out to eat grass. Along with this they gave us ground corn with water and they gave me a man. I was twelve years old and he was a man from another tribe who had a family in Africa. I couldn't understand his talk and he couldn't understand me. He came from South Africa. They put us on block together and sold us for man and wife. We came to the Quarles plantation in this place called Bogue Chitto and here is where I been ever since. The slave masters and overseers beat us for every little thing when we didn't understand American talk. Overseer bad master, want to beat all the time. My husband, he good man, wise man."

She told me how her husband had used his wisdom to keep up with the cotton he sold. She said even after slavery her husband was a sharecropper and raised much cotton. He found that his cotton bales were not being counted correctly, but what the correct method of counting was, he did not know. He began to keep up with the number of bales by putting a grain of corn in a jar each time he took a bale to the white man's gin. At the end of the gathering season, he would not ask the plantation owner how much cotton he had made; he would get someone to count the grains of corn he had laid aside and tell the planter that he had so many bales ginned.

Aunt Sally and her husband gave to America one daughter, seven grandchildren, and many great-grandchildren, a number of them teachers in the public schools, and ministers, laborers, and housewives.

Tuskegee Institute once provided Aunt Sally a joyful moment of poignant memories. Foreign students from all over the world came to the United States, and black visitors were always sent to Tuskegee by the federal government for

courses or training in various industries, especially agriculture. In turn, Tuskegee sent them to observe the method
used by the farm and home demonstration agents. As Dallas
County offered varieties of farming, visitors from abroad
came frequently to us. In 1936, my husband had a visit from
a former Tuskegee classmate—Daniel Kato, from Sierra
Leone, Africa. We took him to meet Aunt Sally, and they
began to talk about Africa in general. Suddenly she
screamed with delight; the two of them were from the same
tribe! This was the first time she had met anyone from Africa
who could speak and understand her language since she
had left her home more than 80 years before. She was filled
with joy.

As they talked about their country, the village, the nearby
rivers, speaking many times in their own language, I sobbed
aloud with happiness for her. This African woman could
not forget her native land and she was never free, though
she knew she was emancipated.

However, Aunt Sally lived in a fearless community, and
she had witnessed many brave acts of its citizens. Less than
50 years ago, one of the Bogue Chitto men refused to doff
his hat to a white man and to say, "Yes, sir." When he went
home, he told his neighbors that some white people were
coming to lynch him. The men got together and that night,
took all the ammunition they had and went to the threatened
man's home to wait. The Ku Klux Klan did not disappoint
them. They appeared out of the darkness and burned a
cross near the man's house. As they approached, the Klans-
men were met with a rain of bullets. They ran in all directions and never since have they visited Bogue Chitto.

Ministers played a very important part in politics in Dallas
County, especially in Bogue Chitto. Many of them did not
know how to read or write, but they had someone read the
Bible to them. Others, with some assistance of day school
teachers, taught themselves. Ordinarily, it was easy for the
white man to indoctrinate the blacks, because he could
read and his interpretation of the Bible was always in favor
of white supremacy. But this was not so in Bogue Chitto.

The ministers made it part of their sermons each Sunday to instill in the youth the importance of becoming registered voters when they reached the age of 21. Their text would be "Repent ye, for the kingdom of Heaven is at hand. Register and vote and pay your vows to the Lord." The youth crowded the church and looked forward to the day when they too could become deputy sheriffs or other officers. How many times have such hopes been dashed through such schemes as that related by the statistician!

Blacks who wanted to do something and gain any sort of power had to leave the area and find other places to work. They moved to Birmingham, to New York, to Ohio, and Florida in hopes of better circumstances. Bogue Chitto thus lost many of its youth and its enterprises. Some of the young people now want to come back and make Bogue Chitto what it should be. With a population of approximately 2,000 and with energetic leaders, the citizens want to see it become a township with its own post office and shopping centers. They want the right to have their own city officials. They worked hard to get the Right to Vote bill; now they want to exercise this right to build up the community.

The people of Bogue Chitto gave solid cooperation when the other blacks of this county were struggling for the vote. Bogue Chitto was one of the few places, as early as the early 1940s, that opened its church and school doors for political meetings and for places to teach people how to fill out applications to vote. Here, at least, the people had a heritage from the days when their forefathers did hold political positions. Community leaders made many trips to Selma, the county seat, to register, and they taught others. But the forms, even though correctly filled out, would be turned down by the board of registrars. They were often the first in line to register, even after driving 20 miles to get there. They were among the first groups to march for freedom and the first to go to jail.

CHAPTER 5

Race and the 'Christians'

Men resemble the gods in nothing so much
as in doing good to their fellow creatures.

—Cicero

During the Great Depression, money was almost obsolete, especially when the banks of Selma were given a currency known as scrip. Some blacks were working for as little as $1 a week. Our family at that time consisted of five: Bill and I, our two sons Bill, Jr. and Bruce, and Leathia, a young lady who had lived with me before my marriage. We tried to help her go to college. With only the income from my husband's salary, we knew it would be impossible to keep Leathia in college, but we were willing to pay for a semester and ask the president of Tuskegee to put her on a five-year plan and let her work her way through.

But the school's five-year program was filled and Leathia could not be accepted on any plan. However, Dr. F.D. Patterson, Tuskegee president, said he had been asked to send a girl to work at the governor's mansion in Montgomery. If we thought Leathia could do the work, he would recommend her. We said we thought she could work in any capacity and a year's work would give her enough money to enter school.

Next morning, we took this very competent young lady to Montgomery. She was accepted right away, but instead of the duties described to her, those of supervising the housework in the mansion, she had to do or assist in all the work. The governor's wife gave orders and the black servants obeyed.

One morning, there was to be a large delegation of important guests coming in for dinner, and Leathia rose early and made all the necessary preparations for the big event. She felt very proud of her work, but it soon became evident that taking such initiative and responsibility was not to be tolerated by the governor's wife. Leathia said she thought that since it was "only a matter of hours before the guests would arrive. . . ." The governor's wife stopped her and said, "*You* thought? Who are you? You are not supposed to think; you are a nigger, and hereafter I am to do the thinking here." She ordered things put back in place, although less than an hour later she returned and directed Leathia to arrange things exactly as she had done earlier.

One weekend, Leathia came home sick at heart. She said she had had enough of it and was filled with revulsion at the disrespect and vulgarity of many of the guests. It is ironic that black women have to fight viciously to keep from being attacked and raped by the same white men who hate blacks. She had an awful time fighting off many of the white men, who sought "night-time integration." She was told by one of the older helpers that this was a common custom of the guests. With this and the disgusting conversation at the table after dinner, Leathia had left, never to return.

She said the entire group of visitors, including the governor, discussed the highlights of the day. After they had talked about the boating on the river and the hunting on the reservation, they got the biggest kick out of telling of the final sport at the Kilby prison. As I listened, I, too, felt sick at heart, and wondered what could be done about such ungodly treatment. For these people's enjoyment, some of the blacks were released from prison, and outside the walls in a large area approximately a mile long with no trees, the prisoners had to race hounds to the woods and climb trees to keep from being torn apart.

One man said, "Did you see the big buck running? I

almost cracked my sides laughing when the hound dog grabbed him by the seat of his pants and he finally got up in that little tree." Another said, "That wasn't as funny as when the guard shot at the black nigger and he thought he was hit. When he found he wasn't, he jumped and took to the woods. That was the blackest and runningest nigger I ever saw."

It is fantastic, the lengths to which the "good" white citizens in the Black Belt will go to stop any attempt at mingling of the races, which might put the blacks on an equal footing with the whites. In some sections, white ministers and their fellow Christians have been forbidden to hold meetings with blacks who belong to the same organization. However, this has changed to a great extent since the 1965 civil rights demonstrations.

Until 1968, there was still no white Protestant Christian group that invited a black or a group of blacks to worship with them or take part in their discussions. This was something talked about but never actually done. The only communication across racial lines consisted in giving the darker brother something which made him dependent; this was just about how far most of white Christianity in the Black Belt went. White ministers had always been invited to fill the pulpits of the black churches, and until recently, the black churches had special seats in the front rows for whomever the white visitors might be. Collaboration in an official capacity of white ministers with black Christians in civil rights movements was dangerous, as will be seen in later chapters. However, there was after 1968 an affiliation between the white and black ministerial associations.

During one of the missionary meetings in the Tabernacle Baptist Church, an annual affair for all the missionary groups in the city during the Great Depression, ladies from the white churches were invited. We were happy to see several of them from the downtown churches there, and thought, "How wonderful it is to communicate." Now we would have an exchange of ideas and thoughts.

The first white speaker introduced herself as the president of a downtown church missionary circle and said she was glad to be invited. Then she opened the Bible and began to tell how God cursed Ham and said his children would be servants for his brother's children (Genesis 9:25, obviously misinterpreted). A poised and intelligent black woman informed the white sister that it was not God who cursed Ham, but his father, Noah, who was so drunk at the time that he pulled off all his clothes and slept naked. "However," she went on, "Ham went out of his father's house and settled on the banks of the Nile, where his descendants were among those who handed civilization to the entire world."

After the beautiful explanation of Ham and his father, many questions were asked of the white visitor. Among them was, "My dear white sister, do you think God, who is gracious and almighty, would be a just God if He made me black and you white and then made me to be inferior because of the color of my skin, yet would expect me to do the same things you have to do to get to Heaven?" This question puzzled the white woman, who was disturbed and embarrassed. She said she had never thought of this before.

Another of the white speakers steered clear of the subject of Ham and Noah. As the discussion progressed, the black ladies referred to one another as they did to the white visitors, as Mrs. or Miss. One of the visitors stood and said, "Don't call niggers 'Mrs.' in our presence!" Then, realizing what she had said, she tried to smooth it over with, "You see, it makes us feel much closer to each other when we can say Mary and Sue or Henrietta, so just don't use the word 'Mrs.,' because we want to feel very close in this meeting." Her cover-up, of course, didn't cover at all. But no one asked, although we were all thinking it, "Then may we call you white ladies by your first names?"

The black hostesses handled the situation beautifully and intelligently, by ignoring her statement and returning to the subject of the evening. They continued to address each other as Miss and Mrs. We continued to invite the whites, because the black Christians realized that, somewhere along the line, someone needed to break down segregation, or at least make the attempt, and where better than among Christians and in the churches?

Each year the Selma City Federation of Clubs, part of a national organization, sets a Sunday aside as "Know Your State Day." The program is built around a different subject of national interest each year, and in 1942 it was "Women's Role in Politics." We invited some of the white citizens to participate, because we felt they could give us much information, since they had been in politics for many years. The blacks in Dallas County were still unable to register and vote.

The first white speaker began her discussion by talking about the Sunday school lesson for that day, impressing upon the women how important it was to go to Sunday school and church every Sunday. She ended with, "God wants you to be good servants. He said in his Bible, 'Servants, obey your masters.' "

The federated group of black women looked at each other and smiled, realizing that the white guest either misunderstood the purpose of the program or thought all blacks were stupid and ignorant. Perhaps it was hard for her to admit to herself that *these* black women were intelligent, educated, experienced, and dignified. She seemed unprepared for this fact.

As usual, when a white visitor saw that the white speaker before her had made an embarrassing mistake in addressing her black audience, the next speaker changed the subject. She chose another avenue of thought, but the object was the same. Her subject: "God loves everybody, but He separated the races."

After her talk, one of the hostesses explained, for the benefit of the white visitors, the purpose of the subject, "Women's Role in Politics," the meaning of the general "Know Your State" program, and the accomplishments of the federation. She then turned to the visitors and told them we were very glad to have them with us and we trusted that their presence in our celebration was fruitful and that they would find a spirit they could take back to their federation. In the future, there would be a real federation of women of all creeds, colors, and denominations.

If there is a people anywhere who is experienced in the Golden Rule or has tried to live a Christian life, either from fear or necessity, it certainly has been the masses of blacks, especially in the South. But the brand of Christianity that many white churchgoers have exhibited in the South is one that can't be found in anyone's Bible. It is unfortunate that those who represent the church organizations and the intelligentsia make such impressions, for we all know that they do not represent the rational thinking of the more Christlike white individuals. Just as blacks vary in their attitudes and beliefs about whites, there are also whites who do not buy the idea of an inferior race.

Almost daily, some employer wastes time trying to impress upon her maid that she is different and, in a way, God's stepchild. Only within the past few years has the black pondered these things in his heart, and decided to speak and think for himself.

A black friend often told me what went on in the white folks' house where she had worked for more than 35 years. One day a neighbor praised Flora for some extra work she had done for her. She said she was going to pray that God would take Flora to Heaven when she died. Flora's mistress interrupted, "Do you think God has niggers in his Heaven? If I thought that God had black niggers up there, I wouldn't want to go." The neighbor lady said, "Why, do you think God has children that he does not love? Blacks are as much human beings and the handiwork of God as we are. He has no prejudice as you and I have, my friend. Certainly blacks will go to Heaven when they die."

The mistress, an important figure in her church, for whose deceased husband a Bible class had been named, replied, "Well, if this is true, I'm through with God and his niggers and his Heaven."

CHAPTER 6

Brainwashed

*There is a limit at which forbearance
ceases to be a virtue.*

In 1936, I had resigned as home demonstration agent to
marry Bill Boynton, and two years later, I began to work
for an insurance company as a debit manager. I needed
someone to help in the house and to be at home when my
young son came home from nursery school. The work was
light, because I did most of it myself. I thought it would be
easy to find someone to come in for about three hours a
day, but I was mistaken. Blacks did not like working for
blacks, and many would not do as good a job for them as
they would for a white employer.

I once employed a Mrs. Smith, who seemed to be quite
attached to the family. She lived less than three blocks away
from me, but it was not long before she left us for a job
more than two miles away, although she had to walk the
distance. I asked her what her duties were, and found she
worked in a white home with a mother, father, three children, and an invalid grandfather. She did all the cooking,
cleaning, and some of the washing. She kept that job for
about two years, working for much less than we had paid
her. Finally, the family had to let her go because of financial
hardship. She then came back to me, but it was not long

before she left again, to go to another white family. The last time I saw her, she told me she had to stop working for the lady because the work was too hard, and the husband of the invalid wife, with the wife's consent, expected her to be his mistress.

She was not half as brainwashed as one woman I invited to live with me when I first came to Selma. Mrs. Johnson was very neat and clean and needed a home. She had been washing for a white lady, Mrs. Wilson, and that was her only source of income, which was not enough for her rent and food. She agreed to take over the house and keep it as her own, as I was never there in the day and would not interfere. This she agreed to only if I would let her wash her white folks' clothes.

Mrs. Johnson, though ill many times, never failed to walk at least a mile to get the bundle of clothes (consisting of uniforms for two people working at the hospital and the clothes of two children, 8 and 12.) It never rained too much or was too cold, nor was she ever too sick to go fetch that bundle, which she placed on her head. Sometimes there would be as many as ten uniforms to be washed and ironed. Her pay would be between $1.15 and $1.50 a week. The work began early Monday morning, as soon as she came back from picking up, and the ironing would be completed sometime Wednesday. Usually she was so exhausted after the clothes were finished, that she would be unable to do anything else.

About this time, my mother came to visit me. She said one day, "Mrs. Johnson, why don't you put that big bundle down and get something lighter to do? The work is entirely too hard for you." Mrs. Johnson replied, "Mrs. Platts, this lady has been too nice to me. She gave me a job washing for her when I needed it most. One day, she knew I needed a foundation garment and she knew I didn't have the money to buy it, so she went somewhere and got three of them for me. They were old fashioned, but I sewed the three together and made myself a good corset." Mother told her she would send her $3 a week if she would put the washing down and just rest. But Mrs. Johnson said she would not dare treat Mrs. Wilson like that.

Mrs. Johnson had been born on a plantation in Dallas County, where her father and mother didn't have to think, because the plantation owner did that for them. There were several children in the family, and there were big cotton crops, but they never kept an account of the number of bales, because their "master" was going to take care of them anyway. They never went to school, because their father was told they were doing fine without knowing how to read and write. If they went to school and learned to read, they might read bad things. Mrs. Johnson's father accepted this and thought the white man could never be wrong. Thus, the children all grew up illiterate.

During Reconstruction, the minister was often the black man's only leader. Often he was handpicked by the plantation owner and in most instances, he was the only literate person in the black community. Few of the country preachers attended any of the political and cultural meetings, because they felt it might conflict with what "Mr. Charlie" would like them to teach their congregations. The black minister is content. He has no fear when his church is in the landlord's cow pasture and his flock abides on the plantation. Some of these ministers who have church once a month have been conditioned to take their sermons to the plantation owner before they deliver them. If there is anything in them he doesn't like, they cut it out. The poor backwoods preacher, like a puppet on a string, preaches what he is told to preach.

Early in 1967, I went to one of these churches. Many years ago, I had seen several like it, but I was shocked that such things still existed. It was hard to find even a road that went near the church. I drove about six miles out of Safford in a dairy section, and came upon a huge pasture with a big gate. I opened it and drove in, although I could see no house or any kind of building, but knew the trail must lead somewhere. I finally came upon a clearing in the woods, where stood an old, dilapidated church with its steps falling apart. Inside, the altar was makeshift, the floor had holes large enough to lose a child through, and the benches were homemade from old lumber. They, too, were falling apart, and were very uncomfortable. The minister and his congregation were as ignorant as they could be, but did not seem to know it.

I found that these people were afraid to move the church or to improve it because Mr. Brooks' father, the landowner, had given it to them about 75 years before, and the congregation didn't want to hurt his son's feelings by moving.

There are still many such churches on plantations where the people fear any change. The starvation income, the large farm families, and the poverty-stricken surroundings are all reflected in the shambles called a church. The only things well kept and prosperous on the place I visited were the cattle and the pasture belonging to Mr. Brooks.

Any black who lived in Selma during the 1930s will remember a very ardent white church member, Mr. Frick, we will call him, who practiced his type of Christianity by having a Wednesday night Bible class named in his honor; he was a great Sunday school teacher and a politician. Mr. Frick was at the height of his career during the Franklin Roosevelt administration and he hated anything Roosevelt did for the poor. He discouraged the PWA and the WPA projects coming to Selma and later, at the time of World War II, made it his business to go out of Craig Air Force Base and call a meeting of all heads of families. He told them not to pay the black help any more than $2 a day at the most, and if one had to work seven days, not to pay him more than $10 or $12. Craig Field had been practically donated to the government, in order to bring revenue into the city, but industries were kept out to prevent blacks from improving their lot.

During the Depression, blacks were actually starving, and the only thing that saved some of them was a federal program for the distribution of staple groceries to those in dire need. A minister of the Brown's Chapel AME Church, the Reverend Mr. Hughes, who helped his flock work with any and all government programs, preached on cooperation one Sunday. He explained to his people the importance of being governed and told them to stick with these programs. He encouraged people who were getting as little as $1.25 a week to ask for more money for their labor.

But his sermon reached beyond his black congregation, for someone took it back through the kitchens and back-yards to the white community. It reached the ears of Mr. Frick, who called together some of his henchmen and went into action.

Reverend Hughes was in his study talking to another minister about his sermon and the mounting hostility of the whites, when someone knocked. Mrs. Hughes, suspicious, said he was not there; he had gone to visit one of his sick members. Frick and his men did not believe this, and asked several questions which Mrs. Hughes answered calmly. The three men left and she hastened to tell her husband, who had heard the conversation and wondered what he had said in his sermon that would cause such anger.

The white men had not really left, but had gone around to the back door of the house. This gave the minister a chance to slip through the front into the church, only sec-onds before the bloodthirsty whites followed, stopping only long enough to question the visiting minister. Reverend Hughes hurriedly climbed the dark and narrow steps to the top of the belfry, where he watched the men below. They searched every pew and every room without success, and finally left. Fear gripped Reverend Hughes as he realized what a close call he had had. The men not only had a car, but pistols, a rope, and a knife.

The visiting minister went to the church to persuade Reverend Hughes to let him take him out of town. Reluc-tantly he came down and they got in the car to go to Burns-ville, the other pastor's home. They traveled a dirt road, and the dust and curves in the road and the deep ravine along it were a blessing for Reverend Hughes. Soon the ministers noticed that there was a car behind them, and Reverend

Hughes ducked down to the floor. Then there were two cars, and a third one. They knew that the road was not often traveled by many cars at the same time, so they sensed that it must be a mob. As the cars gained ground on them, they increased their speed. As they rounded a deep curve with steep ravines on either side, the minister suggested to Hughes that he jump out of the car into the thicket, which he did, and rolled down ten or twelve feet below the road. The other minister continued to speed until he reached his church.

He had barely gotten into the church, when the white mob opened the door, and without any ceremony at all, Frick, who was carrying a pistol, asked where Reverend Hughes was. The minister said he had not seen him; he had gone to his house and his wife told him he had gone to visit a sick member.

The white men grabbed him by the collar and demanded that he produce Reverend Hughes. But he swore he had not seen him, whereupon one of the men took the rope and placed it around his neck and told him he ought to string him up instead. The man was sure he was doomed, but he would never tell what had happened to the Brown's Chapel minister. One of the men suggested that they go back to town and search again around the church. They loosened the rope from around the minister's neck and returned their pistols to their belts, then left at last.

Reverend Hughes stayed in the woods during the night. He knew that only God could save his life. Later, he hopped a freight train and left the region forever. Many of his members wondered about him, but he dared not write or speak of his whereabouts for fear the bloodthirsty mob might lynch him anywhere. Other friends got in touch and helped his wife to join him. Many years later, word came to Selma that he was pastoring a big church in a large city.

CHAPTER 7

The 'Old Days' Won't Do

Many people live in ghettos. The ghetto
does not have to live in them.

Not far from Selma, there was a large plantation which included a store and a small cafe. This was the only store in the community and whites gathered there to talk about their problems, to play checkers, and swap jokes, but always the conversation turned to "my niggers." Some of the tales were gruesome, some were jokes about the field hands, but most dealt with how to keep them on the plantation and of the fear of an uprising against the landlords, who knew the blacks were becoming restless in Selma and elsewhere in the South.

The cafe on the Calvin plantation was operated by one of the black tenants known as "Mr. Calvin's boy." The building had no paint, no steps except cinder blocks, and the walls were bare weatherboarding with bare rafters above. The only bright spot was a brilliantly colored juke box. The cafe was a gathering place for the blacks.

Some new tenants had just come to the plantation—Jim White with ten children, all large enough to work in the fields. Jim was an unusually tall man, with searching eyes and a determined look that showed he would take no foolishness. Calvin was not sure that Jim was the right person for his place, although he needed more help. He had heard that Jim was eager to give his children a chance to go to school and later find work in the city, and this did not please him. Jim's eldest daughter told me the following story.

Calvin, after spending some time at the commissary with his friends, strolled into the dark and dingy cafe soon after Jim White's family came to work for him. The juke box was playing very loudly and the blacks were talking at the top of their voices to be heard above it. When Calvin entered, their voices ceased, the group broke up and stepped aside, and the cafe operator walked over and cut off the music. All the men doffed their hats and caps and some began to grin. Jim White, the new man, looked from one to another and wondered what was wrong. Calvin, in khaki trousers and shirt, hightop boots, and a Texas ranger hat, ambled around the room with fingers stuck in his belt and a wad of tobacco in his mouth, which he kept tossing from one side of his jaw to the other. The blacks made no sound and did not move.

Calvin had come on what he considered an errand of "good will" for good employer-employee relations. He spat a mouthful of tobacco juice and drawled, "Now you all, you boys who have been here a long time, you know me. I always tell a newcomer I want you boys to get along. I want you to tell Jim what a landlord I am. I don't take no foolishness, but I'll go all out to help you boys if I can, if you get in trouble. I want you all to be good boys and work hard."

Looking at the oldest man in the group with a sly smile, he continued, "Now just look at Uncle John over there. Stand up there, Uncle, and let the folks see you." John, bent from work rather than age, forced himself to stand straight and began to grin to please Calvin. Calvin said, "Now John, he's been here since before my father was born. In fact, he was born here. His old grandmammy and pappy came here from Africa to work for my great grandpa." Trying to figure the number of years in his head, he hesitated a little, then said, "That was, lemme see, over 100 years ago. Yes, over a 100 ago. All of 'em was the best farmers for miles around and my folks was proud of 'em."

He continued to entertain the blacks with his family history and particularly the family property—the blacks—and said, "Why, I remember hearing how John's father made up to 60 bales of cotton. He was living in the same house you are living in, Uncle John. I've never had a minute's trouble with Uncle, never had to move him in no other house either. Most of all these young boys kin say Uncle John is their pappy." Calvin leered around the room to force a smile from his listeners, who started snickering. "He ain't never spent a night in jail either. Been arrested a couple of times for a shootin' and knifin' spree, but I got him out of it, didn't I, Uncle?" John hung his head and said, "Yas sir, boss, you shore did."

Calvin had arranged for Uncle John to get a welfare check, all the while posing as his benefactor. He had told one of the other men, "Uncle John has been my good nigger and I want to do something for him. Take him to the welfare officer tomorrow and tell the folks to put him on the welfare and call me. I'll fix up any papers for him. He never knowed his age, but I guess he is nigh onto 80."

In due course the old man had received a welfare check, but he had to take it to Calvin's store to have it cashed. "Now, Uncle," Calvin had said, "Bring your check every month for me to cash. Let's see, I advanced you the money to get ready to go to town for the check, that's got to come out; you owe for groceries and that's got to come out." He had looked cunningly at John and said, "Don't mean to break you." He then took the check, looked at it, handed Uncle John a pen and said "Just make a mark right here, John, and I will write your name for you. You know you owe me a lot of money from your old debts. I been going along with you till you could do better. I'll just take out a small amount each month until you pay it all back. Ain't I good to you, Uncle John?" The old man had said, "Yessir, Boss, thank ya." He then had hobbled out, back to his old dingy two-room shack—with the few remaining dollars allowed him.

Calvin set himself up as a most merciful provider and told all the blacks what he had done for John. He told John he could get everything he wanted out of the store and said, "I'll stand by you all as long as you're good workers and do a good job. You know we all got to work for a living and we don't want no trouble around here. We don't argue wid 'em and we don't take no foolishness either. You just stay in a nigger's place and everything will be all right."

Jim White, the new sharecropper, who had felt contempt for the plantation owner at the first sight of him, was so disgusted he spat on the floor. He was mostly disgusted with the blacks, who thought, or at least acted as if they thought, this white man could do not wrong. Jim made up his mind that he would stay there long enough to make a crop and then would leave the minute he could get away.

What in the world could the children of these slaves (in mentality) do when they left the plantation? They cowered in their shacks and the only partition between them and hell was their landlord.

Joan, Jim White's daughter, was 21, and the eldest child. She left home that year and came to town to get a job. She said there was no such thing as having sheets to sleep on unless they used the fertilizer sacks. There was only one room with a curtain made from feed sacks for a partition. Joan swore she would not live on the Calvin plantation any longer than she had to, for Calvin was a hard and cruel man. She had never had an opportunity to go any further than the third grade. She had heard people refer to her family as "that set of fool children who are too dumb to get out of the rain." She never had any kind of training except to chop and pick cotton.

It was 1964 when Jim White went to that plantation, the year the Student Nonviolent Coordinating Committee (SNCC) sent representatives to Selma and even to that farm to help free the blacks from the pressures they had been subjected to for years. Jim's children demonstrated for free-

dom and helped in their own way to teach the older blacks
how to fill out registration blanks. Their father encouraged
them. Finally the owner found that Jim's children were
helping other blacks and Jim White and his family were
discharged.

CHAPTER 8

How Ridiculous Can You Get?

*No man can put a chain about the ankle of
his fellow man without at last finding the
other end fastened about his own neck.*
— Frederick Douglass

In our fight against segregation, we encountered so much hatred and hostility, as well as fear, that just recounting some of the stories will give the reader a sense of how diabolical and insidious segregation of the races is. No one can justify it, though many try. There are many who in the past have discriminated against blacks and now look back and wonder at the crazy pattern they have woven and why they were so deadly at it.

During World War II, my husband was asked to handle the black division of the U.S. Bonds drive for the county. He knew the various sections well, and organized each beat and appointed a large number of chairmen, so that almost every adult black was personally involved, and many of them bought bonds. Bill would report the bonds to the bank.

One day in 1943, Bill was asked to attend a bond drive in Selma. These were held weekly in the auditorium of the white school. The white officials told him to bring some of the other blacks to the school because there would be seats for them. My husband was accustomed to being segregated, but he said he would come to one of the meetings. Perhaps, we thought, this was a chance for a breakthrough.

Bill and I and our neighbor, Mr. Reid, arrived at the school
in the midst of a whirlwind of white citizens rushing to get
a seat. We stood and wondered in what direction we should
go, and a white official finally came to us and put us at ease
(we thought) when he said the committee for the bond drive
was looking for us, but he asked us to remain outside until
a guide came for us. He disappeared and it was almost five
minutes before another man came and told us we were
certainly welcome, but he too disappeared among the
crowd in search of one white official who would be so
liberal as to escort us inside. Eventually, a third white man
came, asked us to follow, and led us to what seemed to be
a passage of solid darkness. It must have been a secret
passage or a separate exit for the black janitors. Amazed,
angered, and somewhat frightened, I began to revolt. I had
no idea where we were being taken and I didn't like entering
this passage, which seemed to be at the mouth of hell. But
there was no turning back because there was no room to
pass; I was sandwiched between the two men. No one
spoke, and we slowed our pace because we could not see
a single thing—we held to the wall and felt our way forward.
The white leader pulled out a flashlight and said, "This will
give a little light. We don't have so far to go now, but be
careful. . . . Now here's a little step up."

Where in the name of God was this white man taking us?
Was it to a mob crowd? My mind jumped to what course I
would take if this were true. Then I said, "I don't know what
you are going to do, but I'm turning back."

Just then, a door opened and a streak of light hit the face
of the white leader and we found ourselves in the annex
attached to the main platform of the auditorium. This was
a bleak and dismal section, unrelated to the auditorium
itself. The leader found the lights to this annex and then
returned saying, "You all can sit right here." In front of us
were three thick stage curtains that muffled the sound as
well as cut off the sight from the main auditorium. The white
man said, "You won't be able to see because of the curtains

but you'll be able to hear all right. Just don't make any noise."

As he left, my husband said, "I'll be damned." I said, "Let's go from this place before the KKK grabs us. This is an insult and I refuse to take it." Things were getting quiet in the auditorium and we began to whisper. I sat between the two men and we began to figure out where the exit was and the best way to make our escape. Suddenly a cub scout appeared, another, then another, and soon there were at least six of them (all white of course).

Wondering what these youngsters were going to do, I stopped thinking of our escape. They too could not see the main auditorium or hear clearly what was going on, but they were much braver than we were, for they walked to the ends of the rostrum and began to peep from behind the curtain. They were not as quiet as we were and their moving the curtains back and forth caused the guests on the rostrum to be annoyed and they began to look around as their little heads popped out.

The distinguished guest speakers were Congressman Sam Hobbs and Eddie Gilmore, an Associated Press reporter back from the U.S.S.R. I would have liked to hear what was being said, but not at the price of sitting unseen in the back. One of the scouts dropped or knocked down a heavy object, and this startled the platform guests. Congressman Hobbs rose and asked the attendants to raise the curtains and let the boys see and hear. "Open the curtains wide," he said. "Why keep our boys in the dark? They are our men of tomorrow and our destiny will be in their hands. Open the curtain and let them see. We cannot justify our cause by keeping the youth hidden from the truth."

There was a long pause, seemingly for many minutes after Mr. Hobbs spoke, which gave me time to think. Mr. Reid, our companion, said to me, "Now, aren't you glad you didn't leave?" Then there was a rustling of the curtains, a flood of lights from the main auditorium, and a large congregation in front of us. Here were three surprised African-Americans sitting on the platform less than four feet from the main speakers.

I heard someone in the audience say, "We've been tricked," but we paid no attention. This was the first time black guests had had the opportunity to be on the same rostrum with Selma's white citizens. A beautiful backlash. I was proud to break down segregation.

Naturally, there were cameramen from many of the newspapers and magazines. They tried their best to take pictures of the guests and they turned their cameras at every angle possible, but at none of them could they take a picture without getting one of us in it. It was customary for the newspaper to carry detailed accounts of the bond drives, with pictures to encourage the next week's drive to be even bigger. But this time there was no picture in the papers, and no one who did not attend the meeting could enjoy or deplore the involuntary integration on the platform.

Once when I needed a new stove, my husband checked several places and found one at the Alabama Gas Corporation that he thought would suit me. A salesman telephoned and said, "Amelia, this is Mr. S. Your husband told me you need a stove, and I have the very thing you need."

I resented his calling me by my first name. The Southern whites don't think blacks ever grow up; they are either Mary or John, Preacher or Uncle. I hesitated before answering Mr. S., because I had not met him, and his calling me by my first name sounded disrespectful. When I got my thoughts organized, I said, "Oh, Mr. S., when you first saluted me by my first name, I thought you were my brother or a very close friend of the family. I know you are a businessman, but I only do business with people who put a title to my name." Mr. S. laughed and for the rest of the conversation, he called me Mrs. Boynton. I said I would come down and see the stove.

I also needed a refrigerator, and when Bill and I went to the gas company, we selected one in addition to the stove. The bill would come to a little more than $1,000. Mr. S. was pleased with the sale and gave us papers to sign. After Bill signed, Mr. S. handed me the pen and I smiled and bent over to sign also, but just then Mr. S. said, "Sign right here, Amelia." I continued to smile, stood erect, gently handed the pen back to him, and said, "Suppose you take the contract and put it up. My husband and I will talk it over and if we decide to get the refrigerator and the stove, we will call you. You will not have to call me again." We walked out.

We decided not to trade with the company that did not give enough respect, and I went back to my office. In a little while, Mr. S. visited me there and said he had forgotton to tell me that the stove he was selling was the best bargain anywhere; its oven baked, stewed, fried, and broiled. As he talked, I was making up my mind what step I should take to impress upon him my reason for not signing the contract.

"Won't you have a seat?" I said politely, and he sat down opposite me. I permitted him to talk until he ran out of words, before saying, "Mr. S., do you remember the first time you called me at home and I told you I preferred being called either just 'customer' or being addressed with my title? What I said then still stands."

Mr. S. stood up and said, "If you mean I should call you Mrs., I'll never do it." This did not alarm me, but only gave me the opportunity to express myself. I said, "I didn't ask you to call me 'Mrs. Boynton,' Mr. S. I know you have never been taught to respect people whose faces are not the same color as yours. I tried to impress upon you that you call me customer or A.P., but not my first name. You call us by our first names because you want to impress upon us that, in your sight, we never think beyond a child and I resent this, for I am fully grown and I do business as any other grown person does. And if you don't respect me personally, Mr. S., I still demand that you and all other merchants respect the dollars we spend at your company." Mr. S. began to turn and twist as though he were trying to find a way out, but I was not through with him.

He was defensive. "My company respects all people." Then he said, "We don't separate your money; we put all of it in the same place." At least he was confronting the fact that he was prejudiced except when it came to money. I thought of the commission he would have gotten, and I said, "You are a very unwise man. If you had been wise, Mr. S., you would have waited until I signed the contract before calling me anything. That error just pulled more than $250 out of your pocket, but that isn't all. I will inform my friends of your discrimination." Then I opened the door for him and said, "Good day, Mr. S."

Later, I was arranging to buy a stove from another dealer, and the manager said he would send someone out to show me how to use it. I did not need this information, but since the demonstrator was to come from the company where I had refused to buy, I suggested that he send Mr. S. on the afternoon I was to have my club meeting, and I would certainly use my influence to sell his appliance. However, they sent a lady demonstrator.

It was not my intention to get even with Mr. S., but only to make him and others realize that blacks can demand consideration by withdrawing their trade. Since that time, several businesses that refused to respect blacks have gone out of business in Selma.

Merchants of the Black Belt have yet to respect the many dollars they receive from the black community. As much as they hate or hold contempt for the blacks, they will pretend to respect a black person only if he demands it by threatening to withdraw his business. The blacks are beginning to be more courageous in dealing with such merchants, and they are being treated with more politeness. The white man has begun to realize that courtesy doesn't hurt anyone, but there are still those who would die before they would show such deference, and literally their livelihood may depend upon this. Then there are many who will give the blacks courteous service, but raise the price of services or commodities as though to compensate for the damage to their egos.

In the 1950s, a carload of Norge appliances was shipped into Selma to be sold at the old Southern Railroad station.

Ads were broadcast and printed in the papers for several days. As we owned Norge appliances, we wanted to go down to the demonstration and take my mother, who was visiting us. When we arrived, we saw no blacks, only whites. We were intercepted by an officer, who told us we could not come into the demonstration; it was for whites only. My mother had never actually been subjected to this sort of segregation before and she was humiliated. She wanted us to leave the town where the equipment you buy was too good to look upon. Less than a month later, a Norge salesman came to my house to sell some appliances, but he didn't get to first base. I took the occasion to tell him how self-defeating discrimination was and how it hurt his pocketbook much more than it did ours.

The Alabama State Fair held annually in Birmingham was one of the state's largest. Exhibits came from most of the counties and included many related to home economics and farming. These were our fields and wherever we heard of the latest methods being demonstrated, we tried to be there.

Our family drove into Birmingham and we went first to the building set apart for black exhibits. There were crowds of blacks and a few whites viewing them. We hunted up the science exhibits, for our son Bill, Jr. was showing a definite trend in this direction. We saw everything in the building and then walked toward a larger one. The farther away we got, the fewer blacks we saw, until we were far into white territory, where it was evident that no blacks dared go. The white people eyed us as though we were strange creatures from another world. We saw not a single black person, except those cleaning up behind the animals.

Of course, Bill and I had attended many fairs in Montgomery, but we never had a chance to visit the "white" buildings, because we had been so busy working with our 4-H people and exhibits. Here in Birmingham, with the leisure to see everything, we didn't realize at first that we were getting on dangerous ground.

I suggested to Bill that we should leave, but he was so

intent on gathering knowledge, that he was not observing how "far out" we had gotten. Then we came to a sign which read "white only." We had the children with us, and we made an attempt to get some sandwiches, only to be told that blacks could not buy there. We noticed the piercing eyes of a policeman whom we had seen when we first entered the building, but being law-abiding citizens, we thought we had no reason to fear.

We came to the amusement park, where we had heard there was a section for blacks, but we found no black section and no blacks on the grounds. The same officer followed us during our entire tour through the white section; each move we made he scrutinized as though we were convicts. Finally he came to us and asked, "Whar you-all goin'?" We told him we were looking for the black amusement park. He told us there was none, and asked us where we were from. When we said Selma, he said, "I thought you-all wasn't from this part of the country, 'cause niggers don't come here where they aren't allowed. Now you-all go right on back on the other side and I advise you to leave and leave damn quick." We did not tarry, but went right away into the city to the house of a friend.

There we told of our experience, and as we talked, I became more and more filled with fear, humiliation, and embarrassment. The consolation we received from our friend was, "You don't know Birmingham; you are lucky to be alive. They shoot us down here like dogs, and the law says it's justified."

CHAPTER 9

How Stupid Can You Get?

The evil that men do lives after them. The
good is oft interred with their bones.
— William Shakespeare

After such treatment, I would have sudden fears, then my feelings would change and I would become more determined and hostile toward the segregated system. There was no good reason for the dual system practiced in America, I said, and it would have to end eventually. I was often asked why we were so fearless and different from the other blacks in Selma. The only answer I could give was that we were reared to respect people as people, to realize that all people are alike and color makes no difference. This had been true, up to a point, in Savannah, but in doing business in Selma, I found that the line of demarcation was so obvious between the races, that automatically the blacks felt that they had a place, and they stayed in it.

One summer, I realized that I had not had a thorough physical check-up for quite a while, and I took the advice of a friend to go to her doctor. His office was in one of the old hospitals, with a deep lawn in front. I went in the front door, where the receptionist at first ignored me. As I continued to stand there, she asked what I wanted, and I told her I had come to see the doctor. She said I should go through the back of the building where the colored waiting room was.

I turned to leave, deciding that I didn't want to go to the doctor anyway; I would just wait until one of my own doctors could give me an appointment. As I turned to go down the steps to the street, the receptionist confronted me and said, "Just step this way." Foolishly, I followed her, with the intention of leaving as soon as I reached the colored waiting room. To myself, I was thinking it was such an outrageous thing for blacks to always be put in the back of everything, except the battle front and a few other places where they might be first to be killed.

If I assumed the black waiting room would be comfortable, I was soon disillusioned. The room itself was about fourteen by fourteen feet, with several broken-down chairs, an old settee, and a rusty iron bench. It was August, but there was no fan, either electric or palm leaf. There was one window and a makeshift toilet in one of the corners, with only a beaverboard partition surrounding it, and that only halfway to the ceiling. Here the blacks were to produce urine specimens for the doctor.

I stood looking at the waiting blacks, sweltering in the heat. I was unable to turn around and walk out of the room, because the receptionist was standing in the doorway and asking my name. She asked me to have a seat, and I told her "No, thanks." "What is your name?" she asked. I didn't say anything, because I was thinking what name I should give; it would not be my real name, because her doctor wasn't going to wait on me. Finally, I said, "A.P. Boynton."

"What is the 'A.P.' for?" she asked. I shrugged and said "Just A.P., that's all." She looked at me somewhat unbelievingly and said, "I've never heard of a woman being named only initials before. I've heard of a man." I then said, "If I were to tell you, you couldn't spell it, because no one can spell it and few people can pronounce it." She still insisted, so I said, "My name is Armacarmalatecia Bantinnie Pasyiah Boynton. Now you spell it." She looked me over as though I had been transformed into another species, and said, "That's a Spanish name, isn't it?" I hadn't thought of that before, but I agreed. I had begun life in Savannah with the

Geechee accent, and I felt this was a good time to return to it. Her attitude changed, and she said, "Come this way, Mrs. Boynton."

This time I was so surprised that I followed her to another room, which was cool and had an electric fan, a bed, three windows, and was comfortable. She left and in a moment, the doctor came in. He was smiling and had a pleasant personality. I had decided to play the role of an islander. He said, "How do you feel?" I chopped off my words in calypso style and said, "I yum fine un you?" He looked at me with piercing eyes and seemed to search for questions to ask. Hesitantly, he said, "How did you learn to speak English?" He asked many other questions, among them, "How do you like our country?"

This revealed his ignorance more than anything else. My roots are planted deep, much deeper than any of the white people I knew, what with Indian, black, and white blood in my family tree. "Our country" indeed! It was more *my* country, I thought.

My examination was not very thorough, but I was glad to get it over with. Later, I received an enormous bill for the cursory examination, but the experience was almost worth it—that of making a fool of a segregationist.

Those who remember the Depression of the 1930s know how cheap food was, yet how hard it was to find a job and make a dollar. When the federal government created the Public Works Administration (PWA) and then the Works Progress Administration (WPA), people were kept from starving and the doors opened for young children to get proper food.

A block away from our home, there was a colored nursery school operated by WPA. As we kept a garden and had a farm, we could furnish vegetables and fruit for the nursery children. The supervisor was so grateful for our help, that she suggested we send our eighteen-month-old son to play with the other children. We gladly did this, since I had planned on working; their cooperation made me want to do much more for the school.

A request came to some of the parents and friends to send coal to the nursery, because the building was chilly. I went to one of the coal yards to order a ton. The owner, who was acquainted with my husband, was very talkative. He said, "You and your husband are two unusual blacks." I said, "I am afraid you don't know blacks. There are hundreds of thousands of blacks who are like us. You should meet them. We are just average people."

He was used to telling blacks about their faults, and they were afraid to talk back to him. He said, "Know something about your people? They will steal. I had a boy (a man about 40 years old) who had been working for me for nine years, and the other day, I found that he had two sacks of coal covered up under loose coal, that he had taken for himself. Your people would be all right if they just didn't steal."

Of course, this conversation irked me very much, for I was thinking about the many ways people like him had stolen from the African-American through the years. They've exploited his labor, cheated him legally, arrested him falsely, and made him pay extortionate fines and interest on loans, and in a thousand different ways they have stolen from him. I tried to be calm and retain my poise. I said, "Mr. D., you say my people will steal. I dare to ask how much salary you are paying this Negro, because I am sure you aren't paying him what he is worth. This poor man no doubt has a house full of children to be fed and clothed, but do you care anything about that? I will bet you would pay a young inexperienced white boy far more just to stand and watch the Negro. Furthermore, I understand that you are paying all the blacks together here less than one decent salary. Mr. D., I don't know what you call stealing, but when you work people in your kitchen from seven in the morning until five in the evening, doing all the cooking, cleaning, washing and ironing, and pay them $2.50 and at the most $3 a week, I don't call that stealing, I call it *Robbery* with a capital R." After making this statement, I hurriedly left, before I showed further disgust, and I am sure he was glad to see me leave.

Many blacks have found that not all white people are well educated or intelligent or capable of being the superior of the black man. One day a black man came into my office and laughed and said he had been fired. He didn't seem too perturbed about it, and I asked him why.

He had worked in a small factory whose owner seldom visited it to see how the work was being done; he relied upon the supervisors and the straw bosses. This African-American, who was a junior college graduate, had a straw boss who was white but illiterate. When the reports had to be made and carried into the office, the black man always made the report. Whenever the official wanted to know what was going on, the black man had to figure it out for the straw boss, and even teach him how to present his subject matter accurately.

Finally, there were words between the African-American and the office and the African-American was fired. Then the white straw boss quit. The owner questioned others as to the reason for his leaving, and was shocked and somewhat chagrined to realize he had not known that the white man was illiterate and could not write up a report. Also, that the African-American, although getting a much lower wage, was doing all the paperwork for him. The white straw boss did not want the office to know that he was so ignorant, so he left to team up with the African-American elsewhere.

CHAPTER 10

The Seamy Side
of Selma

The man who has not anything to boast of
but his illustrious ancestors, is like a potato.
The only thing belonging to him is
underground.   —Sir Thomas Overbury

There are many Americans whose color identification is
hidden, and only a search of one's family background
could reveal African blood. The black man—and perhaps
the white man too—runs into much difficulty in the South
trying to identify himself racially.

A friend of ours, like many of the offspring of plantation
and domestic blacks (who mostly think "white is right"),
was a product of "night-time integration." Unlike most such
offspring, he was housed under the same roof as his father.
He had all his father's features and was a pure Southern
white gentleman, with even the superior air and soft Southern drawl. Many times I had met him on the street and he
would say something unusually friendly. My first impression, before we became well acquainted, was, "There is a
white man who is trying to get fresh with me," and I ignored
him. Lots of white men used extreme politeness to woo
black women when they did not get into their homes as
salesmen or insurance agents, and lots of black women
were afraid to say no to a white man. But here was a "black
man" who, although his skin was white, did not cross over
into the white race. His name was Jim Dana.

One day, Jim was having dinner with our family and he

told us about his background. He said his mother was fair-skinned and had had a white father. She lived with her mother in the backyard of the Humes family residence, on one of the better streets in Selma. When her mother died, the family was very grieved, and to compensate for her loss, the family made her the cook. She became pregnant at a very early age by the young son in the family. As she had nowhere to go, they kept her, and when her child (Jim) was born, he too was taken care of. His mother died when he was eight. He lived in the home, learned to read and write, and assumed he was one of the family; in fact, his complexion was somewhat lighter than some of the relatives who visited, and as light as any in the house. As far as he knew, no difference was made between him and the other children, although he was taught to do brick work as a teenager, whereas the other boys took office jobs.

When he was seventeen, Jim's white father said,"Jim, I want you to have a house all your own. If you don't know of one anywhere on the other side of town, I will pay all of the expenses and have one built for you, just as you wish it to be." Thinking that this was very generous of his father, Jim went "beyond the railroad tracks" looking for a house. He didn't find one, so his father found a lot and helped him draw house plans. He never once questioned the reason for his father's arrangements, until he found that his half-brothers were not similarly treated.

While the house was being built, the father informed him that he could stay with them no longer, because he was not one of them. "Son," he said, "you will have to leave our home and find a life on your own. You are a Negro, not a white man, and you are growing into manhood. You must go among your own people, the Negro people." For the first time in his life, Jim realized he was not white. He was grieved in his heart, and did not know which way to turn. But later he married, lived in the house his father helped him build, and became a first-class bricklayer.

One day, he took a job in West Selma in the house of a family with a four-year-old child. While he repaired the chimney, the child came into the living room to watch and ask questions. At noon, Jim told her he would be back after lunch and would sing to her. He expected the child to come back to the living room, but she did not. Later, when her mother was out of the room, she tiptoed in and came up close to him and whispered, "I can't come back in here because my mom said you are a nigger."

The child's father was Jim's grand-nephew, and the house he was repairing was on the property of Jim's grandfather.

Discrimination and segregation have been in Selma in every pattern. Not that Selma is different from any other place in the South, or in the United States, for that matter. The blacks who live here and are affected by this pattern are constantly meeting its unhappy consequences, whereas the whites do not even see it—it has been taken for granted so long. There is no secret about night-time integration, which is more prevalent in the Black Belt than in most places. Those who don't want to hear about it turn a deaf ear, but they might just look around and see the blacks who are not very black and do not have woolly hair.

Some cases of racial mixing are stranger than fiction. There were two black women who had babies fathered by two white men on different plantations. As the children grew up, each of the fathers tried to outdo the other in looking after their black sons. They were sent to boarding high school, then to college. The black sons married and each was given land and cattle by their fathers. The fathers often came to the fine brick houses and talked with their sons, letting them know they could depend on them if they needed help. This is the reverse of what usually happens. Much commoner is the incidence of brutal and inhuman treatment of blacks by whites—cruelty that would curdle your blood.

In 1965, two black employees of one of the local Hill-Burton hospitals told me a story which horrified them so, they jeopardized their destiny to make it known. A blacks-only ambulance had driven up to the "Negro" delivery door and several employees ran to attend the patient, who was then wheeled into the hall. The regular admitting process was completed, for she had the means to enter. Then she was sent into the patients' waiting room. Between the severe pains which racked her body and caused her to speak only in monosyllables, she gave the name of her white doctor, who was summoned. He apparently did not realize at first that he had been summoned for a black patient, although the hospital was supposed to admit black patients in a small segregated wing.

He soon came and found her in an advanced stage of labor. The doctor raged, because he had been called to deliver a black baby. He turned to the help around him, saying, "Who in the hell brought this woman here?" He then had them call the ambulance to take her to a black hospital. The black ambulance then took her away in pain and misery to the all-black hospital.

A black woman came into our office one day and mentioned that her children had a white father. She said that she began to cook for this man, a bachelor, when she was a very young girl. Soon he added a room for her with a walk from it into his house. She had been born and reared on his plantation, and felt she dared not disobey his desires, so she became his mistress. She had several children by him, but she never moved from the one house that the plantation owner had built next to his house. When the children grew large enough to do the chores, the other plantation hands were dismissed. They took their place as soon as they were old enough to follow behind the plow. Their education was limited, as they went to school only three months out of each year.

The planter realized he was growing old and feeble and felt he should do something for his common-law wife. He was quite rich and owned much land. He called her in one day and told her she could have all the young calves that his herd of cows dropped. From year to year, the cattle dropped many calves and the mistress's money increased, as she sold many of them. Though her sons were large enough and perhaps wise enough to put the money away, she gave it to her bachelor-husband-employer and asked him to put it in his large iron safe, because she trusted him and believed he would do the right thing.

Later this man died, and his brother, who despised the mistress and her children, took everything and told the family to move off the farm. Although the children had raised the crops and increased the field, not one foot of land or any livestock was given to them. The money for the calves was taken from the iron safe by the brother, just as he had taken all the rest of the property. There was two generations' worth of labor and an accumulation of money, but the woman and her children had nothing to show for it except age.

During my first few years in Selma, it was a common thing to see the black sons and daughters who had white fathers segregate themselves and express pride in having come from the big plantation owner's overseer, or claiming the owner himself as their father. Not only plantation owners, but white men from all classes, rich, poor, high, and low, can claim to have children who are blacks or blacks who are their mistresses. Nowadays, there aren't as many children born to these mixed couples, but many of the women who live this type of life say it is hard to get away from the white man, even if they want to.

One young woman moved to Selma to get rid of her white lover. Though she had several children by him, she was willing to take them and do her best for them without their father, who had a family and had separated from his wife in order to have the black woman. He had warned her that if she ever tried to leave him, he would certainly kill her. She had been in Selma only a short time when he found where she lived and came after her. He had a pistol and she shielded herself with her ten-year-old daughter, thinking he would not kill his own. Pleading with him did no good. He fired several shots and one hit his daughter, causing her to lose an eye. The police ended the case by saying it was done at the hands of an unknown intruder.

Where is the line of demarcation between the races? Who

is supposed to be white and who is colored? All races are mixed, and both blacks and whites can trace ancestry to the Indians, as well as to other nationalities. There are blacks who are whiter than some so-called whites, and there are whites darker than some blacks. Though many white people in the Black Belt have black children and grandchildren, society has drawn the line to such an extent that the father turns on his own to please that society.

PART III

Steps Toward Economic and Social Justice

We must all hang together,
or assuredly we shall
all hang separately.
—Benjamin Franklin

S.W. Boynton

The ballot is stronger than the bullet.
—Abraham Lincoln

The story of the battle for full American citizenship for African-Americans must prominently include Samuel W. Boynton, my first husband. S.W. Boynton, born in Griffin, Georgia in 1904, was the oldest of four children of William and Carrie Boynton. They were the owners of a several-hundred-acre farm and were considered leaders of the community. Bill was a graduate of Tuskegee Institute in agricultural science. He came to Dallas County, Alabama in 1928, as county agent for the Alabama Extension Service, and served in that capacity until his forced retirement in 1949.

As a county agent, whose job involved teaching the latest farming methods to black farmers, he immediately recognized the plight of all blacks, and most particularly the problems of the black farmers, who were victims of a white racist society. He devoted his life to efforts concerning the improvement of their economic and political lives.

That is why my husband and I defied the Southern system from the 1930s until the Student Nonviolent Coordinating Committee (SNCC) came into Selma in 1964, and taught black people to have land ownership and to register and vote.

We dared to go to Washington, D.C. in the 1940s to ask

our congressman to vote to take the voting rights bill out of the hopper and bring it before Congress to be voted upon. His answer was, "If I were to do that for your people, what could you do for me? You are not registered voters and you can do nothing for me." Such a statement from the man we helped put in office (I had been a voter since 1934) made us more determined than ever to help blacks become registered.

My husband and Mr. C.J. Adams worked in the city, where few people made themselves available, and in the countryside, where we were able to get most of the hundreds of people with whom we worked in the extension program to come to voter registration classes. We associated ourselves with political organizations such as the NAACP, Voter's League, and the Selma Civic Association and held offices in all of them.

My husband's accomplishments were many, and his memory lives long after him. During the 1930s, rural blacks could come to Selma to spend their meager monies with white businesses, but were not accorded the courtesy of simple respect or sanitary facilities, such as restrooms, by such businesses. Supported by contributions from rural blacks, Bill went to Washington, D.C. and received a WPA project grant for Selma and Dallas County, Alabama. The federal funds were used to construct a community center, now known as the George Wilson Building in downtown Selma, which not only provided bathroom facilities and a place to rest, but also included the first public auditorium for blacks in the area.

During the mid-1940s, with contributions from rural blacks, S.W. Boynton caused the black 4-H Club of the county to purchase over 120 acres of land with a lake, as a recreational facility for all blacks in the county. This place is known as "Joyland" and the black 4-H Club continues to be the owner of this valuable property, located six miles from Selma.

In 1948, S.W. Boynton received the Merit Award from

Tuskegee Institute, which is the highest honor given to a graduate of that university.

In a continuing effort to cause blacks to become registered voters, he was president of the Fourth Congressional District for Registration and Voting from 1945 until 1963. This district paralleled the actual congressional district, which was comprised of Dallas, Autauga, Coosa, Calhoun, Talladega, St. Clair, Etowah, and Clay counties, with only 1,005 black registered voters, contrasted to 175,000 white registered voters, until the 1965 passage of the Civil Rights Voting Act. During that time, he and others held meetings in homes and churches, where blacks were instructed on filling out the voter registration applications and coached on likely questions that would be asked. He was a registered voter and vouched for black applicants, but his authority was terminated because he brought too many black people to apply for voter registration.

In 1953, as local NAACP president, S.W. Boynton was responsible for causing two black lawyers, attorneys Peter Hall and Ozell Billingsley, to become the first black lawyers to practice in Dallas County since Reconstruction. These attorneys represented a young black man, William Earl Fikes, who was falsely charged with the rape and attempted rape of several local white women, including the daughter of the mayor. Found guilty by a white jury, Fikes was condemned to death in the electric chair. The representation by Hall and Billingsley against the death sentence resulted in the U.S. Supreme Court decision in *Fikes v. Alabama*, a landmark case today on coerced confessions and prisoners' rights. While the decision was won to keep Fikes from dying in the electric chair, his freedom was only achieved after he had spent twenty years in the penitentiary. He was freed a few years ago, being close to death, on application by leading black Selma attorney, J.L. Chestnut.

Foretelling the demise of cotton as a profitable farm crop, and consistent with his philosophy that a black sharecropper who continued to live on the land of a white landlord would become a "white-faced calf," he found available land for sale to black farmers and arranged financing for the purchases.

After retirement from the extension service, S.W. Boynton became the first black licensed real estate and insurance broker in the section of Alabama surrounding Dallas County.

In 1955, S.W. Boynton testified before a U.S. Senate sub-committee concerning the denial of the franchise to blacks in Alabama, which testimony was instrumental in the passage of the 1957 Civil Rights Act.

After one year of a disabling illness, S.W. Boynton died on May 13, 1963. The first large mass civil rights meeting in Selma was held on the night of his death, as a commemoration of his life, at Tabernacle Baptist Church.

The October 16, 1986 *Tuskegee News* reports on the presentation of the S.W. Boynton Lay Justice Award to Ms. Sophia Harris, for her untiring service through the years for the survival and expansion of public day care programs. The award was created to commemorate S.W. Boynton's "lifelong commitment to uplifting the quality of life for blacks in the Selma area," by the Alabama Lawyers Association. Its purpose is to celebrate the bond between the lay and the legal communities.

The Alabama Lawyers Association says of S.W. Boynton, "Mr. Samuel W. Boynton was one of those lay persons who, during times of harsh discrimination, served as a lay advocate in the black community. More significantly, Mr. Boynton, a Selma resident, not only laid the historical foundation for the Voting Rights Act, but also invited the first black lawyers into the black belt to pursue civil rights cases."

Bill and I raised two sons, whose lives, I believe, have borne out the truth that one's home training in one way or another is necessarily reflected in one's children. Bill's family rearing was much like mine, and we tried to give our two sons all of the advantages, so that they might grow up respecting the law of the land and to strive for leadership among their peers.

On Friday nights, when our son William was about nine years old, after dinner we would entertain ourselves by playing educational games, including checkers and dominoes. At the beginning, we would let him win and later we found that he played scientifically and won almost all of the time.

His father liked the country and country life. During hunting season, he took William out to the country and taught him how to fish and hunt. Such sports drew father and son closer to each other.

After having graduated from high school in Selma, William attended Howard University, in Washington, D.C. Each summer was spent in Philadelphia with my mother, his grandmother, whose wisdom and historic background became an everlasting foundation for him.

He kept himself busy with two and sometimes three jobs, including working at the Marriott restaurant in a supervisory capacity, and at the U.S. Post Office in Philadelphia, also as a supervisor.

While living in Philadelphia, he became involved in real estate on a small scale. William is also very interested in the growth of flowers. After getting his flowers planted as he wished, he found that they, like children, needed certain attention he was not knowledgeable about. He now is taking a course in horticulture with a scholarship recently offered him. His home is a showplace for flower lovers.

William's wife recently died, leaving one son, who is the bandmaster in a Georgia county.

Bruce Carver, our second son, was invited to play with the children at a WPA nursing school at age 18 months. This was also good for me, because it gave me a chance to work. However, many of the citizens, knowing that he was not old enough to be in the school, began to complain. After talking with the supervisor, who had permitted us to send him to the nursery school because we contributed heavily to the program, I decided to withdraw him. We asked the principal of a training school on the campus of Selma University to let him sit in the classroom, not as a student but to be with children.

Bruce Carver advanced with the class, graduated from high school at age fourteen, and attended Fisk University in Nashville, Tennessee at age eighteen. He graduated from law school at 21 years of age.

An account of his civil rights case, which outlawed segregation in interstate travel and eating establishments can be found in Chapter 13 below.

Bruce now practices law in his native town of Selma, Alabama and is the attorney for the Dallas County commissioners. He and his wife have five children. Alice Boynton, his wife, is president of BEST (Best Education Support Team), which is running the campaign to improve education for all of Selma's school children.

CHAPTER 2

Our Historic Home

What is life without the radiance of love?
                            —Friedrich Schiller

The home that Bill and I kept in Selma was a magnet for everyone concerned with civil rights. I will never be able to give the names of the many dignitaries who visited our house and later the office. When the civil rights and right to vote movement needed an office, I gave half of my office, which was known as the Boynton Real Estate and Insurance Office, for use by the Southern Christian Leadership Conference (SCLC), and my house was turned over to Dr. King and his staff. Many plans and programs were made there.

Before my husband bought this house at 1315 Lapsley Street, which became so popular during the movement, it was owned by a former state demonstration agent by the name of Mrs. Rosa Jones Ballard, who worked very closely with both Booker T. Washington, Tuskegee Institute's founder, and Thomas Campbell, the first U.S. Department of Agriculture's director for the seven lower Southern states. Both Mr. Campbell and Mrs. Booker T. Washington were among her many visitors. While I lived there, our visitors included the following:

C.J. Adams, founder of Dallas County Voters League
James Baldwin, author

Mary McCleoud Bethune (founder of Bethune College)
Reverend James Bevel, SCLC organizer
Dr. George Washington Carver
Dr. Daniel Cato, Sierra Leone, African Agricultural
    director
Governor Leroy Collins, Florida
William L. Dawson, Tuskegee Choir director
Morris Dees, attorney, Southern Poverty Law Center
Dr. Walter H. Elwanger, president of Lutheran Academy
Felix Gaines, artist (painted murals in Selma Center)
Dick Gregory, his wife, and their three oldest children
Mrs. Jesse Guzman, editor
Ruby Hurley, Southern regional director, NAACP
Emery O. Jackson, founder and editor of *Birmingham
    World*
Dr. Martin Luther King, Atlanta, Georgia
Reverend Bernard Lee
Constance Motley, attorney, NAACP
Mrs. Robert R. Moton, wife of Tuskegee's president
Ed Nixon, Pullman porter, Montgomery's civil rights
    forerunner
Dr. F.D. Patterson, President of Tuskegee Institute
W.C. Patton, Alabama State President, NAACP
P.L. Polk, Tuskegee's photographer
Adam Clayton Powell III (son of the congressman)
Reverend James Reebe
Walter Reuther, labor leader
Dr. Harry V. Richardson, president, Theological
    Seminary, Atlanta
William Seabron, assistant to the U.S. Secretary of
    Agriculture
Reverend Fred Shuttlesworth
C.T. Vivian, SCLC organizer
Aubrey Williams, publisher, attorney, and the first white
    man to come to our house as a sympathizer
Reverend Andrew Young, SCLC organizer, later mayor of
    Atlanta
Congressman Jonathan H. Bingham, New York

Congressman Jeffery Cohelan, California
Congressman John Conyers, Jr., Michigan
Congressman John Dow, New York
Congressman Kenneth W. Dyal, California
Congressman Don Edwards, California
Congressman Augustus F. Hawkins, California
Congressman Charles Mathias, Maryland
Congressman Ogden H. Reid, New York
Congressman Joseph Y. Resnick, New York
Congressman William Fitts Ryan, New York
Congressman James H. Scheuer, New York
Congressman Weston E. Vivian, Maryland

Some day, this house should be placed in the *Historical Register,* because people who made history not merely for Selma, but for the entire country, made history at 1315 Lapsley Street.

CHAPTER 3

Law and Order

*O that my tongue were in the thunder's
mouth! Then, with a passion would I shake
the world.*

—William Shakespeare

Not all of the U.S.A. is like Selma and Dallas County. All white people are not like the judges and juries I have known. There are peculiar tilts to the law that fit this town with its perpetual board of education and there are customs, manners, and methods that would be strange to any other town in a democratic society.

What other place in the United States, "the land of the free," would jail its citizens of color, work them all day on the streets with a white, pistol-carrying overseer, his hand most of the time on his pistol, and ready to shoot at the least provocation, then open the jail doors in the evening and on weekends to let the same prisoners go home for meals, and a bed to sleep in? This was done in Selma during the Great Depression to keep the prisoners from being a financial burden on the city. What other part of our civilized country would arrest a black teacher who had come from another town to visit a friend, jail him on no charge for several weeks, find no violation or blot on his record, but inform him he could not be discharged until he paid board and lodging while in jail? Such strange things, and many more, have happened in Dallas County.

Those of us brought up in some other section of the

country wondered why the blacks in the region were so complacent. From the first day I came to Selma, I could see that fear and distrust hung over the county like a black cloud. It is a cloud that cannot be lifted until black and white extend their hands and hearts across the deep, wide, and dark chasm of misunderstanding, distrust, and fear.

I have heard of so many atrocities that it would take thousands of pages to list them. In the 1930s, there were many beatings, killings, and other cruelties to blacks, and no one dared to say anything. The following two decades were no better, as far as I could see. I heard so many sad stories that I began to hate, then pity, then finally I wanted to do something to help these poor, miserable white creatures who were such cowards, that the only way they could feel important was to "kill themselves a nigger" or take part in some sort of mob violence.

One cool spring night we were awakened by a soft rap on the door. At first I thought I had dreamed the knock, and tried to ignore it, but in a few seconds the rap came again, this time at the back door. I went to the back, turned on the light, then opened the door to three black men who were unusually nervous. I recognized two of them. I awakened my husband and we went into the living room to hear their story. I had heard many tales of mistreatment, but I was not prepared for this one.

The men were too jumpy to sit still, and beads of perspiration dropped from their faces. The oldest, Mr. Raleigh, begged us to keep our conversation secret. "Please, don't let this get out to the white folks or we will all be killed," he begged. I tried to reassure them.

He went on: "Jimmy and us bury John Henry and he wasn't dead."

"What?" I exclaimed. If I were the least bit sleepy before, I was wide awake now. "What do you mean?" I said, and he repeated the horrible words that rang in my mind the rest of the night and several nights afterward. Bill and I looked at each other, both wondering how we could get protection for these people and expose the white perpetrators. We had known John Henry well, because for years he had been attending the community farmers' club meetings. He was a smart, quiet, and just man. He was very frank and believed he was capable as a farmer and as a family man of doing his own thinking.

Raleigh continued, "John Henry's boss, Mr. C., was mad because John Henry didn't turn in all his scrappings of cotton. John Henry was paying $150 for rent at first and Mr. C. would go up on the rent every year, 'cause John Henry would make a good crop—him and his family of ten children."

Raleigh's companions had finally composed themselves enough to say something. One said, "He turned in fifteen bales of cotton to pay his debt and scrapped the field and got two more bales for himself and his children. Dat's what made it so bad. He only turned in the fifteen bales. John Henry was a good farmer."

The third man said, "Mr. C. went and told him he wanted the other two bales of cotton because he owed every bit of it on his bill. John Henry just up and told him he was going to keep the two bales, because he worked for it and his children needed shoes and clothes and he wasn't going to give them up. He would go to jail first. Mr. C. got mad, I reckon, when John Henry said he had made slaves out of him and his children; all the years he lived on his place, and he didn't have nothing to show for it."

Raleigh, who was doing most of the talking, said, "I was at John Henry's house when Mr. C. asked him about the cotton and he talked back. Then Mr. C. said if he didn't turn it in he would have to pay for it."

There was a pause, as though he could hardly bear to go on. The other two men sat with their heads down. "After a while, we heard such a hollering and a screaming that we went to see what was the matter. We saw Mr. C. and five other white men just abeating up John Henry. His wife and children were screaming and couldn't do nothing about it. After a while, John Henry stopped screaming and fell to the ground, then they kicked him and beat him. I was so scared I couldn't say a word.

"When the white folks thought he was dead, they called us. 'You niggers, git this damned nigger out of here damn quick!' They looked like they wanted to beat us if we didn't move fast enough.

"Another white man said, 'Git to moving, niggers, and throw him in this here truck; we're going to bury him.' "

One of the other fellows, seated on the couch, tried to pull himself together enough to talk and finally got out, "He put up a gun and told me he'd shoot my damn brains out if I didn't hurry up and git goin' fast." Then he put his head between his hands and began to moan and sob. But with help from the others, as soon as he calmed himself, he said, "We got all the shovels from around the house and put them in the truck where John Henry was. They pointed the gun at us while we was riding and every time the truck ran over a rut, John Henry groaned. I was scared to tell the white folks John Henry wasn't dead.

"I just couldn't keep still no longer, when we put him in the hole we dug. I said, 'White folks, dis man ain't dead.' The little man with Mr. C. said, 'The hell he ain't, bury him anyway and he'll be dead soon enough. If you don't get a move on you, you'll be dead, too.' They made us bury him wid his eyes wide open."

Later, as I lay in bed trying to clear my mind of the horrors I had just heard, my mind kept going over other miserable experiences people had related to us. I thought of a 4-H Club boy, who left Dallas County with his parents and moved to one of the border counties near Mississippi. He said the segregated school he attended was near a fishing hole in the woods where they often went swimming. It was the only place of recreation they had, because the only parks and playgrounds in the town were reserved for whites. The school had no recreation facilities.

One day, while the students were at recess, a group of white men came through the school yard dragging a black

man behind their wagon. They paid no attention to the
students, and galloped the horse with the wagon through
the yard. The students ran into the building as the wagon
went down the hill. After school, the boys went down to
take a swim and found the body of the black man hanging
over the swimming hole.

Hardly a month passed without our being approached by
blacks who had been taken advantage of, blacks who had
relatives that had been wronged, or others who told of some
killing. I had heard of a black man being killed in jail, and
at first I prayed that it was just a rumor. But the next day I
was visited by a very disturbed woman, who told me what
had happened.

She said, "They killed my son in jail, and I want something
done about it. They told me I could come to you and you
would do something." This was a job for a lawyer and we
didn't have one nearer than Birmingham who might become
involved. But I asked her to tell me about it.

"My son's wife, Eva, worked for a white woman. Eva and
Bill had quarreled and Eva ran to this woman she works for
and told her Bill was after her. The white woman went out
and told Bill to go away and leave Eva alone or she'd have
him arrested. But he talked back to her and made Eva go
home with him. They had fusses all the time, but they always
made up. The two of them settled their differences and went
home together.

"Bill was in the bed sleeping Saturday night late, when
two officers knocked on the door and, when he couldn't get
there fast enough, they broke the door down and come right
in while he was in bed. They told him to get out of bed and
put his clothes on, because he was under arrest. They
handcuffed him and threw him in the car and took him
straight to jail. Then old Alfred Sanders come along."

Alfred Sanders was an ex-officer, known as a most vicious
man, who had the killing of several blacks to his credit. He
operated a filling station under the name of one of his
relatives, and had a loan association where blacks had been
known to pay as high as 700 percent interest. When they

couldn't pay on time, it was a common thing for him to take along some other bloodthirsty white man, who would help him beat African-Americans nearly to death. Why did they continue to patronize ex-officer Alfred Sanders? African-Americans were always in dire need of money, because their wages were so low and living expenses so high. He was cunning; he went to their houses and in their communities with pockets full of money to loan.

The mother continued, "Old Alfred Sanders followed them up the steps cursing and carrying on like a mad man. Then all of a sudden, he pulled out a pistol and shot my son for nothin', Mrs. Boynton." This was the story I had also heard on the street.

The mother then told me that Captain Bankon came to her house and told her that he had had to shoot her son because he had advanced upon him with a knife. She showed me an old broken-blade rusty knife, which could not cut butter, which the captain gave to her, saying it had belonged to her son.

We tried to do something about this case. However, the mother left the state and went to live in Pensacola, Florida. She wrote me that she would rather not press charges, because she was afraid to come back to Selma even under protection.

When an officer of the law says he has killed a black, he is justified, because he *is* the law and can give any reason at all for having killed him. This man, Bill, was handcuffed when taken to jail and handcuffed when he was shot. It was always open season for African-Americans to be killed by officers of the law.

CHAPTER 4

Law and Order II

*If anger is not restrained, it is frequently
more harmful to us than the injury that
provokes it.* —Seneca

In spite of the many people who were involved in atrocities
and who told me nothing would be done even if an African-American took a white man to court, I could not believe
it. But although I knew the white man's ideas of justice were
warped, I saw some things in the courthouse that defied
comprehension.

Almost everybody involved in the major court cases as
offenders was known to my husband or to me. We took
special interest in the cases of those we felt were not guilty
or who had no legal guidance. Many were members of the
farm groups or clubs in the rural section where we had
worked for so long.

One case concerned two 4-H Club boys, Jim and Joe, the
oldest sons of Mary. She also had a fifteen-year-old son who
worked as hard as the older boys in the cotton field of a
colonel. It was customary for the sharecroppers to have all
day Saturday off in order to go to Selma and do their shopping (if they had any money), see their friends, and just sit
and look at the other blacks from adjacent counties. Few
blacks had money to spend, but it seemed to be a *must* to
go to town. That was their only recreation, though Selma
had nothing to offer them at the time, not even restrooms.

Very early on a Saturday morning, the colonel came to the house and ordered Jim and Joe out into the field to chop cotton. The boys said it was Saturday and they were going to Selma for the day. This type of firmness and courage to talk like men (which they were) vexed the colonel. He said he would be back that evening and the work had better be done. Jim said they had worked too hard during the week not to have at least one day off, and if they had to give up that day, they would move. The colonel said, "You heard what I said. I'll be back later this evening and the work had better be done."

About dusk, several white men rode into the yard with the colonel. Jim and Joe picked up their shotguns and went to the wooded section just below the house. The white men went into the house and, without saying a word, began beating the mother and the fifteen-year-old brother, whose cries were heard by the boys. They stood it as long as they could before coming from the woods near the house. They raised their guns and fired into the house, peppering two of the men with bird shot. The men rushed to their car and drove off at high speed. A short time later, the officers came to the house and arrested the boys and took them to jail.

Another case was tried the same day by the same judge: a 70-year-old woman who had been beaten to death in her own house by an officer of the law. This white officer had been carrying on night-time integration with a young black girl, who sometimes lived with her grandparents near Selma. They disapproved of her liaison, but as she was of age, the grandmother could tell the girl that she and her husband didn't want her to live there if she had to see the officer. The granddaughter left.

One weekend the officer came to the home of the old couple and asked for the girl. He was told that she had not been seen for several weeks and didn't live there anymore. He threatened the old lady, who then closed the door and locked it.

Later, the officer was taken to the house by a taxi driver, who happened to be the woman's cousin. (He later turned in the evidence that led to the white man's arrest.) When the old lady opened the door, the policeman rushed in, shouting and knocking over chairs. As he attacked her, she tried to run out of the front door, but he knocked her out with the butt of his pistol, threw her off the porch, and shot her.

The two cases, Jim and Joe and this officer, were tried the same day by the same judge. The black men had a white lawyer to defend them. In less than half an hour, the all-white jury was charged and left the box. Within ten minutes, they returned and read the verdict: "We find Jim and Joe guilty of discharging firearms with intent to kill." The judge called them before the "bar of justice" and gave each 30 years at hard labor in prison.

I sat there thinking, "How in the name of God could a man be jailed for protecting his own domain?" I was too shaken to move from my seat for a while. I went out into the street and breathed God's fresh air, which I felt was the only good thing in this town. I could not go home, because I had to hear the other case, which should have brought more than 30 years to the officer, who killed a black woman simply out of pique.

When the court reconvened, the officer charged with the killing was calm, cool, perfectly at ease. Few witnesses were called. The defendant was never called to the stand, and neither of the lawyers seemed to have been digging deeply into the practice of law. In summarizing to the jury, the lawyer for the defense said, "Gentlemen, this was a poor, old, ignorant nigger. Her days were just about done, she had nothing to offer the world." In other words, he was saying that old people, especially blacks, are rejects; worn-out tools. That was bad enough, but when he ended his summation, I was even more shocked. He said, "Gentlemen, if you find this officer of the law, this fine, promising gentle-man, this white man, guilty, then no white man will have the freedom to go to any nigger's house."

During the 20 to 30 minutes the jury was out, I had a strange feeling—frightened and sick. I could not afford to get sick; I must see this through. Will they give him the electric chair? No, I am sure that would be too much like justice. Would they give him life? I was sure not, because it was a black he killed. But they are bound to give him more than they gave the two brothers, who were sentenced to 30 years each. They would have to give more to justify their discrimination, I thought.

Here comes the verdict, I said to myself. I held my breath, and heard, "We find the defendant *not guilty*," from the foreman. How in the name of God's green earth can a man be found not guilty when his uniform, his gun, and his shoes were spattered and soaked with the blood of the dead woman? How? How? How?

I was as angry as I have ever been in my life and it did something to me inside. It seemed as though it tore from me all trust and confidence I had in the law, the courts, the judge, the jury, and the *white man.* They were all rotten and unjust and I hated all of them now for the first time, and I wished I could go some place where there were no white people at all. Oh, how I hated them! I came out of the courtroom blinded by tears, and started the car as though I were on a race track. I had to get away from the courthouse, which was so stinking with injustice that I was choking. When I got home, I fell across the bed and, to give vent to my feelings, began to cry hard and loud.

I kept crying and asking God where was justice and where was He. The doorbell rang but I gave no heed. Again and again it rang, until I finally pulled myself up and went to the door. To my amazement, there was a priest from the Fathers of St. Edmund's (a black parish). I was angry with him for coming and for being white. Why did he come? He had never been to my house before and I wasn't about to be interested in anything he was interested in.

But I managed to invite the father in and ask him to have a chair. My upbringing would not let me treat him the way I felt. I am sure he realized I was crying and even if he didn't, I couldn't let him get away without lashing out vengeance in words upon him, simply because he was white.

I told the priest that I had just returned from the court-house and I found that the very air there was foul with injustice. It was generated there, with the judge, the lawyers, the jury, and all the whites feeding the flame. Between my sobs, I emphatically informed him that no white man was excused. My body was sickened with hate; I was mad at the world.

"All white people cannot be like that, Mrs. Boynton."

"Don't tell me anything about white people being good," I said. "You are all alike, one way or another, when it comes to blacks. Furthermore, how can a man like you stand by and let white people murder blacks just because their skin is black? Oh, no, Father, you cannot make me believe you aren't like that bunch of crooks in the courthouse."

In his supposedly consoling voice, the priest said, "God is not asleep and justice will overcome evil; just give it time."

"Time," I stormed. "How much more time does justice need? It has had several hundred years. You are just like the rest of them, because if you were to see a white man or woman assault me on Broad Street and we went to court, you as a witness would take the side of the white person against me, even though you knew I was innocent. You, who call yourself a priest, are just as bad as the others. You'd rather keep your mouth closed than to tell the truth, if it happened to be in my favor. What makes you any better than any of the other white people? You will have to show it to me to prove it. The only good white man is a dead one."

He looked at me with pity and said, "Would you do one thing for me, Mrs. Boynton?"

Now that I'd had my say, I listened, waiting for his request. He said, "My request and advice to you is for you please not to go downtown the way you are feeling. Stay at home and cry all you wish. After you have finished, you will feel better, but please don't go out of your home as you are. Your anger will not help the situation at all."

I was too immobilized to say anything more, and he left

without another word. I was glad when he left, and I felt I didn't need any more lectures, particularly from a white person.

When my husband Bill came home, he had already heard about the verdicts and the sentences. He saw I had been crying and he knew how such injustice affected me. We started discussing the horrors of the day, but I could not keep from having outbursts of tears and anger and hatred for the whites. I was so bitter that each time we talked about these things, it was like opening anew an old wound. It seemed that an overflowing fountain of tears could not be dammed up. I became uncontrollable and rude. Bill was doing his best to calm me, but it was no use. We talked, we discussed, and we argued about the treatment of blacks. Bill told me I was wrong to feel as I did about white people and this would bring on more arguments. I could not see why I was wrong, when the whites had made my people hewers of wood and drawers of water, exploited them, used them for immoral purposes, and killed them off like rabbits.

Several hours passed before Bill could get me to talk rationally. He finally said, "Amelia, you have damaged yourself so terribly that your heart seems to be just as bad or worse than those who dish out injustice to our people. Who are you hurting by feeling like you do? Are you hurting the white people or are you hurting yourself? Hatred is one thing that hurts the hater, not the hated."

I now listened to his admonition with an open mind, and I had to admit that I was damaging myself and becoming worse than those who would take a gun and blow my brains out. I didn't want to be like those people; hate caused them to do as they did. I should do differently, otherwise I was a black white-hater, whereas they were white black-haters— and what is the difference?

This was the turning point of my life. I had to change within. Just as all blacks are not alike, certainly all white people couldn't be alike. Little did I realize that, later in my life, I would have such close communication with a different segment of the white race, and that I should learn to love them as my sisters and brothers. Also, I couldn't know then that the hatred I had for the white bigots would later turn into pity—pity because it is an emotional sickness that must be treated with kindness and understanding. I went off to sleep that night wondering what could be done to bring justice to our land and what would be the first step to take.

CHAPTER 5

A Listening Post

Patience is sorrow's salve.

Although after my marriage I no longer formally taught and visited the people in the rural area of the county, the friendships I had made in those early years endured, and my office became a listening post for the affairs of the black community. The intelligent, the well-to-do, the poor, the illiterate—all who needed information or consultation—came for help. They also came for notary service, community service, insurance, and employment. From 1963 to 1965, the office was used by civil rights workers and many of the nation's celebrities and citizens, who sacrificed comforts to contribute all they had—themselves.

Many aged people came to get their birth records and file their income taxes, so that they could receive Social Security. This was a vain hope for many of them, because their work had never been subject to any kind of record-keeping, and their employers had never provided for their old age in any way that was accountable to anyone.

The street on which our real estate and insurance office was located was always crowded on Saturdays with blacks from the rural areas. There was hardly a white face to be seen on the side where blacks had many businesses, except for the white police officers, who constantly patrolled with loaded pistol and night stick. They wove their way through the narrow walk and knocked blacks out of the way when they didn't move fast enough. The blacks dared not utter a word of protest or they would be slammed in jail on a disorderly conduct charge.

There was a liquor store a few doors from my office, where whiskey, until recently, had been sold only to blacks, but only white clerks were employed there. Blacks were routinely arrested by the police for having asked for liquor discourteously, or for refusing to address the salesmen as "sir."

One Saturday, a man staggered into my office and stood, not saying a word. I asked if I could do something for him. Dripping with perspiration, untidy, and with his breath smelling like a whiskey still, he doffed his hat and tried to stand erect. He seemed undecided as to whether he should sit, stand, or run out the door. I pulled out a chair and invited him to sit down. He did so, thanked me, and said, "I ain't heard a kind word spoken to me before in all my life." Though this man was not normal, because he had been drinking, I was interested in his reasons for saying this. He wanted to talk, so I laid my work aside and began to listen.

His was not an uncommon story of having been brought up in the most abysmal poverty: his mother first a field hand and later a prostitute; his 12-year-old sister seduced and made pregnant, later to die in childbirth; growing up in fear and without any real family life, without mother love, let alone any father or father substitute. Then, when he was old enough, he made a bare living by odd jobs and gambling. Finally, he had killed a man and had served 20 years in the penitentiary. At the end of his story, he said, "I did learn to read and write and I even learned a trade while I was there. That was more than the world had to offer me. I had a good roof over my head and I had three meals a day."

I wept for this man and for the many, many children in the world who know nothing of love and tender care. I wept because society, with its discrimination, segregation, and exploitation, was responsible for the destruction of the lives of this entire family. I wept because I had no solution to the many problems of this man and the many others who would grow up as he had, committing crimes that would send their souls to hell, even while they were living.

I wondered, who is to blame for this man's dilemma? I have thought of the many women who have come to my office from time to time, who made only $12, $15, and sometimes $20 a week. How could a mother with no husband take care of a family of four on $15 a week? How can she get food, clothing, pay the light bill, gas bill, rent, insurance, and other bills?

No doubt, this man was conceived because his mother could not take care of her other children by working in the field seasonally, starving the rest of the time. Perhaps someone offered her assistance in paying her bills, and this man, whose story I heard, was a result of such a relationship. Who is to blame for these wasted lives?

In 1968, lives were still being wasted. Tom, a highly decorated war hero, returned to Selma from Vietnam. Many people were praising him for his heroism, and others marveled at his narrow escape from death. He was seriously wounded and was flown back to the United States, minus both legs, but with the courage to live.

Tom would talk for hours about his wife and the baby he saw for the first time on his return home, the experiences he had learning to shoot, and always he would end by talking about having to kill many of the Vietcong, who had wives and babies just as he had. He was restless among his friends and he was ashamed of the tottering steps he took on his artificial legs. He despised having to live in a segregated neighborhood in the worst part of East Selma, with its run-down shacks and its uncollected garbage.

Tom could still drive a car. To show his independence, he bought a new Chrysler and managed to drive as a normal person for a few days without serious mishap. To show his friends how well he could handle the car, he picked up three of them and took them for a ride. But he lost control and he and two of the others were killed instantly; the fourth was permanently injured. The wars we fight on foreign soil come back to us in the minds of the sick and the well, the good and the bad servicemen.

Tom's friend Raymond decided, the Monday after Tom's death, that he was not going to his draft board. He knew that the Army wanted only the best, and he and Tom were considered among the best of the young people in the community. He was a good student, went to church, taught Sunday school, and was a model for the 6- to 16-year-olds in his neighborhood. He held a good job and was well liked. But Raymond was frightened—thinking he might come back home like Tom. Worse than that, he would have to kill.

The Saturday night before induction, Raymond discussed his fear with his friends and relatives. He said he had spent many restless nights, wondering how he could get out of going into the Army. Finally, he stole a car from one of the car lots, drove into a community where cars were parked bumper to bumper, drove at high speed and rammed the stolen vehicle into several cars.

Bleeding, scared, and frustrated, Raymond was taken to the hospital for minor injuries, then off to jail. When he was asked why he broke his good record and tried to destroy property that didn't belong to him, he said, "Anything is better than going to Vietnam."

Should the black man (if he was lucky enough to return) be satisfied with the same living standard that he left in America, after having fought long and hard in Vietnam? God help him to demand that which is truly his. He has fought for it, he won it, and he deserves it. Not a bed in a plush, segregated hospital or the same house with a little paint thrown on it in a black ghetto. There is no doubt that he expects a full, free American life to be lived wherever he chooses, to have his children go to the best schools, and to work at whatever desk or job he is capable of holding. He wants to be and live as a first-class American citizen.

If the black man does not get his freedom, who knows

what the consequence will be. One thing is sure. The American servicemen, white and black, will *take* what belongs to them: full participation in government and jobs without discrimination. They have a right and will demand that which is theirs—freedom. If these men come back to the same ugly conditions they left, with only a promise that "things will be better, it takes time," while the rich become richer, who knows what may happen. These men may use all the tactics taught them and emerge as dehumanized monsters, prepared to take a better life by violence. It is possible that at such time, the poor white man, the black man, the red man, and all others who have been denied freedom will pool forces and change the course of American history.

CHAPTER 6

Early Attempts
at Betterment

*I go for all sharing the privileges of the
government who assist in bearing its
burdens.*   —Abraham Lincoln

For many years, black leaders have tried to arouse African-Americans and get them to realize that they are taxpayers and citizens who have the right to vote. For many years, we urged black citizens to call on the local governments of Selma and Dallas County and ask for these rights. But it was like swinging the pendulum offbeat. We got no substantial results until 1965.

During the late 1920s, a group of Selma and Dallas County black citizens formed the first city-county organization that unified them for one common cause—becoming registered voters. But the Dallas County Voters' League (DCVL) went to sleep for lack of enough interest.

It was revived in 1936, just before election time, when the DCVL members were called together by my husband Bill, Mr. C.J. Adams, Henry Boyd, and P.L. Lindsey, and another attempt was made to serve the black community. C.J. Adams, a railroad clerk, was elected president again. He was truly the most dynamic person Selma had, but most blacks were afraid to follow him. They knew he was right, but the point was to please the "white folks," or they knew their lives would be in danger.

Mr. Adams was finally forced to leave Selma because of

the economic pressure imposed by the whites, and afterward Bill became head of the League. He continued as president until his death in 1963. The harder the DCVL worked to get blacks registered, the harder the county, city, and state worked to throw up barriers so high as to make registration impossible. In 1963 there were only 180 registered blacks in the county, though clinics and schools had been held for several years. We found that other methods had to be used to break the complacency of the adults. If we succeeded, other parts of the South might do likewise. As blacks gained political strength, they would certainly be able to gain more of their constitutional rights.

At that meeting in 1936, because of the small overall number of black registered voters and the still smaller number attending the meeting—Mr. C.J. Adams, Henry Boyd, S.W. Boynton, P.L. Lindsey, Dommie Gaines and A.G. Carroll—it became a committee meeting with reference to the grave concern they had about the city and county's public educational system. To call the attention of all citizens, the Selma Civic League, a subsidiary of the Dallas County Voters League, was organized.

It is incredible to think that it was not until 1946 that the first public school was established in Wilcox County, adjacent to Dallas. Dallas County was little better, as far as taxpayers' money being spent on schools. There had been private schools since 1880, including Lutheran College, Selma University, Payne College, and Knox Academy. The only public school was Clark, which graduated blacks at the eighth-grade level.

A petition was sent to the board of education, asking for the following: a high school through the twelfth grade, a decent new building for Clark, and at least one truant officer. This was perhaps the first petition ever sent to the city fathers by organized blacks.

After studying the petition, one of the board members, in conversation with a porter, wanted to know what was wrong with "his people," and suggested that he should get into the organization and "straighten them out. Your people don't know what they want," the board member said, "It's dangerous to educate Negroes."

The Selma Civic League's petition was completely ignored, because we had asked for a new building as well as twelve grades. Instead, the old white high school was turned into a junior high school. Clark school, which was already overcrowded, added on the ninth grade as the final level of public education for the poor. A few months later, the city announced that Selma would build a bigger and better high school for white students only, which would have the most ultramodern equipment, including a planetarium.

Knox Presbyterian School, which was once a black high school, was condemned by the Selma Board of Education because it was unfit for human habitation. However, twelve years after condemnation, the old, dilapidated, broken-down Knox Academy got a new coat of paint, a few new boards to prop it up, a few new window panes in rotten sashes, and in 1945, the school was opened to blacks through the tenth grade. The next year, eleventh grade was added, and in 1947, the first public high school was opened to blacks.

The third floor of the Knox Academy was off-limits for students but not locked. One day, three curiosity-driven boys ventured up the steps of the third floor. Below where the boys were, a teacher was imparting her knowledge to a class of 50. Suddenly, as though in a fairytale, the ceiling opened and one of the three adventurers descended to the teacher's feet. This episode was reported to the board of education, but the teachers as well as the students were simply told *not to discuss this under any circumstances.* Naturally, no one discussed it. Several years later, conditions remained the same. Other buildings on this campus were still being used until 1968, for handicapped children.

Many programs given in Dallas County brought African-Americans together in large numbers. One of the first was the community sing held annually in the 1930s. Communities throughout the county competed for a trophy that was presented to them by Dr. F.D. Patterson, president of Tuskegee Institute, and William L. Dawson of the famous

Tuskegee choir. This community sing was held in Selma at the municipal athletic field, Block Park.

In 1936, the white citizens were rather skeptical about the large numbers of blacks gathering at Block Park and feared their togetherness might make them realize how badly they were being exploited. So they began to find fault with the annual community sing.

As county agent and home demonstration agent that year, Bill and I distributed programs for the biggest community sing ever, only to be informed by the county officials that it had to be canceled. This was a bad blow, for the sing was the only affair all the African-Americans in the county could enjoy together. We asked why we would not be allowed to hold it, and were told that traveling on the highway was rather hazardous to the black person and some of them might be injured or even killed in a wreck. It was true that blacks used any type of travel, including trucks, cars, and homemade buses. But since when had the white people become so concerned with the African-Americans' welfare that they did not want him to be exposed to danger? Thus, the only annual enjoyment the black citizens of the city and county had was canceled.

The community sing was the first step toward chipping off the wall of fear. Believe it or not, the white citizens formed a community sing of their own the very next year. Later it became a statewide affair—segregated, of course.

The rural people particularly were anxious to work together. As there were only two of us to work with approximately 15,000 African-Americans at that time, it was hard to be in touch with most of them, except by having programs for which they could all gather. There were no phones in the rural district for blacks and few modern methods of travel. The agents had to make personal contacts and use the mail, though many blacks could not read.

In spite of all these handicaps, the blacks would seek information from us and from their neighbors in order to join any group and work together. Among the successful programs were the farmers' conference held at Selma University every year, which brought together people from all parts of the county, and had national leaders as speakers. Then there was the Ham and Egg Show, always a great event, which created much interest, because it was one project which represented the small farmer who was not under a landlord. The first 4-H Club poultry show brought hundreds together. It was a mammoth thing, housed in a building half a block long and exhibiting nearly 1,000 chickens. The cash earned by this project was in some cases the first money the girls and boys had ever had to call their own.

Late in the Depression, there was an alleged shortage of soda (sodium nitrate). As it was very important to have this to get a good yield of cotton, the independent black farmers applied at the various fertilizer plants in their counties, but were turned away. However, the blacks who were share-croppers and tenants could get soda because their land-lords were white and their crops went to them.

County agent Boynton called all the independent black farmers together and asked if they would be willing to buy their soda from the producer and pay for it wholesale. They agreed and asked Bill to make the arrangements. Within a few days, many boxcars of soda were side-tracked to such places as Marion Junction, Orrville, Browns, Bogue Chitto, Minter, Plantersville, and other railroad switches, so that black farmers, working together, were able to save their crops.

At that time, blacks owned many more farms than they do now, and had mortgages on them. The mortgages were often held by white men, who encouraged the black owner to keep buying until he had bought more than he could pay for. We later found that soda was really not that hard to get, and if really necessary, the fertilizer dealer in the county could have brought in carloads, as the black farmers did. The real objective of the shortage was for the blacks to have a failing crop for lack of soda and for the white mortgagers to foreclose. Bill's plan to save the farmers did not help him to gain favor with his white co-workers and with the white mortgage holders.

CHAPTER 7

How Stingy Can
You Get?

Against such stupidity the very gods
themselves contend in vain.
                           —Friedrich Schiller

A s Selma was the shopping center for six counties,
business was pretty good in spring, fall, and winter.
The doctors, lawyers, and merchants all depended on the
income of the farmers. On Saturdays, which was the only
time off for the farmers, African-Americans would bring
their families to town by whatever means were available—
cars, trucks, buses, and wagons. In spite of the influx, the
merchants provided no place for them to sit, no shelter
from the sun and the rain, let alone cold, and no restroom
facilities. Often the merchant would drive them out of the
store after they were served, regardless of the weather.

They were often beaten and jailed for blocking the streets,
when the streets were the only place they had to go. My
husband and I were greatly disturbed by the treatment that
came from those who lived from the bulk sales to those
farm hands, and by the brutality of the officers. We went to
the local merchants and asked them to go to the city officials
and make some provision for these people, but they were
not concerned. We talked with many of our leaders and
they were in sympathy, although most said it would take
thousands and thousands of dollars to put up any kind of
building.

WPA and PWA were building the new city hall, so we contacted the officials in Washington to see if something could be done about a community center. We were encouraged when we found this was possible. Our next move was to contact the blacks in the county and the city to raise money; the reception was very good. Then we talked to the mayor, who wanted to know how much money we had raised. We told him what we had, and here is where the project began to get the runaround.

The official we had written to in Washington was now out of office and his successor paid no attention to our pleas for funds. The city fathers said they had no money and no place for such a building. We did not want to put it out of walking range of the stores, because this would not serve the people who needed it most. No place we suggested was agreeable to the city council or at least some of its members.

Then we appealed to Dr. E.W. Gamble, the rector of the white Episcopal Church, and one of the blacks' best friends in Selma. C.J. Adams, P.L. Lindsey, my husband, and I went to see Dr. Gamble and showed him our plans, with a sketch of the proposed building. He was enthusiastic and had even thought of the same thing himself. He began to front the project for us and there was a decided change in the federal government's attitude, although the city was still giving us the brush-off as to a place to locate the building. We next raised a special fund to send Dr. Gamble to Washington. With the plans drawn, the survey and records complete, and Dr. Gamble speaking for us in Washington, we knew the building would be a reality soon. At least, this is what we thought.

But at meeting after meeting with city officials, we would present requests and each time some of the members would block it. We continued to raise money and prayed that there would be some way for the building to go up. Finally, one of the main objectors to the project died of a heart attack, and within a few days another one died, then another. Heaven knows whether or not this was indirectly an answer to prayer, but anyway, the city council decided not to stand in the way but to buy a piece of property and permit the government project to proceed. Our dream came true.

There was much gratitude to Dr. Gamble, and to this day one hears echoes of "What a wonderful thing Dr. Gamble did for us when he opened the way for us to have a community center." True, his presence turned the tide. There was much struggle and sacrifice in time, energy, and money on the part of the blacks also, but it is partly a result of the long years of unquestioning submission, and the associated idea that many African-Americans have, that if there is anything good coming, it has to come from the white people.

The building, which at last materialized in 1937 (two years after we started to arouse interest in it), was a third of a block long and half-block wide and had waiting rooms, an auditorium, a room for the home demonstration agent, a kitchen, library, and recreation rooms, as well as restrooms.

It was once the pride of south-central Alabama, where all the big bands like Duke Ellington, Earl Hines, Nat King Cole, Fats Domino and others came to play for the black servicemen from Craig Air Force Base, near Selma.

The building still stands today, though most of it is used to store city hall junk. A small portion of it is used to house federal agencies. The toilets are still open to the public. But the beautiful murals by Felix Gaines, a product of the WPA artist program, are closed off to the public and can no longer be seen.

No provision was ever made for parks or playgrounds for blacks while I was living in Selma. State and local officials were asked about a swimming pool, but there was little response and no suggestion as to where one might go for further information or encouragement. Bill Boynton thought of the Sampson farm, where we once held our Movable School. The place had hundreds, perhaps thousands of acres. It was thickly populated with blacks in rundown shacks and was a quail-hunting reservation. The owner and dignitaries hunted there in elaborate style. The place had many trees and grasses, cool streams of water, and plenty of feed for the birds. The soil was poor, and all blacks on the place contracted to plant peas, corn, and other grains in return for a place to live; they paid no rent. For the blacks, however, it was only a little better than starvation.

Mr. Sampson had no close relatives, but he was intensely interested in the welfare of the white men on his farm, if they treated his dogs right. One man he seemed to trust completely, to the extent that he placed the entire farm in his care, with special instructions that the dogs came first, and to hell with everything else. This overseer, Dan Kratchet, had had a black mistress who bore him three children. He seemed to think of them as being his own flesh and blood, but he would only go near them at night.

Bill Boynton went to New York to see Mr. Sampson and asked him to donate a swimming pool and bathhouse to the 4-H Club area, to be named in his honor. Mr. Sampson was very pleased with the idea and was willing to donate the money for this worthy cause, which meant that the people on his place would have use of the facilities. Then we were told that the money would be given only if the overseer Kratchet approved. We thought the greatest hurdle had been overcome, for surely a man with black children would not only approve, but hasten the building of the pool. Mr. Kratchet said he thought it was a good idea and he would certainly talk with Mr. Sampson about it.

But a few weeks later Mr. Sampson wrote us that Mr. Kratchet disapproved of his giving funds for a swimming pool and bathhouse to the 4-H Club camp, and for that reason he could not sponsor it. So that was the end of that.

Slowly and reluctantly, Selma's power structure began to realize that depression and deprivation of any type of recreation in the city created discontent and juvenile delinquency. When all sorts of crimes began to emerge in the white community, attention was directed toward doing something for the youth of the city. There were a YMCA, a municipal golf course as well as that of the country club, a memorial park and a ball park, but the underprivileged whites and the black community still had little or no place for recreation in the city. The city government decided to build some fish ponds.

In the 1950s, bulldozers swung into action in East Selma, and three fish ponds were excavated. Around the first two ponds trees were planted and seats and tables were built. At the third pond there were no trees, no tables, and no seats. Within a short time the signs were up. The cruel words for the first two were "White"; the third sign said "Colored."

The white people fished in their ponds, ate at their tables, and sat under their trees. The blacks fished in their pond, sat on the ground, and were baked on their backs by God's sun. The blacks graciously thanked the city fathers; that is, some of them did.

After the blacks had been fishing in their pond for about two years, one or two white people tried the blacks' pond and found the fish bit better there than in the other ponds. More white people came to fish there. One fine spring day, when everybody would have liked to be out of doors, there suddenly appeared a new sign at the blacks' pond. It said "White." The blacks, thinking that the sign had been switched by a prankster, paid no attention and began to fish. Then a city police car appeared and, as usual when cops are around, the blacks became frightened and froze to the ground. An officer strolled over to the blacks and said, "Auntie, what's catchin'?" The black woman lost some of her fear and said, "Fish big enough for a meal." The policeman said, "Well, I just wanta warn you that you can't fish here no more. This here pond is now for white folks and we gonna dig you-all another one right quick." Thus ended their fish pond. Later another was built a block away to take its place, but of course fish in it were not large enough to be caught until after two years.

In 1939, my husband Bill realized that wholesome recreation for rural people was a must. Besides the community center, which was controlled by white city hall officials, there was little recreational outlet for rural people.

He began to contact various white people, whom he

thought might sell a piece of property to blacks. He was directed to a doctor who owned a former white recreational center, which had not been used in many years and was overgrown in bushes and weeds. Only nine miles from Selma, it was a 120-acre strip of land, with a fish pond and a lovely thicket of graceful, tall pines. The owner wanted to sell it at a bargain too good to turn down.

Bill immediately contacted his farm leaders and members of his local club, the Chesterfield Club, and interest took root and grew. The decision was made to buy the land for a 4-H Club campsite for boys and girls. The farm people began to raise money by selling fish, candy, and anything else saleable, and giving programs in the churches to raise money. Bill had already personally, out of his salary, put an option on the property, and there was no turning back.

Then began another flurry of raising money—entertainments, dinners, and other projects. The blacks were very proud of their cooperative ownership. Within a few months the land was theirs and free of all debts. We began to raise money to place benches on the grounds, to clean out the fish pond, and to keep Joyland, as we called it, in good condition, free of weeds and underbrush.

White citizens began to get curious and somewhat skeptical about the blacks getting together so often. Tenant farmers were questioned by their landowners about their meetings and most of them were cautioned and told they would be sorry if they weren't careful about attending such meetings. Some whites feared a conspiracy and feared for their own safety. Most of them refused to realize that the blacks were only seeking proper facilities for themselves, because the state, county, or city had made no provision for parks or playgrounds for blacks.

It happened that there was a white man who liked the campsite and wanted very much to own it. He met Bill on the street one day and expressed his wish. Bill listened politely and with a smile, said, "Is that so?" and went on about his business. Bill saw the man again a while later and told me, "Mr. Smith asked me again about selling Joyland but I don't see how he can be in earnest about buying. He seems to know everybody on the board, the struggle we had to pay for it, and everything else. I wonder how he happens to know so much about what we are doing?" I said, "You've got someone in your ranks who is feeding information to him. I can't believe this is for any good reason." As is always the case whenever there is a group surging forward, there can be found at least one person who will do anything to get a few dollars, or who is so sadly conditioned that, like a robot, he will do anything to please a white man.

Next, Mr. Smith called the house and in an imperious tone said, "Boynton, I have approached you before about selling me Joyland. The doctor told me that I am sick and must get out into the country for my health and I must have a place. I want to buy Joyland. You niggers can buy land somewhere else with the money I am going to pay."

Bill said, "Mr. Smith, I cannot sell you Joyland because it doesn't belong to me. It belongs to the Negroes of Dallas County." Mr. Smith came back angrily, "You can use your influence to get them to sell. I've got to have that place." Bill said, "Mr. Smith, under no conditions would I urge or use my influence now or ever to encourage the Negroes to sell the only little spot of earth they own for a recreation center in this county. Please don't ask again." But this was not Mr. Smith's last attempt. He was determined, and he went first to one African-American, then another. Each came to Bill and told him about the conversation.

Finally, Mr. Smith talked to an African-American who was more white than black, and whose white father was still living in the house with him. He was promised $500 if he could cause the blacks to sell the property. Being perhaps more concerned with being white than black, as well as being conditioned to think the way the white controller wanted him to think, he set out to convert board members into selling Joyland.

During this period, Bill Boynton as county agent had much pressure placed upon him by the white community, because he was teaching the blacks to register and vote, buy and own land, and stick together. He had a slight stroke, but as soon as he was able to get back on the job he succeeded in turning the tide and made sure that Joyland continued to belong to the black people.

While he lived and was county agent, there were annual countywide picnics, private gatherings, and recreational events for the smaller children, as well as swings, merry-go-rounds, and see-saws.

Since Bill's death, with the exception of building a shed to shelter from the rain built under the supervision of Bill's successor, who served for approximately 40 years, nothing has been done but the sale of timber, to build the rain shelter. The land has become overgrown in weeds and bushes, and what is left of the fish pond is only a memory of a once-thriving recreational center.

A terrible sadness fills my heart when I think of the time, money, headaches, struggles, and battles against racism, which my husband fought almost single-handedly (after others either died or had to leave for their safety), to obtain these facilities for a people who knew not where else to turn.

CHAPTER 8

School Desegregation

*Iron rusts from disuse; stagnant water loses
its purity and in cold weather becomes
frozen; even so does inaction sap the vigor
of the mind.*   —Leonardo da Vinci

The white man, as a rule, has always tried to keep the African-American "in his place," like a robot who would come at his call. Those who would keep him ignorant are also the first to say the African-American is incompetent, incapable, shiftless, and lazy.

One of the biggest civil rights problems is the segregation of schools. Apparently the idea has been to continue to keep the African-American only half prepared even though he lives in a world which requires more and more training of the mind in order to survive. Apparently some white men find courage to stand up and be men themselves only as they can manage to keep the African-American inferior. The black schools in Dallas County and in the state of Alabama are inferior and will continue to be as long as they are segregated and cut off from better equipped buildings and teachers.

Until 1970, integration was moving at a snail's pace all over America. The whole process was a farce that was making a fool out of the government that had ordered it. About half the time for a generation to populate the world had passed since the 1954 Supreme Court decision. White heads were continually bumped together to come up with some kind of law that would circumvent implementation of the long overdue desegregation decision. Such people as Governor Wallace brazenly and publicly denounced the laws of the country. In 1956, Wallace denounced the federal government and dared to place his little body in the door of a great structure, the University of Alabama, just to keep one little African-American girl from entering its halls, in quest of the education her people had been denied for so long. He should have been ashamed of himself for impeding progress and making such a spectacle of bigotry before the eyes of the world.

When Lurleen Wallace became governor she cut down the state appropriations to the two black land-grant colleges—Alabama A&M in Huntsville and Alabama State College in Montgomery. Tuskegee Institute appropriations were cut out entirely. White college funds were increased. The scholastic rating of the black schools, of course, went down. Later, appropriations were restored and Alabama State acquired university status, but in name only.

The methods of integration through 1969 were actually only a form of segregation. There were few African-Americans going to white schools and most of these were either very bright or the children of middle-class families. The poor and less apt children remained at the black schools; the feeling was that they were not good enough to attend the better schools. They thus developed further their inferiority complexes, while the black person who attended the white school developed a superiority complex toward his own race. Only when the schools are mixed completely can we say we have integration.

The first few months I was in Selma there was a great effort made to teach illiterate adults to read and write. I could not understand why there was such a rush by the Alabama Department of Education to give only a short course with a decisive deadline. I learned that the 1930 census was to be taken and the state wanted to increase its literacy rate—for the record. After the census, the adult training program was dropped.

Almost every black teacher, whether she held a master's degree, was working toward a doctorate, had years of teaching experience, or was a college graduate teaching for the first time, was taken out of the field in which she was trained or had been teaching for many years and was placed in another subject. This meant she had to work overtime to prepare, and the school did not have the benefit of her past experience.

Many African-Americans have been born in houses which leak when it rained; they wear cast-off, second-hand, hand-me-down clothing, and clothing from cheap stores; they attend inferior, one- or two-room schools with wooden shutters and pot-bellied stoves. They've graduated and if lucky, attended the most inferior state-supported colleges, set aside for blacks only. Too long have the governing bodies allowed poorly educated teachers to return to the shuttered classrooms to start another generation with no better educational foundation than the teachers themselves had.

There were no white one-teacher schools in the county, but many black ones. A few of the black teachers had not finished high school, but most held a Bachelor of Arts degree or were working toward it. Many communities had no school buildings; classes met in churches. There was no transportation for the children, and many had to walk as many as seven miles to school.

As home demonstration agent in Dallas County, I worked with the women and girls, going into the homes to teach better homemaking and into the schools to organize 4-H Clubs. For the first time in my life, I recognized the true meaning of segregation and discrimination. The term for the African-American schools was three months and the community supplemented this by paying an additional two months' salary to the teachers. Because the people were very poor, the teachers were often paid in produce, such as sweet potatoes, peas, meat, syrup, or chickens, although the families were actually denying themselves when they gave food away.

Because crops had to be gathered on the big plantations,

often the makeshift schools would not open their doors until the last of October or the first of November. To prevent one black group from getting ahead of the others, all the black schools had to wait until all farm chores were finished. In November, December, and January, attendance was almost 100 percent; the only ones absent were those without shoes. February's roll call would find the attendance dropping. Older students would be absent day after day because they were working in the fields. Their classmates were promoted, leaving them behind. Finally, the older boys would drop out, never to return to school again. African-American renters or landowners would try to keep their boys in school until it closed. Sometimes they made great sacrifices to send their children to the city to get nine months of schooling.

One would think that teachers' salaries should be enough to set their living standards above those of the community income in general. But most salaries in the 1930s were $20 a month, although some few who worked in the city system received $25 a month. Certainly teachers living on these salaries alone could not afford cars or luxuries—only bare necessities could be squeezed out of such stipends.

As late as the 1950s, there were no desks in many of the schools and the students sat on hard benches, hewn out of rough lumber by the men of the community. The men also hauled wood for fuel. The classrooms were often built of just weatherboarding, unsealed inside, with a stove in the center. The boys brought water from the spring and spent almost half their school time in this kind of drudgery. When the weather was cold, the shuttered windows had to be closed and all had to endure the smoke and the dark.

Mrs. Lorene Stewart, who had a masters degree, taught in such schools until the 1960s. She recounted the conditions to me. There were large cracks in the floors. To keep the schoolroom warm, she brought pasteboard boxes from the city and tried to line the walls to keep the cold air out. Since there were two teachers in one big room, she also made a partition of the pasteboard. She had as many as 105 students at one time. At first the school had no toilet, so the boys cut some poles and built a makeshift outhouse.

One day I met the principal of one of the county schools. She had a masters degree and was considered one of the best instructors in the county. She was telling me of the overcrowding in her school and said, "Do you know, I have only five classrooms, eight teachers, and nine grades, and nearly 500 students." I said, "How do you manage?" She said the arrangements were five classrooms, five teachers, two teachers with the blackboard between them in the auditorium, and one on the platform of the auditorium. She told me that she had gone to the board of education for some desks and had been given some old, broken-down chairs, most of them with the arms off. She took the boys out of school, got some materials and went into the chair-making business for the school.

Even in these "modern" times, the teachers in the rural areas are responsible for the maintenance of their school building. They have to pay the janitor and the heating and electrical bills, and furnish school supplies. This means that the teachers and students are constantly selling, giving parties, showing movies, and using almost any other method that is legal to raise funds.

The best schools have usually been those run by church organizations. Wilcox County had its first public schools for African-Americans in 1946; the only black schools there before that were private. In Dallas County, several private schools for blacks were established between 1880 and 1924, including a Lutheran college and Selma University, both of which are still in operation. Most African-American students certainly could not afford to pay for private schooling. Payne College, founded by the AME church, moved to Birmingham in 1932. Knox Academy, established by the Reformed Presbyterian Church, was closed down during the Depression.

I don't often allow myself to become involved in a heated argument, but once, in the early 1950s, I became so involved and hurt that I was sorry I went to the meeting. I was hurt because those who were supposed to be leaders could be so easily satisfied with the pacifiers given them by the city officials. All were teachers at this club meeting except me, and we began to discuss the school situation in Selma. One of the black schools, Payne Public School, had recently been remodeled and a new building added to its campus. From the outside it looked nice, but quite small; it had only ten rooms. I had visited a classroom and found the students' heads unusually close to their books, though the only light—a ceiling light—was on. The cement floor was gray; the cinder block walls and ceiling were also gray, and had absorbed all the light available.

I felt awfully depressed as I stood in that room, which seemed to have smothered the students. I said nothing then, but later, thinking what the little African-American children had to go through to get a start in life, I decided I had to mention it to someone. The old school on the campus was bad enough, and one would expect it to be depressing, but not a new building. I told the teachers the new building was a makeshift to fool the people who might pass by. One of the teachers was enraged at my criticism and said, "Don't talk about our school; we think it's fine." I could not allow this to pass, because I had visited white schools and I knew the pleasant atmosphere which surrounded the children there. The motivation to study that was so necessary, the light and color that would make the rooms so inviting— these were missing in this gray, dark, dismal dungeon.

Our conversation became a debate and grew more and more heated. Finally, half the members were on my side, realizing for the first time that the schoolroom was far from being good for the students. We ended on a sour note with one of the teachers saying, "If you had been teaching in a roach- and rat-infested building in a basement that was damp more than 75 percent of the time, you would welcome anything that was better."

I replied, "I would never welcome anything that was thrown together carelessly and pushed on me. The hundreds of thousands of dollars collected each year in taxes are used for the improvement of white schools and salaries.

Little or none has been used for the African-American teachers or schools' improvement."

Knowing the fear that guided the very destiny of most African-Americans who depended on white officials for their living, whether through the board of education or from working in their kitchens, I ended the discussion by saying, "Blacks will always be confined to the worst schools and houses if they don't cry out against such mistreatment. You can take what you want from the white man and what he throws at you if you wish, but as for me, I'll fight against this short-changing until I die." My club members looked at me as though they thought I were crazy. We left for our homes, hot and indignant over the questions I had raised.

After the Supreme Court decision of 1954 to desegregate schools, my husband and I were advised by the NAACP to contact leaders and those who would understand and prepare for the new day. The white people gathered on every corner to discuss what could be done. The blacks also discussed and wondered how they were going to be able to enter the schools.

The cold, cunning eyes of the state, county, and city officials betrayed an attitude that told the African-Americans that they were prepared to use their most powerful weapons to maintain segregation regardless of the cost. The African-Americans were lied to, bypassed, and discriminated against. The federal government was blinded by the scheming and delaying tactics of the South—or so it seemed. This is a charitable view. In too many instances, the federal government was as responsible as the states for maintaining segregation.

School doors opened, the bells rang, and buses began to roll in Thomasville, Alabama, as in other sections. Parents, both white and black, put their children on the buses to be taken to the white, supposedly now integrated schools, and the blacks prayed that there would be no violence for their young ones and lived in hope that this small town would become a model of integration. But they were never so wrong.

There are communities in Thomasville where black and white families live side by side; therefore, the children went to school together on the same bus that first day. Forty first-graders with black skins returned happily to tell their parents about the day. The second day, the black students and the poor white students again gathered at the bus stop at 7:30 a.m. Then it was 7:45, 8:00, 8:15, and still no bus, nor at 8:30 or 9 o'clock. Black children were taken home by their parents or older sisters and brothers. There was no bus the next day or the rest of the week.

Then the black people called a meeting. The situation became more complicated when it was revealed that the school, although ostensibly integrated, was still segregated by classrooms; black students with black teachers and white students with white teachers.

In Dallas County, black parents were sent threatening notes if they attempted to send their children to a white school. Some of those taking their children to the white Plantersville school were refused entrance and told to go back to the black school to get other instructions. When they were returned to the all-black school, they were sent to the superintendent's office in the courthouse, who told them they had to fill out other papers, to be obtained at the black school, and so it went.

CHAPTER 9

The Destiny of the Black Man

*Truth ... never comes into the world but
like a bastard, to the ignominy of him that
brought her forth.* —John Milton

For the "excellent service rendered to the county for nearly 25 years," was the citation given to the county agent, Samuel W. Boynton, with the Meritorious Service Award from his *alma mater,* Tuskegee Institute, in 1943. This was the first award of its kind conferred upon anyone by this great school.

During Bill's service as county agent, he devoted his entire time to the elevation of the blacks, especially the farmers. Through a new standard of scientific farming, a wider program of farm ownership, of greater partnership and participation in cooperative actions with a desire for human dignity, he raised the black man's standard of living.

The citation was given not only because he gave himself unselfishly to his work, but because he went far beyond the call of duty in uplifting humanity. Teaching the farmers to raise more corn and cotton, and training them in better methods of raising and caring for the plantations' cattle always brought him a pat on the back from the white community as a good black, but when he taught the hundreds and even thousands of blacks how to gain political, financial, and educational strength, he was considered by whites to be a dangerous black man, who would get blacks in trouble.

Whites and blacks alike realized that such awakening would destroy the white man's way of life (his caste system), for the African-American would cease to be exploited. Unfortunately, many of the middle-class blacks were also disturbed and wished we would leave the city and leave them alone. They were doing fine and why should anyone start anything to cause white people to think they were going too far? Many times raising the standards of the black was like trying to give a child a dose of medicine while he was fighting against you.

Whites would say, "If the Negroes would behave themselves and stay in their places, there would be no trouble." Such statements stuck in the minds of the poor blacks. Another statement was added to make the African-Americans fearful: "Don't rock the boat, this is the white man's country and he is always going to run it as he sees fit." Nothing exasperated me more than to hear such statements by teachers, businessmen, and professionals. When Bill brought up the subject of race or mistreatment of an African-American among his club and fraternity members, he would hear this kind of talk and the only consolation he had was the cooperation, the confidence, and the trust of the rural people and their desire to work with him for the good of the race.

After the building of the community center, the cooperative purchase of Joyland, and the training of people to become first-class citizens, Bill turned most of his attention toward persuading blacks to buy land. He was born on a farm and knew the value of ownership. His father and grandparents on both sides were large landowners. His ideas irked the white people, who had a place for blacks that did not include their owning anything, not even their children, if the white man desired to take them away from him.

"The destiny of the Negro lies in education, possession, and the ballot," Bill insisted. He urged the people to buy property and his daily word to the farmers was, "Ownership makes any man respected. Living on the plantation makes a man's family a part of the owner's possessions. The time will come, ladies and gentlemen," he would say, "when the only way you are going to stay on this white man's place is to turn into a white-faced cow. Soon your farm will be turned into pastures or rented to the government and you will be turned out to graze elsewhere."

Within less than five years after Bill retired in 1953, blacks were told in large numbers that the farm didn't need them any longer, that they had to leave the plantation because the land was going to be fenced in and cattle would be placed on it. The part used for farming needed little labor because of mechanization. That rented to the government gave clear profit to the owners, who were financially nestled in feathered coziness after exploitation of the black man.

Some of the African-Americans rejoiced because they had bought land, taking Bill's advice. Thousands of acres had been bought in Dallas County through his assistance. However, in many instances the white people would not sell when they found blacks to be land-conscious.

Although the federal government's agricultural program with its subsidies was geared to help the farmers, those who needed it most did not receive any benefits. I questioned officials in Washington, "What chance does a farmer have to receive benefits from this program—one who has worked all his life on someone else's farm, but who owns nothing?"

I was told emphatically that there was nothing he could receive from the program, because it was for those who owned something. There was nothing for the dirt farmer; he was outside all government programs, and all he could hope for was a handout from welfare agencies. Through that subsidy program, the blacks were cheated, exploited, evicted, and beaten, not by the government, but by the landowner.

Where did these blacks go? Some followed the instruction of their leader and bought land; many moved into Selma, but the masses of human beings who had been used as implements, with their backs bent from toil and their fingers numb, bundled up their families, the only possessions they had accumulated during a lifetime on the farm, and went to the big city ghettoes, minus education or skill, to be placed on the welfare lists.

The question has been asked many times, "Why did he leave the farm?" Here is part of the answer. The shack in which he lived was not new. It had housed three generations and nothing had been done to it since it was built. He had patched some holes in the floor to keep the wind from coming up under the house. There had never been a toilet, even outside. His family had to go to the woods because the owner said he could not afford to build a toilet. The question has been raised by those who do not understand the psychology of the black poor, why did these people not build their own latrines? Such questioners do not realize that this sort of initiative, enterprise, and ambition for self-improvement are the very qualities which were denied the black. In fact, when such traits began to emerge, his very life was endangered.

The land that the African-American's father used to cultivate as a boy has grown up in bushes, weeds, and poor timber. If he could only buy a few acres of it . . . but it is too good for the black man, whose parents and whose children made the owner the wealthy man he is today.

Many people, even the poor and illiterate, realize that the government dragged its feet by keeping only white people in office—people who are trained to keep African-Americans in what they call "their places."

Mr. and Mrs. Harvis Jiles of Orville owned 90 acres of land that produced fine crops each year, including fruit. They sold enough cattle and hogs to take care of a portion of their expenses. Both drew Social Security checks. They were in excellent health and the parents of twenty children. Each year the Jiles family borrowed money from the Farmers Home Administration (FmHA) for fertilizer and each year when the crops were gathered the money was repaid in full, on or before the deadline.

Their house needed repairing badly—it was a typical Black Belt black home in the country. They went to the FmHA office in Selma, reported the condition of the house and asked for a loan for a new house. The administrator, who knew their ability to repay a loan, talked with them at length, and left them with the impression that they could get a new house.

Days passed into weeks, and weeks into months, and the frustrated couple traveled back and forth, signing papers, bringing deeds, and waiting patiently. Months became a year, and then two years, and they still lived in hopes of getting a new home. Then, they were told that they had to take out a fire insurance policy with a certain agency. This new stipulation, along with other papers to sign, gave them courage.

Months later, Mr. and Mrs. Jiles went in again and reported that their old house was falling in, the roof was partly blown off by a storm, and the porches had fallen through. They were told that the loan had been processed and that $3,500 was available for repairs to the old house. They were disappointed, but decided to accept the loan for repairs. They were told that provision would be made for the contractor to get the money and they were also told that they had pay $29.50 a month, beginning the next month.

Each month the couple went to the office and paid on the loan. As time went on and no repairs were made, Mrs. Jiles asked, "Why has the work not been done on our house?" The administrator answered, "*Your* house? You do not have any house, that house belongs to the government." Dejected, they walked out and wondered what was the next step.

They came to my office and told me their story. I called an official of the Department of Agriculture in Washington, who agreed that something should be done. The next day, I received a call from Mississippi from a man under orders from the office of the Secretary of Agriculture.

When we went to the Jiles' house, Mrs. Jiles told him not to come in; she had been deceived by so many white people she could not trust any of them. But she finally admitted him and told her story. This is one story with a happy ending. Mr. and Mrs. Jiles got a new house and lived happily in their declining years.

What happened to the FmHA administrator of Selma? He was moved to another section, perhaps to continue processing applications like those of the Jileses, if the client happens to be black. How can the African-Americans make progress under a system which is given to such people to administer?

CHAPTER 10

Continuous Harassment

Our actions are our own. Their
consequences belong to Heaven.
                              —St. Francis

My husband was continually made aware of the political pressures working against him in his struggle for the rights of the African-Americans, and this constant pressure took its toll on his health. He came to realize that he could do more good outside of a state-supported post and, in 1953, he resigned as county agent, forestalling what he felt would sooner or later be dismissal.

Not long afterward, a white salesman, Mr. Fitts, came to our house one night and asked if I would like to handle a fire and casualty insurance agency. He knew I already managed a life insurance office. Bill and I listened attentively as Mr. Fitts explained the responsibilities involved, although I said I would not be interested. He turned to Bill and said, "How would you like to start an agency?"

In my heart I wanted him to take it. I prayed that he would; it seemed to be God-sent. Should I encourage him to take it? No! If it failed, I would blame myself. Yet, what would he do with himself? He had been cut off from the rural people he loved so well, and this would be a chance to make a comeback. He accepted the proposition to represent the Southeastern Fidelity Fire Insurance Co.

The state insurance commissioner of Alabama permitted

many newly formed companies to be established with a requirement of $10,000, to pay off any claims that might arise from automobile accidents. These were the weaker liability and comprehensive insurance companies we were allowed to work with, but most of them were short-lived. Within a year or two, they were closed by the state commissioners and much of our customers' insurance protection had to be transferred to other weak companies.

We made preparations for an agency, which could occupy space in my already-established life insurance office. An advertisement was published through the churches and rural districts. The people were very glad to talk to Bill again, and came to see us in large numbers.

At this time, the State of Alabama passed a law that all cars must have either liability insurance or $1,100 set aside for damages that might occur. Most of the people wanted auto liability insurance, but Southeastern Company did not write it. We could not turn them down, so we let them fill out applications anyway, and agreed to let them know if we could get liability policies for them. We then went to see one agency after another in Montgomery, Mobile, and finally Birmingham. At one of the Birmingham offices, the official seemed interested, but we were turned down for the usual reason—color. But the president of still another company saw our 100 applications, accompanied by the money, and this was more than he could turn down. So all our business was turned over to the Southeastern and Texas Mutual Co., and we had places for all the applications that came to us. For three years we had smooth sailing.

Then came calamity, with a letter from Texas Mutual, saying we must stop writing all insurance, because the company was going into the hands of a receiver. This was indeed a hard blow. How could we take it? My husband, who had always been so dedicated to his people, did not want to tell them the company had gone down; those people had confidence in him. There was $10,000 worth of business going down the drain. What could he do? What could he tell them? We talked it over that night and I said that, since he had several other companies asking him to write insurance for them, why couldn't he take all the policies and set them up with the other companies? It would mean a loss to us, but he said he would rather take that loss than lose our good name. So we transferred all the business we had to other companies. They would not take it on a *pro rata* basis and we had to pay the difference.

Every time we placed policies with another company, it would go bankrupt, and we would transfer them to still another. We did not do as the white agencies did; when their companies went down, they told policy holders, that was it. We talked with some of the people from the white agencies and they said we were fools to absorb all the responsibilities of the defunct companies.

We found we could not resort to any strong company, but the weaker companies were glad to have us do business with them. One company wrote us, saying, "Don't write Negroes $500 medical payment." We canceled the few policies we had with that firm and placed them with another. We not only could not deal with people who discriminated against us, but we would not work with those who would use us to discriminate against our own people.

All of this was too much pressure on my husband, and again he had to go to the hospital with high blood pressure and a slight stroke. But again he recovered in a short time and was back at the office. He was lucky to have some part-time secretaries who could carry on in his absence. Furthermore, some of the secretaries who came into the office had an aim in view: to make money to go back to college. It did Bill a lot of good to know that he had made some contributions to these girls, who would have had no other way to finance their education.

There was an elderly man named George Tate, who owned and operated one of the largest insurance agencies in Selma. He loathed the idea of an African-American having a business like a white man. He could not keep his hatred to himself, and he picked an opportune time to unleash his vengeance—the day Bill got out of the hospital and came back to the office.

Tate walked into the office and burst out, "You dirty, lowdown, black nigger. I hate you. I am going to take this stick and kill you." I jumped up. My husband was amazed and could not understand what was going on; he had never come in contact with this man before. As Tate lifted his cane to strike Bill, I grabbed it from him. If Bill had not been there, I think I would have given Tate a good licking that he would never have forgotten. I made an attempt to strike him, but Bill said, "Don't hit him, don't hit him!" Just then two blacks who had seen the drunken real estate broker come into our office and who knew how vile and nasty he was, came in behind him.

One of them could take his cursing no longer and said, "Get out of here, Mr. Tate, before we throw you out." I knew the white people would take advantage of these men if they got into it. I said, "You don't have to throw him out, because I am going to take his own stick and beat him half to death." I was really angry, but my husband warned, "Don't touch him!" His voice was calm, which caused me to be more rational.

I realized this could cause a fine, fat lawsuit against us, so I told the men to gently lead him out and not to hurt him. I calmed down and reflected that a man in his condition could not take care of himself. However, I would like to have given him a sound whipping, remembering the many blacks he had insulted, kicked, and beaten. Bill said the man was sick—sick with hate and prejudice. His mind and soul were corroded.

When Tate got out on the street, he remembered that I still had his cane and he began to scream and curse and demand that I give it to him. I threw it out to him and relocked the door. At this point, there were dozens of blacks and whites out there laughing at him. To give vent to his feelings, the man beat the front glass door down from the very top to the very bottom. The officers did not come until he had finished the job. I was just waiting for him to come back in, and nobody would have had to help me throw him out. This was one time I would not practice nonviolence.

Black lawyers would not take the case and found all kinds of discrepancies that might have come up. I felt that changes *had to* be made if we were to live together. There is a chasm of misunderstanding; overconfidence that the whites could do no harm on the one hand, and lack of confidence on the other, with whites thinking the black man cannot and will not do right. This is almost a perfect job of indoctrination, which has been done by the so-called good white folks for more than 300 years.

Doing insurance work often took me to homes, and sometimes the policy holders would be out and I would see them in public places. One day I saw a client downtown in the shopping center during rush hour, when many white people were on the street. She approached me with a friendly hello. She wanted to pay her insurance, and it took me a few seconds to write a receipt. She quickly thrust the money in my hands, saying, "I'm so nervous, I don't know what to do. Here, take this money quickly before the white folks see me. They will think I'm giving you money for the NAACP." When I looked up to say something, she was gone, leaving me with the money, receipt, and change due her.

It had been whispered around that our friends were afraid of us, not for us. Instead of the usual smile and hello, as we approached some of them on the street, we got a cool and hasty "hi," or they would pretend not to see us in passing. One of my friends and club members, who rode to club meetings with me, began to give excuses each time I called for her, for not letting me take her. Later, she told me she was actually afraid to let white folks see her with me. She was cautioned by many of her co-workers to stay out of the Boyntons' car and that the white people might take her job away, if they saw her being friendly with us.

For a long time, I wondered why the club members had changed so toward me. I wondered why, as I entered the door of a place of meeting, everything seemed to be so frozen. I found later it was because my car was parked in front of their door. It was even worse when the meeting was to be at my house. A club member would call with regrets that she could not come. Then another and another would call with some excuse, until more than half the members would be absent.

During a meeting, if the doorbell rang, the members became fidgety and jumpy. I could always tell there was something wrong, but I did not want to believe that the trouble was fear of losing their jobs or being questioned by their white employers or the principal or superintendent of their school, as a result of being seen with me. A few walked unafraid of their positions or their white creditors. Mostly these were outsiders, who had come to Selma to work. We found also that the African-Americans living in the country had more determination to be free than the city blacks, and much of the courage we saw to keep on working came from these people. My husband and I would say to each other that we were living for the day when African-Americans would feel free enough not to get nervous in the presence of a white man.

However, the accomplishments, the good that was done, the victories won (although they barely scratched the surface) soon dispelled the uncomfortable feeling my friends had when in my presence. Many of the younger people we had taught in the rural areas went away to school and came back to take positions as leaders in Selma and the county. They had learned to live fearlessly, rather than as cowards. These 4-H Club leaders had learned the skills of leadership and were accepting responsibility. As time went on, many confessed their fears, which were well grounded—they knew personally what had happened to so many people who had protested against the system.

Joe Yelder was a young boy in the country in the 1930s, who went to school only after the crops were gathered, but he was bright and eager to learn. My husband asked him to be a 4-H Club leader and gave him special instructions. He took him to Tuskegee Institute to the 4-H Club short course.

Later, he enrolled at Tuskegee as a regular student, received his degree, and came back to Selma to teach. We were proud of him, and he said that, had he not been given the chance to go to Tuskegee, he no doubt would still be in the country trying to eke out an existence on the farm. But he always said this when my husband and I were the only ones around.

One day Joe came to me and said he had to get something off his chest. He praised Bill for having helped him to make wise decisions, but he just could not jeopardize his job by visiting him in the hospital or at home any more. He was afraid some white person would see him and he feared the reaction. He confessed that there were many days when he saw Bill on the street and would cross to the other side to keep from having to speak to him, hoping Bill would not notice him. Bill once saw him walking and waited to offer him a ride to his home, but he hastened by.

My husband often said, "I will fight for Negroes until I die, for Negroes really don't know that they should be free. They don't know their strength, but once they know it, this will be a different section in which to live. They will be happier because I have put myself out on a limb for them."

More black-owned or -operated businesses were needed in Selma, at least to keep up the standard of the average black businesses. The pressure placed on the black businessmen, the white merchants who operated in black communities, and larger chain stores, which forced little merchants out of business, rendered the African-American unable to compete on an individual basis. For a long time, the Boynton Real Estate & Insurance Agency was the only black business of its kind. However, African-Americans began to organize for cooperative business.

When it was whispered that some men had gotten together for the purpose of establishing another black-owned real estate and insurance agency in the city, we were glad and we discussed it at length. My husband said it would be a good thing, because more African-Americans would patronize black businesses. Because the doctor's orders

were that he must cut down on his activities, I suggested
that Bill offer his agency to the corporation that was opening
up.

After deciding to streamline his activities and confine
himself to promotion of registration and voting, he contacted the head of the corporation, offering his business for
little or nothing, only to keep it in the black family. It was
bluntly refused by the new agency's spokesman. When the
new agents went to Birmingham to get information on setting up an office, they were told to come back to the Boyntons, but they did not.

This mistrust of us was a perfect illustration of the lengths
to which the undermining had gone. The men who went to
get the license wanted no part of Boynton's Real Estate &
Insurance Agency, because there were many whites in city
hall and elsewhere who disapproved of the Boyntons' activities. Some white city officials did everything in their power
to keep the African-Americans from patronizing us. Because
of the fear and dependency of the white man and the use
of blacks as a cat's paw, blacks were often pitted against
blacks by whites to drive their own out of business.

Ironically, the establishment of the new agency was a
boost to both offices—there was a great increase in our
business, which proved that competition is a healthy thing.

CHAPTER 11

The Need for a Scapegoat

*Indeed, I tremble for my country when I
reflect that God is just.*
— Thomas Jefferson

There is a traditional and widespread fear in the South among some white women—a fear of being raped by a black man. This fear has been analyzed and discussed in various books, fictional and scientific.* It is a fear often perpetuated and seemingly even encouraged by a society which is a remnant of feudal times and sees itself as representing the height of chivalry toward its women—its white women—while reading into the despised black the lustful instincts it does not want to admit to its own consciousness. These fears and scapegoat tactics manifest themselves every so often, and invariably the black takes the consequences, regardless of how unjust, inappropriate, or farfetched. Most blacks know of the dire consequences of even looking at a white woman directly in a friendly way, no matter how innocently, and are on guard against any behavior that could possibly be misconstrued. But once in a while, someone is naive enough to believe that the usual

---

* For a thorough and objective discussion of this whole subject, see Dollard, John, *Caste and Class in a Southern Town*. New York, Doubleday & Company, 1937.

cordiality of a white woman is sincere, and he walks into a trap. Such, I believe, was the case of James Smitherman.

Mr. Smitherman had a store to which a Mrs. Hancock delivered milk daily. They usually had a friendly chat, and one day she said that her business was taking an upward trend. Mr. Smitherman said, "Tell me how it's done. I seem to be going down instead of up." She said, "Really, would you like to know?" He said he would and she said she would be glad to tell him. He then made the fatal mistake of writing his phone number on a piece of paper and asking her to call him some time when they could talk.

Mrs. Hancock took the paper, went to the police, told them Smitherman had made advances toward her, and she wanted him arrested. The officers thought they could trap him by having her call him while they listened on an extension. Smitherman said, when she reached him, "I just wanted to know how I could improve my business and have more trade than I have." Several of the officers listened in and she kept saying, "Is that all?" Smitherman said, "Yes, that's all." She asked him again, "Are you sure that's all you have to tell me?" He said, "Yes, ma'am, that's all." The officers did not see anything that would call for having this man arrested, and most of them dropped the case.

But one or two of the men were not satisfied and took matters into their own hands. The first thing they did was pass the store, to "spot him out." Smitherman rode a bicycle back and forth to work. One evening, a carload of white men wearing hoods rode slowly through the black community several times, and when they saw a man on a bicycle, they kidnapped him and carried him fifteen miles into the country. The man finally convinced them he was not Smitherman, but they left him in the country to walk back to Selma.

Smitherman received phone calls with threats to burn his house, but he was determined to try to protect himself instead of getting out of town. He bought guns and ammunition.

The "avengers" fumbled again, this time throwing a match into a gallon can of gasoline at the corner of what they thought was Smitherman's house. (It was next door.) The next week, bullets were fired into Smitherman's home and all the evidence pointed to these same officers. Newspaper accounts told about each of the episodes, and afterward one of the officers committed suicide.

But the threatening phone calls kept on, and various delivery trucks stopped supplying Smitherman's store. His only recourse was to leave the city and establish residence elsewhere. As he had three children who were barely teenagers, Mr. Smitherman felt that taking a chance in a bigger city would allow them to become educated and prepare them for a better tomorrow.

In the spring of 1954, a story in the local paper said a black had entered the house of a white woman and raped her. When the officers got there, she could give no accurate description whatsoever, only that the man was black. Then followed a wave of hysteria over other alleged rapes, but never was a man found who could be identified and accused. Finally the police resolved to find somebody to pin this recurring crime on, and they declared a curfew for black men only.

One night, a black man named William Earl Fikes, who was a filling station attendant in the next town, and who did not read very well and didn't know about the curfew, came to Selma and ran out of gas on a street between the black and white communities. He walked down the street to find the nearest filling station and, of course, was conspicuous because of the curfew. He soon became aware that a white man was following him, and began to walk a little faster, then turned into an alley and began to run. Fear dominates the African-American much of the time and he works against himself and arouses suspicion even when his conscience is clear. The white man caught up with him and collared him.

When the police arranged a lineup to identify the black

man accused of the latest rape, the only black in the lineup was this man Fikes. The one woman (of doubtful reputation) who appeared named him as her assailant.

Fikes was quickly tried and given 99 years. It was then that my husband Bill resolved to do something about it. It was impossible for any one man to have gone from one side of the city to the other, molesting five to ten women in three or four nights, as was rumored. Bill did not believe this and he thought no one else did. Fikes was merely a scapegoat, captured to stop the rumors.

The first thing the prosecution had done was to see to it that no blacks were on the jury and that very few were witnesses. One was the mayor's stableman (the mayor kept riding horses). The white owner of the filling station where Fikes was employed testified that Fikes had worked there and had made a good record, and at the time of the crime he had not even left town. Other times when he was accused of being in Selma he was either at home with his family or working in the filling station.

Bill went to Birmingham and persuaded two black attorneys, Orzell Billingsley and Peter Hall, to enter the case. He also contacted the NAACP Legal Defense Fund. The black citizens became alarmed and, for the first time, felt they could give liberally to free this man from what they knew was a trumped-up charge. But no two persons had hundreds of thousands of dollars worth of property to go on bond for Fikes while the case was appealed, so he remained in jail.

Fikes was then tried on another charge brought by the daughter of the former mayor, Mr. Rockwell. The circumstances related were ridiculous and impossible. The jury in both trials was all white, although the defense tried its best to get blacks on the panel. We followed up this case, and my husband's speaking out determined his own destiny. When the court was getting ready to choose jurors and the defense lawyers were trying to have African-Americans included, the jury books were brought out and the African-Americans called by the defense were asked to examine them to see if any African-American names were listed. My husband was asked how many blacks he knew in Dallas County and he told them he knew practically all of those in the county. He had retired from extension work only a short time before. They handed him the jury book and he was sent into one of the adjoining rooms to examine it. It was an extensive piece of work, and when the court closed, he had to stop before he had finished.

The next morning, Bill was given the book again and after a time, was called back to tell what he had found. He said there were three names of blacks on the book that were not there the night before when he had turned the book in. This upset the court, and caused the whites to feel they had to get rid of that black man or he would cause trouble. A conspiracy then formed to put Bill out of business.

Meantime, the Rockwell-Fikes trial proceeded. Although the testimony was ragged, inconsistent, and almost fantastic, Fikes received the death sentence. However, on appeal to the U.S. Supreme Court, the death sentence was thrown out for lack of evidence and Fikes was freed after spending thirteen years in the penitentiary for a crime he never committed.

CHAPTER 12

Economic Squeeze

*O what a tangled web we weave, when first
we practice to deceive.*

—William Shakespeare

The first jolt came when Bill picked up the paper to read about the Fikes case. There was his name on the front page. Everything he had said in court was there, plus the assertion that it was he who had brought these black lawyers into Selma. Blacks never made the front page in Selma, except when the article was not complimentary to them. Bill could not understand at first why there was so much credit given to him in the papers when the white citizens were against him. But the objective was to put him on the spot.

The next day, an officer came to Bill's office and said, "Boynton, I have a judgment here for you."

Bill said, "Judgment? What kind of judgment?"

"It seems you owe a bill," was the reply.

Bill looked at the judgment and found that some of the insurance policies that he had transferred to another company had not yet been paid out completely. An amount of $1,600 was yet due, although he was continuing to keep up the current bills of this particular company. A white man had found that he owed this money and had gone to the agency involved and said, "Don't you want to get your money from the Boynton Insurance Agency?" Of course they said yes. So a judgment was issued. Bill signed the papers immediately and said, "I will take care of this very soon."

The next day, there were bold black headlines on the front page of the paper reading,"S.W. Boynton, former county agent, arrested for embezzlement." The accompanying article contained every detail of his participation in trying to get blacks on the jury in the Fikes case. Only one small paragraph mentioned the $1,600 owed to the insurance company. This was all a scheme to discredit what Bill had been doing, in order to make him unpopular with his own people and to deepen the hate and distrust of the whites. The judgment was satisfied, and we decided from that time on to stop dealing with the company involved.

But the harassment did not stop at mere defamation. The next step was to try to keep African-Americans from doing business with Boynton's agency. Every day, some African-Americans called or came to the office and asked for their policies to be canceled. Those who had mortgages with white people were questioned about their insurance and some were told they must cancel whatever policies they had with Boynton or their mortgages would be foreclosed.

One day, a taxi driver came in to make application for insurance. We took the application and received a partial payment, which was requested by the company, then gave him a receipt. He went across the street to city hall to get his license renewed, but the person in charge told him he could not take that receipt or give him the license unless he canceled it and took out insurance somewhere else. The man at the bureau proceeded to use all kinds of profanity and threats as to what he would like to do to "that nigger Boynton." These things were very hard. Our own people were so paralyzed with fear of the white man, that they didn't have the courage to stand up and say, "If I can get it from some other place, then why not at Boynton's?" This man went elsewhere, paid the same amount of money and received his license.

My husband made application to represent mutual funds. A company official came from New York City and gave him the required examination, which he passed without any trouble. However, he was not cleared by the state attorney general, who said that there was a judgment against him and that he was too old. He was 51 at the time. We tried to get the attorney general to give us one specific reason why there should be such a report from Selma when the judgment had been settled. We called attention to the amount of other business we had had with that company over a long period, but to no avail. The attorney general only shrugged his shoulders and said, "This is the record that was sent to me."

I pointed out that the attorney general was not taking into consideration what he really knew. I reminded him that the former county agent, S.W. Boynton, was considered a hero in the many crises we had in Alabama. He was considered the best county agent in the state and other Southern states, but as soon as he began to work to free his people from the bondage of plantation slavery, to get them to buy homes and to register and vote, he became a menace to the white society. More than that, as soon as he used his influence to bring black lawyers into Selma, to fight for a man being given a death sentence because he was black, then suddenly he became the worst man in Alabama. I am sure my talking to the attorney general made him realize the extent of hate and prejudice that enveloped his profession—a profession dedicated to correcting injustices.

After the state refused to approve my husband as an agent for mutual funds, I asked the examiner to let me take the test. I was allowed to take it and passed with a better than B average. I received the company's congratulations, but never heard from the state. I asked why I had not been notified about my standing, and was told that a county official would inform me. That day never arrived.

To add to our economic and social injury, the Dallas County Board of Registrars took my husband's name off the voucher list. Many African-Americans at last decided, after this further discrimination against Bill, "If this is what they are doing to our county leader, our former county agent, the man who is making such a sacrifice for us, we are determined to register and vote."

Our farm was between Marion Junction and Browns, Alabama. It was not on the highway nor was it on a decent road. When we first bought the place, the county commissioner saw that a road was put in that section and was kept up fairly well. My husband was the county agent at the time. But when it developed that he was interested in helping blacks in ways other than better farming methods, the commissioner decided not to bother with the road. We would ask that it be scraped, but nothing would be done, or perhaps a little dirt would be placed in the mud holes. When it rained, it was impassable.

During the winter, a man in one of the families near us became violently ill and had to be carried out on a stretcher by some of the neighbors because a car could not get through and the wagons bogged down as soon as they started out. The neighbors got him down to the public road, and a car rushed him to the hospital.

We tried sending a petition, and a group of us and our neighbors talked with the board of revenue. There were seven families in the area, with 27 people, nineteen of them children, many of them supposed to be in school. The small children could not get out to school when it rained, but the older ones wore boots and went through the mud. When they reached the big road they took off their mud- and clay-caked boots and left them at someone's house, going to school with or without shoes. Despite all our requests and all the reasons why the road should be worked, the commissioners did nothing, and I always felt it was because we, "those uppity Boyntons," had the farm back there. Many of the African-Americans who had property in the section didn't live on it because of its inaccessibility.

In 1967, four years after Bill's death, the road was partly worked, but as soon as the supervisor found that the machines were working the road to our farm he turned the machinery around in another direction. A very good road was built, more than a mile long, in a section where no one lived. The road was soon covered with grass. Our farm road was not worked until 1968, when some refugees from Resurrection City (from the Poor People's Campaign in Washington) came to Selma.

There was another sign that the Boyntons were being systematically shut out whenever possible. We had a man come in and cut timber. He hauled quite a few loads out, but as soon as the buyer found that the timber came from our place, he refused to accept it. This was one of many such acts of economic pressure.

No wonder my husband had high blood pressure and had to be hospitalized several times. But nothing under the sun could stop him from fighting for his people. He said more than once that he had one life to live and one death to die. He tried to buy land in a section where blacks could have decent homes, but nobody would sell him any. Still, a white salesman came to the house to talk to him about a beautiful cemetery lot. His answer to this was, "It's funny you white people don't mind seeing us die and be buried in a decent, respectable place. But you don't want to see blacks live in a decent place. I am not interested in dying just now. If you have a decent place you can sell where my people can have a home, I want to know and I will try to buy it."

We had borrowed $10,000 to buy our farm and had not yet paid it all, but because of his part in the Fikes case, Bill found that he was surrounded by all the people to whom he owed money. Some arrangement had to be made at once to pay them. It happened that the mortgager who loaned us the $10,000 died and immediately the administrator called on us, because he had to close the estate. We knew not where to turn. I was resigned to giving up everything if we had to, and to beginning somewhere else. My mother was going out of the real estate business at that time and she wanted us to come and take over in Philadelphia. I pleaded with my husband to let everything go and move up there and start again. His answer was, "I don't want to go, I want to stay here and help my people." I told him his people didn't care anything about him or about me either. He should realize that if he left, he could better the condition of his children and himself. But his answer was that although that might be true, if he stayed he would be able to better the conditions of 20,000 blacks in whom he had already invested his best years. I felt ashamed of myself for trying to talk him into running away from trouble. I could not continue to urge him to sell a place that gave him his only breath of freedom, after his years of labor. The only thing I could say without bursting into tears was, "If that's the way you want it, that's the way it's going to be."

Bill suggested that we go to the Pilgrim Health & Life Insurance Co. and ask for a loan. That we did, and to my surprise we were given the loan and we paid off all our debts. Our business had fallen off quite a bit, so much so that we did not see how we could keep the doors of the agency open and pay the secretary. We had to act quickly in order to survive.

We were determined to start an employment agency through which we would send girls to New York to work. I went over to the license bureau to ask about it. There was no precedent for this kind of business in Selma, so the matter could not be settled right away. I went again and was told I'd have to call back when they could get a ruling on it.

In the meantime, a man came to town from New York City who was interested in our proposed agency and I sent him over to the bureau to inquire further. He was told he would have to look up the record and find out for himself what arrangements could be made. The next time I went to the bureau, the clerk told me the license would be $300. I didn't see how this could be, when in the city of Montgomery a similar license was only about $75, and in Birmingham it would be about $100 or $125 at the most. We knew then that these were deliberate blockages put in our way to ensure that we would not enter the business.

But we made it over this hurdle; we raised the $300 and bought the license in May 1954. The next January we again had to pay $300—a total of $600 in less than a year. This was the price paid for an employment agency license to operate in a country, one-horse town, Selma, Alabama.

A white man once asked an African-American I knew, "How in the name of God do the Boyntons still live in Selma, when we have done everything we could to run them out?" When the black told us about this conversation, Bill said, "Well, we're going to stay here and nothing they can do will run us out. When we get ready to leave, we'll leave, and not before. I've given everything I have to this section and have lived here longer than anywhere else. I believe I will be here until the good Lord takes me home." And that was the way it was. He died in Burwell Hospital, May 13, 1963 after a long siege of illness.

CHAPTER 13

The Treatment of the Educated Black

*Nonviolent action, the Negro saw, was the
way to supplement, not replace, the process
of change. It was the way to divest himself
of passivity without arraying himself in
vindictive force.* —Dr. Martin Luther King, Jr.

Our son, Bruce Carver Boynton, launched the first test
case of the Supreme Court ruling that outlawed segregation in interstate travel. His case cleared the way for the
first freedom riders to test the law. In December 1958, he
was en route from Howard University Law School in Washington, D.C., to Selma to spend the holidays. The Trailways
bus stopped at a station in Richmond, Virginia, late in the
evening. Bruce went to the segregated lunchroom and found
it was crowded. Passengers were begging to be waited on
before their bus would leave and Bruce saw he would not
be able to get anything to eat in time, so he went to the
white side of the restaurant.

As he approached the counter, a white waitress asked
him, "What you want?" He asked for a cup of coffee and a
sandwich. The waitress said, "I cain't wait on you, you'll
have to go on the other side." He told her he was in a hurry
and would gladly take the food outside if she would be so
kind as to serve him. Instead the waitress went back and
called the manager, who came and said, "We don't serve
niggers in here. You'll have to go around the other side."
Being a law student in his senior year and having a bit of
his mother and father in him, Bruce said he was not going

anywhere, but was going to remain until he was served or find out the reason why.

Within a few minutes the manager returned with officers, who questioned Bruce and carted him off to jail for trespassing. While in jail, he was given the opportunity to call an attorney. He was released on bond, and allowed to continue his trip to Selma.

If those concerned with the arrest of Bruce Boynton had known that the case involved more than trespassing, there would never have been an arrest. The case went to court and drew much attention, with Howard Law School and Georgetown University law students becoming involved, as well as others in the profession, both white and black. This episode was one link in a chain, whose upshot was that the Supreme Court outlawed segregation at all lunch counters, restaurants, and eating places of any description for passengers traveling interstate. This was also later a subject of the Civil Rights Act of 1964.

Selma and Alabama were not proud of the part our son Bruce Carver Boynton played in the Supreme Court's decision in desegregation of interstate travel and eating places, and they tortured him in every way they could. Graduating from Howard University Law School in 1960, he began to study to take the bar in order to practice in Alabama. Often when going downtown he would be confronted by whites about the court's decision and while studying one night, someone shot in the house and cracked a large plate glass window, inches from where he was sitting. The day he filled out his application, he was asked if he had ever been arrested. He said yes and explained what happened, but did not tell the final results, because the Supreme Court had not acted on the case. When it did, he was taking the final examination and the students from the Alabama State College went into many segregated restaurants and cafés and sat to be served. Later, he did not hear from the board within a reasonable time, though he made second to the highest average ever made. He contacted them and he was informed, "because you did not reveal all the truth of being arrested in Virginia, we refuse to give you your license."

We were all very disappointed about this; however, he decided to take the Tennessee bar, for which he sent an application. The application called for the sheriff and two practicing attorneys to vouch for him. The sheriff, Jim Clark, would not fill it out and would not return it to him. He later contacted the president of the Tennessee Bar Association and told him what had happened. He was permitted to take the bar, but later was told that a letter was sent by some Selma white citizens, asking them not to pass Bruce because his parents were troublemakers and were trying to break down the Southern way of life. He was told that he made such a high score in the Alabama examination that the bar could not say he had failed.

All the family realized that the fight for civil rights meant we were treading on dangerous ground. We knew that it would take guts, blood, and determination to help America be the America that we so proudly hail and sing about, as "sweet land of liberty" or "the land of the free and the home of the brave." We also realized that militant leaders, both white and black, must fight and strike down segregation and discrimination and free every man, woman, and child. It took something besides determination, though; it took love in our hearts to overcome the hatred and discrimination of those who tried to destroy freedom.

You might say that Bruce learned the lesson about discrimination in interstate travel at a very young age. In 1940, when Bruce was only four years old, he and I were traveling from Philadelphia to Selma on the Atlantic Coast Line train. I had a seat in one of the integrated coaches, where there were many people of mixed races. Having ridden the train before, I knew I had to change in Washington, D.C.

Before reaching Washington, the pullman porter came through the car and said that the coach on which I was then traveling would go as far as Atlanta, Georgia. Soon the conductor came through saying, "All passengers going south get out of the coach." Everybody left but my son and me. The conductor returned and I let him know I was en route. He said, "This coach is going to be pulled. You will have to get in another coach." Believing the pullman porter,

I remained in the coach. When the conductor realized that I would not leave, the empty coach, with only my son and me aboard, was taken down to Richmond and filled with African-Americans. Segregation began in the capital of the United States.

In 1954, at the time of the Alabama State College student demonstration in Montgomery, when the Supreme Court outlawed segregated eating places in interstate travel, Mr. Sultan Moore owned a thriving grocery store and gas station in a black community nine miles from Selma. He had two sons in college, one in Montgomery and the other in north Alabama.

A member of the White Citizens' Council visited the store and said to Mr. Moore, "Sultan, you've been a mighty good boy and Ah don't know nothing bad about you. But Ah understand your son is a student at that thar Alabama State school."

Mr. Moore said, "Yes, he is."

"Well," said the WCC member, "I heard that he done become involved in the demonstrations."

Mr. Moore said, "I think he was."

The visitor said, "Well, tha's jus' whar he done messed up. Sultan, that boy is gonna get you in trouble yet. Don't ya know better than to let him get out thar in them demonstrations?"

Mr. Moore replied, "I didn't give him permission to get in the demonstrations. You know and I know that we train our children as far as we can, but when they leave us and go out into the world, having had better educational opportunities than we have had, they have minds of their own and they usually do what they want to do. So that was something he wanted to do. I didn't have to give him permission."

The white man warned him, "Well, Sultan, the white folks are mighty mad about what he did and I am mighty 'fraid he's gonna git you in trouble, boy. You better be mighty careful, 'cause I hate fur the white folks in this county to turn their backs on ya."

A few nights later, the Moores received an anonymous phone call saying, "Get out of the county. If you don't get out damn quick, we're gonna burn that store down to the ground and you in it." The next midnight, Moore heard a car stop near his house. He told his wife no one should go outside for anything. A few minutes later, another car rolled up nearer the house, then another. He peeped out the window and saw at least eight men moving about on his premises between the store and the house. He gave his larger children guns and he and his wife took pistols and waited for the mob to attack. One of the white men came on the porch and Sultan said to himself, "This is it. If I have to die, Lord, let me take others with me."

The man on the porch called him to come out. Sultan answered, "If you want me you will have to come in here and get me, because I'm not coming out." The fellow left the porch and consulted with the others, who stood around their cars. After a time, they pulled off.

That was just the beginning. The next week the truck delivering Coca-Cola passed the store and did not deliver the drinks. Within hours, the Pepsi-Cola truck passed, then the bread truck, the wholesale grocery truck, and the produce truck. In spite of the nakedness of his shelves, Moore decided to keep his doors open as long as he could sell gasoline. The next week, the gasoline truck drove up and the driver came into the store. He expressed his sincere regret that the white dealers would not sell him products. He said it was low, evil, and certainly discriminating. Mr. Moore asked him if he would use his influence to persuade them to do the right thing, but the man said he could not; he would be out of a job if he interfered. He had been told not to put any gas in Mr. Moore's tank, and as sorry as he was, he could not replenish it.

Mr. Moore went to some of Selma's leading businessmen to ask why he was treated thus. Each time he contacted one of them he was told that nothing had been said about stopping of the trucks to *him*. He then went to Sheriff Jim Clark's office and said he would like the trucks to continue to serve his store. Clark said he had heard that Mr. Moore owed a deal of money to the various firms.

Mr. Moore said this was not any more than the bills they

had carried over a long period. Clark then said, "I will be glad to personally see that every truck begins to roll and supply your store again, but you will have to do something for me."

"I will do whatever I can."

Clark then said, "Find out what meetings the Boyntons are having, what they say, and what the other leaders of the niggras are telling the people. Give me the names and let us know where the meetings are being held. If you will do this for me, I will personally see that the trucks will fill your shelves again."

Moore was stunned. He was surprised that the sheriff thought he would be so weak as to squeal on his own people. He declared, "Well, Mr. Sheriff, the trucks will never roll again, because I don't know what is going on in the meetings and if I did, I would never give my people away."

Dejected, worried, and broke, Mr. Moore sat in his house on Highway 22, wondering what would be the next step. A few years before he had been considered one of the most businesslike African-Americans in Dallas County. He had two sons in college, had paid for several acres of land and two buildings on the highway, a large pasture, and a fine herd of pure-bred cattle, and had looked forward to the time when he could educate all his children and retire. Now that this had happened, all out of the blue, without provocation on his part, and all was at a standstill, what would he do? Only a few years before, his wife was the only African-American postmistress in the Black Belt, and perhaps in the state. But because of white influence, the post office was closed and the black community's mail route was divided among other post offices.

Mr. Moore said, rather than have his children starve and be deprived of their education simply because they wanted freedom too, he would pull up stakes and leave the section. Within a few months, he sold his cattle and his property, and took his children out of college and left for Minnesota. I have heard they are all doing exceptionally well.

Dallas County

Leader Attacked By White Man

The Selma Alabama Citizen

"Serving The Heart of The Black Belt"

PRICE **10c** Per Copy

PRICE **10c** Per Copy

Selma, Alabama, SATURDAY, JANUARY 7, 1956   S Edition

BOYNTON, POLITICAL LEADER, ATTACKED BY WHITE MAN

By Mozell Talbert
Alabama Newspaper Association

SELMA—S. W. Boynton, Dallas County political leader and businessman was physically attacked in the office by George Tate, where police real estate and insurance man, Monday of this week.

A detailed complete details of the affair have not been released.

[remaining column text illegible]

Funds were raised by Amelia Boynton's play "Through the Years" and other benefits to build this Selma Community Center, still standing at 23 Franklin St. Today the Center is largely unused, and the beautiful murals (see following pages) are locked behind closed doors.

(Below) Coverage of the 1956 attack upon S.W. Boynton by a white Selma real estate agent

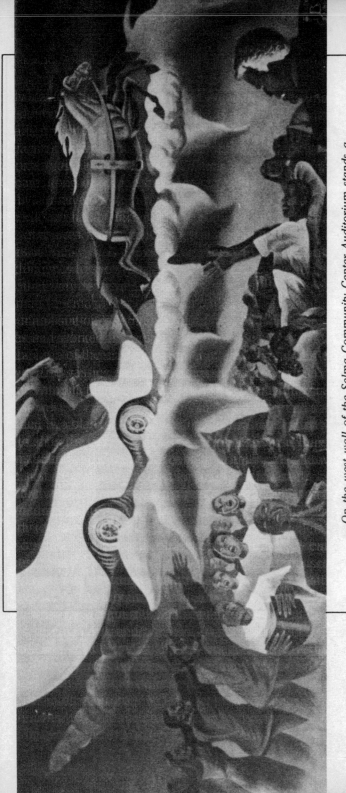

On the west wall of the Selma Community Center Auditorium stands a mural approximately six by eight feet. In the background is depicted an old grey-haired slave on his deathbed. At right there is a slavery-time choir. In the foreground is a more modern choir standing beside the man. The dying man has hands outstretched toward a chariot drawn by three powerful horses—black, white and red—depicting the old Negro spiritual, "Swing Low Sweet Chariot, Coming for to Carry Me Home." Both murals are by Felix Gaines.

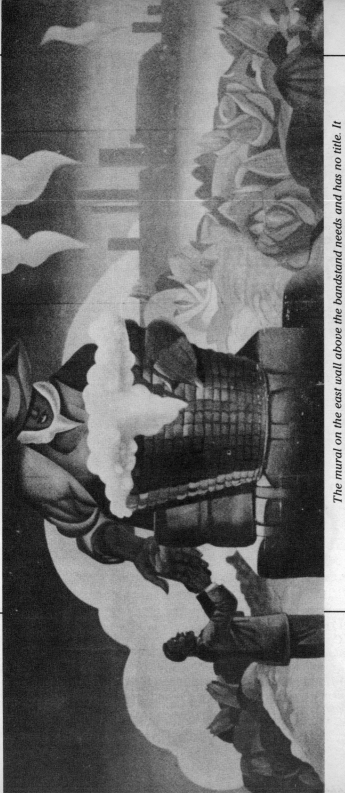

The mural on the east wall above the bandstand needs and has no title. It depicts the diminution of the South's huge cotton crops and the increase of diversified farming. Dr. George Washington Carver is handing to the farmer peanuts from which over 300 products, from face powder to pavement, have been produced. Note the factory in the background.

(Above) The Boynton Insurance Agency was in downtown Selma. This was the SCLC center during the March on Montgomery. It was also the place where African-Americans came to air their grievances.

(Below) The home of Amelia P. and Samuel W. Boynton at 1315 Lapsley St. Dignitaries from all over the world visited here during the Selma civil rights battle.

Dr. Martin Luther King, Jr. came to Selma on Jan. 2, 1965 and set up SCLC's headquarters at Amelia Boynton's home and office. Though he was not present at Bloody Sunday, he led the subsequent March on Montgomery on March 21, 1965, which led to passage of the Voting Rights Act.

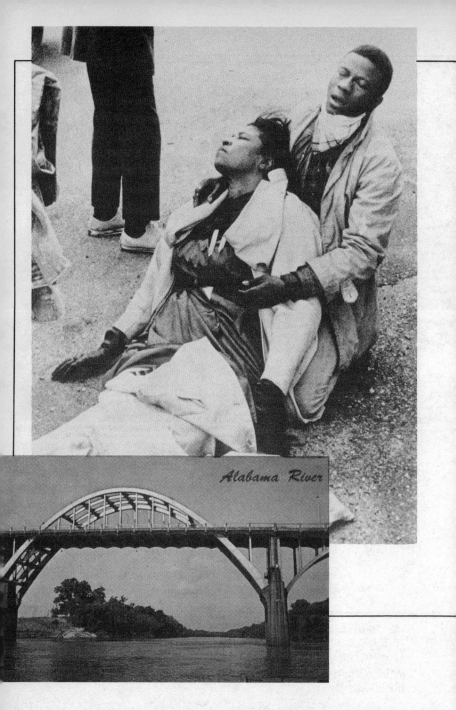

Bloody Sunday, March 7, 1965. Amelia Boynton, unconscious, after being beaten and gassed by Alabama State troopers on Edmund Pettus Bridge.

Negro Woman Is a Candidate

By Sue Cronk

THE FIRST NEGRO WOMAN in the history of Alabama to run for Congress will oppose veteran Rep. Kenneth A. Roberts in that state's Democratic primary on May 19.

"I'm going to Selma businesswoman Amelia Boynton told the Washington Post yesterday by telephone.

Mrs. Boynton is the only other woman candidate facing Roberts. He has represented the Fourth District since...

If she wins, she will become the first Negro representative from Alabama since Reconstruction.

Despite her optimism, the possibility of being unseated by a Negro, male or female, is high. The population of the County, of which the seat is some 57 per cent Negro, yet few per cent of Negroes of voting age are registered.

This doesn't daunt Mrs. Boynton, who has been in the state urging Negroes to register since her husband, L. S. Boynton, started a voter registration drive in 1930.

THIS CRUSADE culminated in the Selma march last October, five months after...

...Boynton's death, when the Student Nonviolent Coordinating Committee launched an intense campaign to train Negroes to pass Alabama's highly complicated...

...enough to run for Congress," she added, admitting that the time people probably would not support her politics.

SINCE her husband's death...

...registered to vote for 30 years, Mrs. Boynton belongs to the Alabama Coordinating Association for Registration and Voting, is chairman of the Civil Liberties Department of the Alabama Temple of ... is chairman of the ... Division of ... Association of ...

Mrs. Amelia P. Boynton *Birmingham World* 4-1-67

Democratic Primary Candidate Cast Light In Ala. Voter Registration

SELMA, Ala. — (SNS) — Mrs. Amelia P. Boynton, candidate for Congress from the old 8-county Fourth Congressional District in the May 5 Democratic Primary, has attracted national attention for the spotlight her entry into politics has cast upon voter-registration in Alabama.

She is opposing incumbent Kenneth Roberts in the zig-zagged, gerrymandered, far-rambling Fourth Congressional District. The district embraces these counties. St. Clair, Calhoun, Talladega, Clay, Coosa, Elmore, Augusta and Dallas.

Jet magazine has carried a feature on Mrs. Boynton regarding her candidacy for Congress. Educational Television has prepared a film documenting activities of Mrs. Boynton. Her candidacy has become news partly because of her residency in Selma, the centralization of voter-registration litigation, obstacles in the way of Negro suffrage, and resistance.

About half of the counties in the Fourth Congressional District are in the Alabama Black Belt. However in each of the old nine Congressional Districts the percentage of Negro voters to the total electorate is about the same, based upon 1962 figures.

Candidate Boynton has been busy completing her platform and mapping plans for speaking en-

MRS. AMELIA P. BOYNTON

gagements. Campaign leaders are expected to be appointed up in each of the eight counties.

Likely Mrs. Boynton will be given an important spot on the program of the Alabama Democratic Conference when it meets in Mobile, Ala. April 11 and 12. She is one of the potent leaders in the organization.

In 1964, Amelia Boynton became the first black woman in Alabama history to run for the U.S. Congress. This brought her instant notoriety. She won thousands of votes, including a sizeable white vote in her Fourth Congressional District.

MERIT AWARD RECIPIENTS — Tuskegee's 1965 Alumni Merit Award recipients are: Mrs. Charlotte Moton Hubbard (left), deputy assistant secretary for public affairs, Department of State, Washington, D. C., and Mrs. Amelia P. Boynton, civil rights leader from Selma, Ala. Mrs. Boynton was cited for her contributions to the struggle for full equality of all races." Mrs. Hubbard was cited for her outstanding achievement in public services.

Mrs. Boynton pictured in the Selma Times Journal *in May 1965. She received the Tuskegee Alumni Merit Award for "contributions to the struggle for full equality of all races."*

PART IV

The Civil Rights Struggle Comes to Selma

I just want to do God's will. And He's allowed me to go to the mountain. And I've looked over, and I've seen the promised land.

—Dr. Martin Luther King, Jr.

CHAPTER 1

Memories of
Martin Luther King, Jr.

*If a man hasn't discovered something that
he will die for, he isn't fit to live.*
—Dr. Martin Luther King, Jr.

Long will we remember that great nonviolent leader Martin Luther King, Jr., the man who taught nonviolence to the Western world. He first came to Selma in January of 1965. I have many fond memories of working with Martin and Coretta Scott King, both in Selma and elsewhere. Perhaps this is the best place to put those memories down in writing, as well as the living memories embodied in the Martin Luther King Center for Nonviolent Social Change, of which I am proud to be a board member.

Having a best friend, my sister-in-law Annie, living in Montgomery, Alabama, and the largest shopping center nearby, I found myself in the 1950s visiting Montgomery frequently. As a dedicated church-worker, Annie often encouraged me to accompany her to church. Each time I attended I enjoyed the message brought by Reverend Gregory and other ministers, and the singing of the choirs of Dexter Avenue Baptist Church.

In spite of the Reverend Vernon John's methods of conducting the services, he was very practical and real in what he said and did. He was a self-made man, highly educated, outspoken about his opposition to the white establishment, and fearless. And he was a farmer at heart. His parishioners, being business and professional people, many of them faculty members at Alabama State College (now Alabama State University), felt that he was too outspoken and earthy. When one day he brought fresh fish for sale in his truck outside the church, in addition to the vegetables he usually brought, that was it. His subsequent termination led to the hiring of a new pastor, Dr. Martin Luther King, Jr.

Later Annie told me of the new pastor, whom she enjoyed so much. She wanted me to hear him and meet his lovely family. In June 1954, I met Mrs. King and the following Sunday I met Dr. King.

Dr. King was not a self-made leader. He was one like Moses who was chosen by God. He reminded us many times of the most meaningful Negro spiritual, "When Israel was in Egypt's land, let my people go. Oppressed so hard they could not stand, let my people go. Go down Moses, way down in Egypt's land, tell ole Pharoah to let my people go."

Dr. King first came to national prominence with the Rosa Parks incident, which sparked the successful Montgomery bus boycott. Day after day, week after week, month after month, and year after year, men and women had been arrested on the buses for the least provocation and nothing was done about it. Why? The handwriting of the Almighty had not yet been shown.

But one evening, December 1, 1955, after an unusually hard day of work and after standing at a bus stop on this cold and bleak day, Rosa Parks finally boarded a bus in Montgomery, Alabama and sat down from sheer exhaustion, as the bus continued to take on passengers until it was full. The bus driver, seeing a white man standing, came to the middle of the bus where Rosa sat and demanded that she stand and give the white man her seat, which she refused to do. Thus the nonviolent war against injustice began.

After Rosa Parks was arrested, Dr. King was very concerned. Going into his private chamber to pray, he wanted to know what to do in this strange land, where he had come to lead a small segment of Montgomery's most educated and refined black people. "What can I, freshly out of the university, do in a situation like this?" he thought. "The universities I attended did not teach me how to deal with even one violent person. Dear God," I'm sure he said, "I depend upon Your guidance. You must show me the way."

I learned more about what actually happened much later, in 1985, approximately four months before the death of E.D. Nixon, a veteran civil rights fighter in Alabama. I met Ed Nixon in the doctor's office. After asking him how he was doing and one thing and another, the conversation drifted to the Rosa Parks incident and subsequent bus boycott.

"God always sets the stage for us to march forward, if only we can identify it when we see it," he said. "Yes," he continued, "we had had other people arrested for the same reason as Rosa Parks, but somehow it was time to move. When Rosa was taken to jail, she called me. I had just come off the railroad and finished my dinner. I went to my office and then the jail, accompanied by Attorney Clifford Durr (a white attorney), got her out, and called all of the ministers I could think of to meet and tell others. Joan Robinson, a civil rights activist, began to go into action. On the Monday of the trial, at 7:00 p.m. at Holt Street Baptist Church, we had the first meeting. We settled on the name Montgomery Improvement Association."

Having heard some dissension about electing a MIA president, I said, "Since Montgomery had so many heavy-duty ministers, how did you go about electing one?" Ed Nixon said, "In the midst of the confusion and talking about who is to be what, one of the laymen from the floor said, 'I nominate Mr. Ed Nixon as president.' I tell you the truth, Ms. Boynton (he never stopped calling me that), I was too old to be in all the confusion, so I said, 'Gentlemen, I'm too old and you've got so many young people who can lead. I decline in favor of this new young preacher, Reverend Martin King.' " Immediately the vote was carried without a hitch, he said, but throughout the entire conversation, Ed Nixon mentioned being terribly hurt because he was passed over and ignored.

With strong supporters like Reverend Ralph D. Abernathy, Ed Nixon, Robert Nesbitt, Johnnie Carr and many others, the MIA was founded. Thus the most active, progressive, workable, energetic embryo grew, served as a nucleus for Montgomery, and then splintered off into an arm—the Southern Christian Leadership Conference (SCLC, of which I served as second state secretary after Mrs. Adair), which soon became a national organization.

After talking at length with Ed, I attended a board meeting of the Martin Luther King, Jr. Center for Nonviolent Social Change and I spoke of his hurt feelings, knowing for decades he had been the bulwark upon which civil rights had been based in Alabama. I also spoke about the forgotten civil rights activists who had been cast aside. I was asked by Mrs. King to contact Ed and ask him to be one of the grand marshals at the celebration of the first national holiday of Martin Luther King. I called him, and by his voice I could tell that he was happy and appreciative, but he asked me to inform Mrs. King that he was appreciative, but physically he was unable to attend. A few days after that he died.

Dr. Martin Luther King, Jr. did not fear death. He felt it long before it happened. I will never forget May 31, 1965, when Tuskegee University (Tuskegee Institute in those days) awarded me the Merit Award, the highest honor to a graduate. Dr. King delivered the commencement address.

After the commencement and reception were over, Dr. King, Andy Young, Bernard Lee, and I left the campus en route to Selma. As we approached the city of Montgomery, Dr. King marveled at the improvement of the highway. At the intersection of Atlanta Highway and the street going to the Montgomery coliseum, a white male, apparently in his late twenties or early thirties, rolled up beside us and stared at our car, to the extent that everybody noticed it. At the next light again he drove beside us and stooped as though he were getting something off the floor. At that moment Bernard Lee shot past him. Going down a different street, we finally lost him. The conversation drifted to the purpose of the fellow chasing us and that his purpose could have been to shoot Dr. King. Martin said, "I don't think that was his purpose. If it had been more than one man, I might have thought otherwise. I know I'll have to die some day, but one man won't do it."

I had the following dream during the trials and tribulations I experienced while I was working with Dr. King in Selma. I have always remembered it, because of the powerful impact it had on me.

In pursuit of a beautiful blue bird that I thought was wounded and needed first aid, I tried to catch or coop it, to give it tender, loving care, until it was able to become independent. The bird painfully chirped and hopped from the road into a thicket of woods, with me behind it. It seemed to be so pitiful. I surmised the hunter's dogs had tried in vain to kill it, as there was a trail of feathers.

While keeping a constant eye on the bird, and attempting to shield it from further harm, I soon found that I was in a deep, dark, and wide forest. The ground was covered with vines, gullies, ridges, dead leaves and, of course, reptiles and rodents. The flickering lights from a far distant city cast ghostlike shadows from the trees, representing everything that was evil, both large and small, hissing and screaming at me in an unknown tongue. The wind not only whistled but hissed, causing the very trunks of the trees to bend and bow, as though they were walking toward me to smother me to death.

I was terribly frightened. Realizing that I did not think while pursuing the little bird, I said to myself, "Where am I and what am I doing here? The poor little bird will soon die and I'll forget all about it." The forest became dark and only the fluttering of the bird's wings made me know I was still on its trail. Suddenly, the moon came from behind a thick black cloud, as I found myself beside a small tree. Hearing the sound "tweet, tweet," and seeing the pursued bird, food in her mouth, feeding her little dependent family, I gave a sigh of relief for both the bird and me.

I sat up straight in the bed, rubbed my eyes, and said to myself, "What's happened? Thank God that was only a dream."

Not being able to go back to sleep immediately, I re-hashed the previous few minutes in my mind, realizing it was not like me to complete a dream. Surely this dream is telling me something. "What?" I said to myself. I thought of the Biblical story of Balshazzar, the handwriting on the wall, the interpretation of his dream, and the statement, "Some men dream dreams, some men have visions." My dream was constantly on my mind for many days.

I have since tried to interpret this dream, because of the intensity of its impact on me. There had been some dark days since my husband Bill had passed. His last words to me were, "Amelia, I want you to see that all of Dallas County's Negroes are registered." This, I think, is what pursuing the bird meant. I tried to carry out his wish, despite the attacks from Jim Clark and the ostracism from my best friends. I believe the density of the forest represented that fear.

In response to my determination to help to get African-Americans to vote, the coming into the city by Bernard Lafayette, Dr. King and others represented the light from the moon in the dream, and of course, after night comes the day—the day that President Johnson signed the Right to Vote bill.

CHAPTER 2

No Resting Place for Travelers

*Injustice anywhere is a threat to justice
everywhere.*
—Dr. Martin Luther King, Jr.

The fight against segregation began, as I have said, many years before Dr. King came to Montgomery and Selma, Alabama. It began in little ways all over the South, as African-Americans, spurred by the initial successes of the nascent civil rights movement in the 1950s, awakened to their rightful heritage and began to fight for the rights which were guaranteed them in the U.S. Constitution.

In 1961, I had the urge to take a trip to the West. I had a credit card for gasoline, and the company advertised widely its courteous and efficient travel services. I asked the filling station operator if he would map out a route to Los Angeles, with hotel and restaurant stops available for myself and three friends. (We of course knew that not all places would be open to us.) The operator looked puzzled, amazed even, for the task was one he had not done before. He then was chagrined at his inability to chart the route for us and his color changed from pink to red and his voice became indistinct and stammering. Finally, he threw the card on the counter and said, "I don't know anything about travel arrangements. You'll have to do that yourself." I thanked him, took the courtesy card and walked away.

We had more than one courtesy card, so we went to

another filling station operator. He looked at the card, then at my dark skin, and his eyes began to dance wildly, as though we were playing a joke on him. Finally, he asked that we give him a few days to make some contacts. When we went again we found that the rigged-up route he gave us would have us drive all night through Mississippi, Louisiana, and into Texas, arriving there in the early afternoon. The stopover would be a black school, and this was summer, when all schools were closed. The next stop would be the next afternoon at Tucson, Arizona, at a black church. The man said, "You're on your own from there." Frantically, he thrust the badly written, crumpled, and soiled paper into my hand, while his eyes seemed to say, "Drive on until you drop dead. I'll read about you in the newspaper."

The route was not practical, so we turned to a friend, who had recently been to California. This was somewhat better. My friends, Robert Reagin and his wife Rose, their sixteen-year-old son David, and I set out on a clear June morning. We had to leave the highway every time we searched for a night's lodging or something as simple as a sandwich. Things got better the further West we went, but we had a much tougher time coming back East.

We left New Mexico early one morning, stopping several times to get water, drinks, and ice, as well as to have the car serviced. As long as this was all we needed, everything was all right, but the minute we asked to use the restroom or to be served a meal in the café that was annexed to the filling station, the operator would say in a loud voice, "Naw, we can't serve you here," as if to make his stand clear to other men who might be loitering around. Sometimes we would hear, "We don't have colored restrooms," or "We don't serve colored niggers here." We also heard, "We ain't got around to having a restroom for niggers yet, but when you come back, maybe we'll have one built."

This particular day was a long hard drive for David, who was on his first driving adventure, and for me. The other two occupants of the car were not well, and certainly this stretch of the journey did not help them any. Robert had recently had an operation, and Rose was under a doctor's care. On and on we drove, with no malice in our hearts, but pitying ourselves for not having the use of what are supposed to be public facilities, on a government highway, in a government-taxed car, using government-taxed gas and oil.

As night fell, Rose said she was tired and if she could only stretch out on a decent bed for a few minutes she would feel better. Robert was nervous and aching from his operation and needed a hot meal. I drove on with more speed, hoping to get out of Texas as quickly as possible. At midnight, we were still driving and I prayed to God not to let anything happen to these elderly people. The tears began to roll down my cheeks as I became frightened of what could happen. The road seemed to stretch longer and longer as I read the sign "50 miles to Shreveport." "Oh God," I prayed silently, "how long will it be before we can get to a toilet?" The next sign said "10 miles to Shreveport" and the time was 1:20 a.m.

We saw a young African-American walking along the street as we approached Shreveport and we called him to come to the car. He was rather hesitant, as Bob was fair-skinned and he didn't know whether to run or not; injuries might follow, or he might be ordered to get in the car for a "death ride." He began to hurry on, but we drove beside him and I called to him, assuring him that we only wanted directions to the African-American community. I was almost exhausted, my feet were swollen from driving, and Bob and Rose were growing more and more tense. We found the African-American section, where the Saturday night crowd was milling around, but no one could help us find a place to stay.

We went back on the highway to hunt a motel that would take us. My face would get us nowhere, so Bob tried, and the manager was about to arrange accommodations—until someone came to get the luggage and it was discovered that we were blacks. What were we to do? By this time it was about 3:00 a.m. I think all of us cried because we were so tired, we needed to go to the restrooms, and we had had nothing to eat for hours and hours. We finally ended up driving the car into an abandoned filling station, parking there for the rest of the night, and praying that we would not be attacked by hoodlums or outlaws. Later on that day, we drove into Selma, thanking God that we were able to reach home safely.

Such treatment through the years made me and thousands of others realize that the government was too slow in making justice prevail for its citizens and unless we cried out with a loud voice, with demonstrations and other agitation, we would always remain in this condition. This standard pattern of bigotry in the South was like a noose around our necks, dangling us over a sea of fear.

In the fall of 1962, the time came to cry out and to whip into consciousness the necessity to open the eyes of America. The only way for us to bring our injuries before the government and the American people was in nonviolent direct action. Courageous citizens of Birmingham threw their bodies into the streets amid the fast traffic and were bitten by dogs, beaten, clubbed, cattle-prodded, and gassed by officers of the law. This brought our situation to the attention of the government. Rights that were promised us in the U.S. Constitution we had not received, and such rights meant very little unless we were able to claim them.

The Civil Rights Act became law in August 1964. It fell to my lot to test this law, apparently, although I certainly hadn't planned it that way. Since I ran an independent insurance and employment agency and did not fear being fired by the white man in Selma and Dallas County, I was immune to his abuses and felt that, through the years, he had done all the damage he could to us. I had taken a stand to let no man drive me from my home. My being in the insurance field and having to go in and out of the city often gave me a good chance to test the Civil Rights Act.

Before each of the following episodes, I had notified the Justice Department, in order that there would be someone to tell the story correctly if I were mobbed or killed.

In August 1964, I was invited to speak at a church about 60 miles from Selma. My family of four accompanied me—Bruce and his wife and my two teenage foster daughters. I drove a 1955 Chevrolet that had been in the garage for repairs off and on for several years. As there were several good fishing places near Demopolis, my children could fish in the river while I would do insurance work the next day after my address.

First, I called one of the Demopolis motels and made reservations for Sunday at 9:00 o'clock in the evening. A very kind and lovely voice came over the phone saying, "Yes, Mrs. Boynton, I have your reservations confirmed, and we will certainly be looking forward to having you." After the church program, we went to a friend's house for dinner. We told the friend we were going to spend the night at the motel and she was very nervous about it; in fact, she expressed fear for our lives. Knowing her husband's position and knowing that it depended upon the attitude of the local whites, I did not discuss our arrangements further. She said as we left, "Be sure to call and let me know how you make out."

At 8:35 p.m. we went to the motel. As we got out of the car, I saw white people on every side looking at us as though we were beasts in a cage. My son and I walked into the lobby and the clerk quickly arose and said, "What can I do for you?" I told him I was Mrs. Boynton and that I had made reservations for my family. He looked somewhat puzzled. Quite a few whites had gathered around.

I explained to the clerk that I had made the reservations several days ago, and he finally said to me after a great long pause, "I'm sorry, but your reservation has been canceled."

I said, "I'm sure you must be mistaken, because this reservation was confirmed several days ago."

He picked up a card and said, "Yes, it is canceled." Then, he turned and said "The person who makes the reservations must be here before 7:00 o'clock in the evening."

I said, "Not 7:00—the reservation was made for 9:00 o'clock and it is now 8:35. I am ahead of time."

He said, "Oh, no! Anybody who stays in this motel will have to be present at 7:00 o'clock if they are to stay here any time at night."

There were so many curiosity seekers around, I thought we'd better leave, because I didn't want my son to say anything. I knew that prejudice is more against the black man than the woman. We left and drove away, wondering what to do next, as the car was old. Even when we had come into town in the morning, the motor had gotten so hot I thought we'd have to take it to a garage. We decided to phone the friend who gave us dinner, and we stopped at a phone booth.

Meantime, I noticed that a police car was cruising around. The officer didn't see us, but he was looking for us. I said to my son, "Something's up." We left the phone booth without making the call, I got in the car, and went down into the African-American section. There I got in touch with a young man who had an insurance policy with me and explained our situation to him. He said he could arrange for two of us.

I went to the house of another friend, who called a lady across the street, and said she would go over first, then come back for me. She came back about two minutes later, out of breath, and was terribly frightened; officers had surrounded her house. They asked what she was doing with us in there and she explained that we were looking for a place to spend the night. The policeman told her to get those people out of that house, and quickly. I could see how afraid she was, and I told her we would go. But first I would talk to the officers myself.

There were *four* police cars, all with two or more officers in them. As I stepped to my car, the chief of police came up to me and said, "What are you doing in that woman's house, making trouble?"

I said, "Officer, we are not making trouble. We are just trying to find somewhere to stay and she's arranging it."

He said, "Oh no, you aren't! You are making trouble.".

My son, who had not been in Selma for several years, said, "We tried the motel and were turned down."

The officer looked accusingly at Bruce and said, "What are you doing here? What is your name?" Bruce told him and said he was an attorney. Finally the officer said, "I want you to get in your car and get out of town and get out quickly."

I said, "Officer, I am an American citizen and I came from a church. I am to work in this area tomorrow and I am not going back home tonight."

He said, "Oh, yes you are. You're not gonna stay here or I will put you in jail."

I said, "Officer, if you put me in jail I certainly would be glad, for we cannot find anywhere to spend the night and I have to work here tomorrow."

He said, "You're not looking for anywhere to spend the night. I called back to Selma and I know about you and what you do. You're just here to make trouble and we're not going to have any troublemakers around."

Mr. Leonard, who was visiting in my friend's house, lived several miles out of the city. He came to me and said, "Mrs. Boynton, if you will accept the simplicity of my home, we would be glad to have you. I know my mother would welcome you." I accepted his generosity and we all got back into the car. As we went out of the city, three of the police cars escorted us—one in front of Mr. Leonard, one between his car and ours, and one behind us.

Back in Selma a few days later, I went to a white café with a friend. We sat in a booth and waited for someone to come and give us a menu. Instead of a waitress, one of the proprietors came over. He was thin, tall, and elderly. He nervously drummed his fingers on the table, and the moisture on his face told me that he was more than nervous and only needed the support of the other white men in the café to whip up a fury. His fellow employees looked at him as if to say, "If you start the riot, we'll do our part."

His jaws snapped and his teeth chattered as he said, "What y'all want?"

I said, "We would like to be served dinner."

He said, "We can't serve you." He shifted from one leg to the other, as though he were trying to keep from falling before us and finally said, "Y'all better go." I tried to tell him we wanted only to be served, but the poor man was so nervous it seemed nothing could be gained by arguing further, so we left. The FBI and Justice Department were notified before each of these visits.

Later, when I went to the same café with white friends, we found mimeographed leaflets that informed the customers that, "due to circumstances beyond our control, we are compelled to conform to the federal laws that have been forced upon us. We ask that you bear with us until everything returns to normal." I picked up one of these sheets as a souvenir.

My white friend paid the cashier, who looked at her with disgust and contempt. The third time I went to the café, the hostility was weakening. The only discrimination was that the cashier said "thank you" to the customers before and after me, but she accepted my money without saying anything. This was a very small matter and it was not long before the same "thank you" courtesy was given me too, with or without white associates.

CHAPTER 3

We Try the
Boycott

Nonviolence is the answer to the crucial
political and moral questions of our time.
—Dr. Martin Luther King, Jr.

In December 1963, Dallas County Voters League (DCVL) committees had been formed, to learn what percentage of the customers patronizing certain stores were blacks. We knew that in some stores patronage was predominantly African-American, although the owners employed no black help, except in menial jobs.

After the survey, three of us visited the manager of a store near a black housing project. We found him sitting in the back of the store and, as we approached and introduced ourselves, he hardly looked at us.

"Mr. Honor," I said, "We are here from Dallas County Voters League and we wish to talk with you."

He turned around for the first time and looked at us, then said indifferently, "What do you want?"

I said, "There has been a survey made and we have found that 76 percent of your business comes from blacks. In order for these people to be well represented in your store, we are asking that you please put on, during this Christmas season, and for the future, one cashier and one stock clerk who are black."

Mr. Honor thought a moment, then said, "Well, I don't

know. I might consider that. But I'm not going to fire any of my white employees just to give a Negro a job."

I said, "We don't expect you to fire anyone; we want you to add them to your employment. This is the Christmas season, and I'm sure you will need extra help."

Then he said, "You know, the White Citizens' Council sent a committee here to me and they told me they wanted me to fire the niggers I do have." He began to rage, talking loudly, moving things around on his desk and wheeling back and forth in his swivel chair. He said, "I'm not going to add any more niggers. I've got one employed as a stock clerk and I've got niggers down on my farm who are raising vegetables for the store. Before I employ another one or let you or anyone else tell me how to run my store I will close it up. I'll close my doors to all niggers and see that none of them come into it."

Knowing the racists as I do, I didn't become alarmed nor did I lose my temper, but the student on the committee was terribly hurt, and ran out of the store in tears. She didn't understand the bigots and couldn't take their arrogance. Other stores were asked to hire African-Americans, but none of them responded.

A few days after these visits, a conference was called, then we had a mass meeting of citizens. They voted to boycott all the white stores, although the Christmas rush had started. They held their purse strings and informed the youngsters that there would be no Santa Claus that Christmas. Then the merchants began to feel the pinch. Mr. Honor, who had said he would close the store before he would hire African-Americans in white-collar capacities and would even close the store to black customers, led all the other merchants in contacting black leadership to come in and talk to him. He begged them to use their influence to have the black buyers return. Of course, he blamed me and my committee for having diverted the trade, but he apologized for his rudeness to us and asked the group to do all they could for him. However, the committee had to tell him that at this point we would not be able to turn back;

it had been decided that the African-Americans would go through with the boycott. The boycott was so successful that we learned it was the most effective method we could use to demand respect.

Selma was so used to blacks being mistreated (and to their taking it) that they could not understand why black people had turned away and had begun to resent being used like animals. In view of all the hostility of county and city officials toward African-Americans and the fact that African-Americans were still trying to get along with the whites, we thought it would be a good thing to call a meeting of the white people, since they would not call a meeting with us.

Captain Wilson Baker and the mayor agreed to a meeting; we had a series of them, in fact, but each resulted in no agreement. I could not attend all of them, as I was out of town part of the time. When I came back to the city I attended one and as they began to talk about what was going on and what would go on, I asked, "What have you done and what is concrete that you are going to do?" Then came heated discussion.

Mr. Baker said, "We were doing fine until you came, and now you have sabotaged the meeting." This was his interpretation of my trying to pin the officials down to something concrete, so we could have something to depend on. He finally said, "You demand too much." I said it wasn't a matter of demanding too much; after all, we were citizens of America and of Selma, and had paid our taxes as did others. We felt it was our duty to get as much as anyone else and to demand respect also. With that, the meeting was dismissed.

Several days afterwards, one of the black citizens called and said, "We have been invited to come to the mayor's office for a meeting, but the permanent committee is not invited. We are calling all the former committeemen to let them know what the mayor has said. We would like for you to come in just about the time they begin to talk about what they are expecting of us."

Those called to the meeting were the Reverend C.C. Brown, Calvin Orsborn, Dr. Sullivan Jackson, and Warner Reid. They all notified us that they were going. At the meeting, the mayor and Mr. Baker informed them of what was expected of them and that they were to carry on the ideas "that were those of the city." They also told them what they were going to do and what they couldn't do, and certainly any plans did not include giving black citizens their freedom.

The meeting was almost over when the original committee walked in the door and the city fathers looked at us and froze, their faces as red as beets.

Our purpose was to show that the city fathers could not pit one African-American against the other, for the African-Americans now had a solid front. We intended to fight segregation until every segment of it had fallen away in the city and in the country.

CHAPTER 4

The Race for Congress

*In the construction of a country it is not the
practical workers but the idealists and
planners that are difficult to find.*
                                    —Sun Yat-Sen

In 1958, Bill and I had gone to Montgomery and testified
before the Civil Rights Commission, telling of the many
atrocities the African-Americans had endured and how they
were afraid. We told about the African-Americans who had
to get off the plantations because they tried to register. We
told how some were beaten because they went to voter
registration clinics my husband had held in the counties.
We told them of the blacks in the city who had lost their
jobs and the officers who would constantly walk by the
meeting places and intimidate the people.

Many of the men of the Commission complimented us
on our courage but were afraid for us. This was five years
before Dallas County's civil rights struggle was known to
the nation. They advised us not to go home on Highway 80
but to take the back road, which we did, leaving Montgomery early enough to get to Selma before dark.

Keeping the registration fires burning was no easy task.
Six years later, we staged mass meetings in the county or
the city nightly and often, because of the crowds, we had
them in two or three places the same night. Black people
came from surrounding counties to hear how they could
win their freedom. They felt they couldn't afford to stay at

home, although their day's work was hard and the hours long. This was particularly true of the farming people in spring and fall.

Teaching the black people to hold up their heads, stand tall, and be counted, kept an ever-increasing flow of young people attending the meetings. They were easily convinced that something needed to be done about their parents' civil rights and they placed themselves in the line of duty. Convincing the black ministers that the time to help their people was now and the place was right here was harder. Almost all ministers had to be begged to let us have meetings in their churches (we could not go to the armory, schools, courthouse, and other political places) and after we persuaded them, the church would be opened by the sexton but the ministers would conveniently disappear at meeting time.

During these trying times of getting the Selma and Dallas County African-Americans together, I was often greeted with sneers and jeers as I came home late at night. For weeks, I received anonymous phone calls all night long. The callers would let out a volume of the worst curses and threats I have ever heard in my life. But such threats were not new; during the Fikes trial the phone rang one morning about 3:00 o'clock and when I answered, a heavy voice said, "Nigger, we ain't gonna have you all trying to change things around here. Git out of town and damn quick." Later the phone rang again and my husband answered but said nothing to me (I had gone back to bed and to sleep without disturbing him). I finally asked him who it was and he said, "Don't worry, it was some crackpot who said our house is going to be bombed." He also went back to sleep. This kept up for weeks and I hoped no one would dare set foot on the premises, for my husband was a good marksman, who could hit his target from any angle and almost any distance.

All these threats made me more determined to fight for what I knew was right. Not once did I become frightened nor did I fear going into my own home. There were many friends who stood guard at all times and they gave me strength to continue. But more than anything else, I depended on the guidance of God, who I felt had groomed me for this struggle. The struggle of the African-Americans was also that of the white man, and far beyond my expectations, from across the country there came black and white people to help us.

Bill foresaw the African-Americans being registered in the South and even predicted that I might some day run for U.S. Congress. I asked what about himself and he ignored that question, saying, "I'm not joking, you might run for Congress."

I often go over in my mind the conversations I had with my husband when it seemed he was talking about the impossible. Yet, a short time after his death, this dream began to materialize. During his last days, although hospitalized, Bill continued to campaign for better times. He was paralyzed, but he would station his wheelchair in the hospital's doorway and talk to all who came by, urging them to get registered to vote. At the time he could not get twenty Selma blacks to attend a local meeting on registration. But Bill died May 13, 1963 and the first significant mass meeting in Selma began the night of his death—he smiled as though he knew blacks at last were unified, a sight he had longed to see. A new chapter was opening in Selma history, and somehow, for me, the sting was removed from his death.

In January 1964, I spoke at Tuskegee Institute at a regional meeting of the Women's International League for Peace and Freedom. As I sat in this integrated, interfaith group that was working for human rights, I felt I would like to become a part of it and work with others for a common cause. I was impressed by the organization's fight against the war, poverty, and for civil rights. The following year a team led by Reverend Anna Lee Stuart, former national president, and Mrs. Margaret Hatch came to Selma and organized a branch of the league. They plunged into such things as a door-to-door campaign for voter registration; helped distribute food and clothing sent in from across the country; called on white ministers to enlist support; and trained, by the

Laubach method, those who would in turn teach other adults to read and write.

That night at Tuskegee I told them about Selma, the Black Belt, the struggle, and the African-Americans who wanted freedom. My husband's words came back to me and at the end of my talk, I heard myself saying that I might run for Congress this year from my district. That was the first time I had taken the idea seriously, and I had no plans or platform. This was the eleventh hour for candidates' closing. After the meeting, many people said "Why don't you? This is a very good idea. Good luck to you. Blacks should run for office." Then a lady from California gave me a check for $10 and said, "This is your first contribution; I bid you Godspeed." How could I turn back then?

I gave the matter more serious thought and wondered why I had made such a statement. Since I had made it publicly, I couldn't just let it go. I didn't expect the idea to take root and grow right away, but at a mass meeting the following Sunday night, I announced that I might run for Congress. The audience stood up and applauded. Though they were not registered voters, they wanted to see representatives in office who were interested in their rights and welfare.

I wondered how such a campaign would go. Less than 5 percent of the blacks in the district (which included eight counties) were registered voters. For an eight-year period through 1964 only fourteen African-Americans were registered in Dallas County out of a potential 13,000 of voting age.

Two of the most backward counties are Wilcox and Lowndes. In 1965, there were 8,709 people in Wilcox County over 21, of whom 6,885 were African-American. No African-Americans were registered to vote. There were 2,974 white voters registered—113.2 percent. Lowndes County, where the potential black voting population was 5,122 (with none registered), had 2,314 white registered voters, and the official figure was 121.8 percent registered. How could this be? Could tombstones and trees vote?

There was much fighting to do for both black and white poor, who had not exercised their rights. The poor whites were unaware that they too were being taken advantage of politically, almost as badly as the blacks.

I knew I would be a target for the white racists and those blacks who feared thinking any way other than according to the white man's signals.

A black man approached me and said, "Mrs. Boynton, you are crazier than I thought you were. What do you think you are doing? This is a white man's country and it's his politics. You are going to be a target for the white man now."

I smiled and said, "What have you and I been all these years but a target?" He was not a registered voter yet he was one of the black professional men of his county.

By running for Congress, I hoped to accomplish two things: First, to release the African-American from his fear of the white man and get him to go down in large numbers and register, recalling that he is a tax-paying citizen; and second, to arouse the African-American to awareness that nonviolent resistance and going to jail were God-given rights, be he black or white. If the African-American reclaimed his duty to fight to register and vote, bad government could be voted out and good government put in office.

In spite of the threats and the ugliness, I had made up my mind to get on the ballot. On February 29, 1964, the last minute for the candidates to qualify, my attorney, Orzell Billingsley of Birmingham, and I drove to the office of Judge Mayhall, the Democratic chairman. White men loitered inside and outside the building. As we went up the steps, we realized that the crowd was following us. Those inside were whispering and pointing to us. I paid the $450 fee to qualify to run in the Democratic primary, and the news traveled fast; before the day was over, every radio station was reporting my move.

My plans were ridiculous, but now I was in the race willy-nilly. Kenneth Roberts was the representative of this Fourth Congressional District and he spared no time or literature letting his constituents know that he would do all in his power to keep politics white.

I had in my favor the interest of the untiring workers of the Student Nonviolent Coordinating Committee, who offered their services, their encouragement, and their Atlanta office personnel. This was our first affiliation, organizationally, with the Southern Christian Leadership Conference, of which SNCC was the youth group.

The Fourth C.D. consisted of eight counties. My husband had been president of the Fourth C.D. for registration and voting for several years, and I was secretary. The counties were Autauga, Dallas, Coosa, Calhoun, Talladega, Clay, Tallapoosa, and St. Clair. In the entire district there were fewer than 1,500 registered black voters and 190,000 registered whites.

Many friendly white people, as well as many African-Americans, knew the purpose of my running and offered any assistance they could. The blacks had become aroused and, as announcements were made in the local churches, both in town and in the rural areas, many went down to register. Few passed the tests however. SNCC sent a young lady from Washington, D.C. to do the clerical work and John Lewis, James Forman, and others came down to offer their personal service as well as financial support. Special mention should be made of Dick Gregory and his wife and of James Baldwin, who were involved in the Selma struggle long before it became popular, fashionable, and relatively safe to do so.

People of good will were alerted, but so were people of hostility, among them the Ku Klux Klan. I received a letter from Leonard R. Wilson, executive secretary of the Alabama White Citizens' Council. Its many questions, I felt, were better handled by an attorney. Had I tried to answer, perhaps I would be misinterpreted. The list of questions from him, with my answers, was mimeographed by my son, attorney Bruce Boynton, and distributed to all the churches and organizations. The list was also sent to the local papers but was never printed.

One day, as Bruce drove down the street in my car, officers stopped him and placed him under arrest. This made headlines as the papers, radio, and TV announced, "Boynton Arrested by City Police." The article stated prominently that Bruce was the son of the black candidate for Congress in the upcoming state Democratic primary. The objective was to reflect on *my* character. The case was never brought to trial of course; there were no grounds, but the mere arrest had served the purpose of character defamation by headline.

The March 23, 1964 *Selma Times Journal* reported that a television crew from the University of Georgia spent three hours on March 22 at the home of Amelia P. Boynton, shooting a sound film. The crew was hired by National Educational Television Production in New York. Sheriff Jim Clark was interviewed, proudly stating that he and State Trooper Captain Robert Moore halted the three-vehicle, seven-person convoy shortly after it left the Boynton house and asked the members for their identities, which are listed. He said, "Members of his department kept the filming under surveillance from six to nine p.m. Sunday."

The article identified me as the "first female member of her race ever to seek a seat in Congress from Alabama." I was also the first woman, white or black, to run on the Democratic ticket.

Anything I did at this time was called to the attention of those determined to block my progress. I had to have some repairs on my house, and after weeks of suffering along with an unreliable workman, who kept charging me as he did each piece of work, I decided to hold back $70 he was asking until city inspection could be made. He then went to a lawyer, who got an injunction issued against my property. The inspector, whom I called, told me that he had found the place could not stand inspection, but would see to it that the work was finished properly.

After receiving the judgment, I had my attorney take the case to set the matter straight, with the information that the city inspector had refused to okay the house. But I might have known the matter would not end there. A few days later I picked up the local paper to see the headline, "Officers Impound Boynton's Vehicle." I didn't recognize what this was all about at first and then read further: "The Dallas County sheriff impounded the personal automobile of Negro Congressional candidate, Amelia P. Boynton, on a circuit court order growing out of her failure to pay a plumbing bill. . . . Sheriff Clark said the woman's car will be held in storage for the time set by law or until the judgment has been satisifed. If the judgment has not been satisfied within the legal time, it will be sold at public auction to satisfy the debt. The woman is a candidate for Congress against Representative Kenneth Roberts."

One of the more deplorable aspects of this episode was the fact that the plumber was an African-American, and I had mistakenly assumed I would be encouraging "black enterprise." But it was only too apparent that he was a "good nigger, only he half does his work," in the words of the inspector. The "good nigger" was one who could be used, even against another African-American, to suit the white man's purposes.

I was determined not to pay the bill until the work was satisfactorily completed, and I again called the inspector, who promised again to straighten things out.

The old 1955 car was parked on one of the streets where it had developed engine trouble. If it were to be sold to pay for work that was not done, I then thought I had a good chance to bring to court the unjust inspector, who allowed inferior work to get by because it was done for a black militant.

Soon the sheriff's deputies came to my house saying they were sent to attach my property, if they could not collect the plumber's money. I explained the reasons, but got no-where. I said I would not pay the bill, even if I had to go to jail and one of them said, "You would not like to miss being a congressman, would you?" He said he would have to attach something and I told them to take the house. They said they would have to put up a large sign and I told them to go ahead and I would take a picture of them doing it and spread it over every paper in the country. They said they would take the furniture, because the car was not worth the money and I said this would be great, because such a picture would be even more interesting to the readers. However, they did not carry through.

In spite of all the attempts to discourage African-Americans from voting, I knew I was winning the hearts and minds of black Americans in Alabama. Election day arrived, and I received more than 10 percent of the votes in the district. Many precincts with no blacks gave me a goodly number of votes. My campaign motto, which was also posted as a sign in our office was: "A voteless people is a hopeless people."

CHAPTER 5

First Steps Toward Freedom

Man must evolve for all human conflict a method which rejects revenge, aggression, and retaliation. The foundation of such a method is love. —Dr. Martin Luther King, Jr.

In October 1962, Bernard Lafayette, a former Fisk University student active with SCLC, came to Selma and spent a few weeks studying the condition of the black community. On Thanksgiving of the same year, Bernard left and returned with his wife Colia. She was a college student, young, smart and outgoing, with the gift of vocal communication and a wisdom superior to her age.

Colia drafted a plan to touch every black home in Selma and as far beyond the city limit as her transportation permitted her. No sooner was her plan drawn up than she began to implement it, calling students, girls and boys from thirteen to sixteen years of age, and sending them in teams to contact occupants of every house. They had them fill out forms, asking name, age, address, occupation, and whether the person was a registered voter. These survey sheets were filed for later use by older surveyors, and thus laid the basis for the survey of the entire city.

In late 1964, students interested in the whole civil rights movement were gathering after school at the home of Mrs. Margaret J. Moore, a teacher, where Bernard Lafayette lived. At this home, the young people were getting acquainted with African-American history and the search for identity,

and they were learning freedom songs. Students filled the
house at all times.

During this period, the city police, the sheriff, and his
deputies constantly patrolled the neighborhood, picking up
the youths after they left the house and jailing them. Finally,
Mrs. Moore gave one of her rented houses for the activities.
Many of the girls were harassed by white men as they
walked down the streets in groups. As word spread of the
mistreatment, more interest was created among the blacks,
and the black crowd seeking justice grew still larger. The
First Baptist Church was opened by the Reverend M.C.
Cleveland, Jr., and Tabernacle Baptist Church, pastored by
the Reverend L.L. Anderson, took care of the overflow. Both
churches were open day and night, and both held teaching
sessions on nonviolence and the filling in of applications
for voter registration. This was before Governor Wallace
changed the applications every two weeks and made them
several pages long.

The first church in Selma permitting us to have voter
education training was that of Reverend Hunter, pastor of
the AME Zion church on Lawrence Street. The church was
small, but we were warmly welcomed. The second church
was First Baptist, followed by Tabernacle Baptist on Broad
Street. The participants were so numerous by the latter part
of 1964 that, Brown Chapel AME Church being nearer the
heart of the city and near First Baptist, the adults were asked
to assemble at Brown Chapel, while the youth remained at
First Baptist Church. People from the rural sections were
much more advanced in voter education, being exposed to
their right to vote as well as land ownership for many years
by their county agent, S.W. Boynton.

Another phase of the meetings was the teaching of self-
control and Christian methods of handling discrimination.
During one of these meetings early in 1964, the streets
around the churches were patrolled by Jim Clark and his
deputies. Their aim was to break up the meetings and send
people home in a fright. Clark sent men into the church to
pick up the leader of the meeting but the men did not know

him and came back without him. Then Clark himself went in, while the young Reverend Bennie Tucker was on his knees praying. He walked up to the young man, collared him, and dragged him while his deputies cattle-prodded him to the waiting sheriff's car.

Early the next morning, black adults about 400 strong went to the courthouse to register. The courthouse doors were locked and guarded by men with bayonets and shotguns. The people were not allowed to get out of line or hold conversations with passersby or even with the persons next to them. To inconvenience them more, the restrooms were locked and the prospective registrants were not allowed to step out of line at all or they would lose their place in line. Sheriff Jim Clark informed all who were standing that he would jail them for disturbing the peace if they talked.

The sun was hot, the pavement was hard, and there was nowhere to sit. But instead of falling out from exhaustion, they stood like soldiers, hoping, praying, and wishing Jim Clark's heart would soften and that he would open the doors for them to go into the courthouse and register. At 3:30 in the afternoon the people left, not one having had the opportunity to register.

Every day that the books were open in this spring of 1964, long lines of blacks would brave the wind, the cold, the rain, or the hot sun, only to be humiliated, turned away, or jailed. One hot day in May, while several hundred people were waiting to be registered, a committee including James Forman and John Lewis of SNCC, Marie Foster, and other workers prepared sandwiches and punch to serve the people who so patiently waited. We took the lunches to the steps of the federal building just across from the courthouse.

I walked over to where Sheriff Clark stood and asked him to permit me to give the people sandwiches and something to drink. He turned as though I had struck him. After he recovered from the shock, he said, "No, I'll be damned if you do." I told him they had been standing in the hot sun all day, and I wanted to at least give them water. Again he shot back at me, "If you bring water or anything, I will arrest you for molesting."

I was as shocked at his using the word molesting as he was at my approach to him, and I said, "Molesting? If giving human beings something to eat when they are hungry is molesting, then mothers molest the babes in the crib." I turned to walk across the street and I heard a white man in the crowd say, "Git 'em!" White people were running toward two blacks who were being beaten by officers. I saw the officers handcuff the blacks and push them into a waiting bus. Then a tall white man went into the bus and cursed the two black youths loudly and shook his finger in their faces. The youths had brought all this on by trying to give an old man a sandwich and a drink of water. The white man who left the bus walked slowly down the street observing every person in line. Later I heard that he was Mr. Dunn, co-owner of the Dunn Rest Home.

The hundreds of people in line included teachers, ministers, professionals, and businessmen and women, as well as domestic workers and housewives. There were also two nurses' aides, who worked at the Dunn Rest Home; their names were Elnora Collins and Annie Cooper. As Dunn passed them, he paused long enough to be sure these were his employees. Mrs. Cooper then said to Mrs. Collins: "There goes Dunn," and Mrs. Collins replied, "And there goes our jobs."

The following day was Mrs. Cooper's day off, but the secretary of the Dunn Rest Home called her to say her services were no longer needed. She had expected this.

That night, the 40 or more employees of the rest home called a meeting and asked me to attend. They decided to ask for the return of Mrs. Cooper or they would all leave. In the petition they drew up there were other grievances, including need for a raise in salary (they were paid only $16 a week), work hours to be cut from twelve per day to eight, and provisions for sick leave and insurance. The petition was typed, signed, and given to one of the nurses, who was spokesman for the group. The time to hand Dunn the petition was to be 10:00 o'clock the next morning. Meantime, Dunn sent for Mrs. Collins to come to his office. She also was expecting the call and went to receive her dismissal for trying to register to vote.

Dunn gruffly announced as she walked in, "Elnora, you're fired. I don't need you around here any longer."

Elnora smiled and said, "Thank you, Mr. Dunn." (His employees usually respectfully addressed him as "doctor," although he had no M.D. degree.) She left to inform the others, but before she could get to the other workers, Dunn's secretary again called her and told her that Dunn wanted to see her again.

She found him standing in front of his desk with a camera. He told her to face him so he could get a good picture. She knew this was the method used by whites to keep the African-Americans from being hired by anyone else, and she held her purse up to her face and said, "I'm not going to let you take my picture, because I know just what you're going to do with it." Dunn then put the camera down and picked up a cattle prod he had used on one of the janitors. Before Mrs. Collins could get away he beat her over the head, across the shoulders and on her back, electrifying her entire body and inflicting painful bruises.

She ran screaming out of the office, down the stairs, and into the street. Her alarm brought the rest of the workers from their posts and all left the rest home. The woman who was to deliver the petition remembered it just in time and handed it to the secretary as she passed her in the hall.

This all happened early in the morning, and at about 7:30 a.m., there were 40 nurses who came to my house to tell me what happened. My first impulse was to take Mrs. Collins to a doctor and have the entire group go with us. We did this, and Mrs. Collins was treated for burns and bruises. The Justice Department and the FBI were notified and many sworn statements were taken by them.

What happened to Dunn, superintendent and part-owner of the Dunn Rest Home? The same thing that happened to all white people who mistreated African-Americans. Nothing, except a pat on the back from other racists.

(Note: By late 1967 Mr. Dunn had passed to his reward and the Dunn Rest Home had become integrated.)

CHAPTER 6

Backlash and Frontlash

*Those who profess to favor freedom, and
yet deprecate agitation, are men who want
crops without plowing up the ground, they
want rain without thunder and lightning.
They want the ocean without the awful roar
of its many waters.* —Frederick Douglass

During this time, when the blacks began the struggle to register and vote, there were more than 550 out of jobs, fired because of their participation in some phase of the civil rights movement. No one would hire them, and many were heads of families. This created a grave problem, with the families hungry and half naked, bills long overdue, and eviction threatening.

A plea was sent out across the nation by SNCC, asking for food and clothing for those who were feeling the backlash from the Selma movement. Other sections of the Black Belt were experiencing the same fate, as their attempts to register brought on white retaliation. Food, medicine, clothing, and other supplies began to pour in.

Many blacks in the middle class as well as others, who steered clear of the movement for fear of the whites, realized they could no longer walk on the other side of the street to avoid those involved. This was the struggle of every black man, woman, and child, and they began to join the others, swelling the mass meetings to overflowing.

Songs and poems were written to be used in the mass meetings. Sharon and Germaine Platts, twelve and fourteen years old respectively, and Arlene Ezell, fourteen, wrote the following song.

Chorus:
Freedom is a-coming and it won't be long
Freedom is a-coming and we're marching on
If you want to be free, come and go with me.

1.
We are marching on to freedom land
So come along and join, hand in hand
Striving on and singing a song
I hope we're not alone.

2.
We are striving for our equal rights
So come on and join hands and fight
Striving on and singing a song
I know we're not alone.

It was heartwarming to have the doors of the churches open to us, although the ministers were still uncommitted, in spite of the pleas of their deacons and other church leaders for them to take an active part. The grassroots people we were most concerned about showed their profound interest and were determined to work with us. At the opening of the meetings they threw themselves into singing "We are climbing Jacob's ladder . . . Soldiers of the Cross. . . . Every rung goes higher, higher, Soldiers of the Cross."

This made the most faint-hearted and discouraged feel the reality of the struggle, and the progress being made for white and black alike. Every round of it moved them higher into the realm of first-class citizenship. They knew that God was with them and they could feel the slackening of the mental chains of slavery that had bound the race for hundreds of years. They could feel freedom overcoming lawlessness, ill treatment, disfranchisement, poor housing, unfair employment practices, segregated schools, and many other evils.

One evening my tears flowed freely as I looked into the faces of these people, who believed that freedom was coming. I said to myself, "If only the white citizens of Selma would come and see the faces of the new blacks and hear them lift their voices to God in song and prayer, praying for their white brothers as well as themselves, one would think they would have a change of heart and would realize that, as the black man progresses, so will the white."

But this was no time for tears. We had a job to do and it had to be done now. We had to find jobs for the fired people and give them something besides words of consolation.

I called the Employment Bureau of Alabama to let them know that we were sending women for employment, but they were given the brushoff. Some were told they had to be high school graduates and, when they produced their diplomas, they were given a card to hold until they were called, which of course never happened. This was because when they filled out the information sheets, they had to tell about their local activities, including meetings they attended. They had been dismissed because they dared to break the traditional pattern of the Southern way of life. They wanted to register and vote! They wanted a fair share of America because they had worked for it and so had their forefathers.

I asked myself, what could we do for the people right away?

For more than 30 years my sister Elizabeth Smith and her family, who lived in Philadelphia, had operated a small factory in their basement. The large clothing factories kept them supplied with thousands of garments each week. The rough work was done on them and returned to the factory for finishing. Many of the operators they employed were people fresh from the South and others who could not find work elsewhere. Some were given work to take home but most worked eight hours a day and made as much as $80 a week. If this plan could work in Philadelphia, why not in Selma?

Mrs. Marie Foster and I called together other friends who

were willing to give time, and the idea took hold. We realized that help and encouragement had to come from outside the city because the white citizens who sympathized were afraid of becoming outcasts. Mrs. Ruth Lindsey, Mrs. Geneva Martin, Miss Idell Rawls, Mrs. Foster, Mrs. Gloria Maddox, and I set the project in motion when we brought the plan before the Dallas County Voters League and asked for sewing machines. The First Baptish Church offered its basement and its minister, the Reverend M.C. Cleveland, who was one of the most liberal and cooperative ministers of the larger black churches, offered whatever services he could give. The Reverend Ralph Smeltzer of the Church of the Brethren began to make contacts for us. He made provision for Mrs. Martin and Miss Rawls to go to Maryland for a training course that would teach them to train others. Other white friends sent sewing machines. Applications for working in the project came in by the hundreds from people who were happy to get the chance. They were able-bodied people, who wanted to retain their dignity and self-respect as well as to be independent.

As we began to make progress in training women to sew on high-powered and ordinary machines, the good white people of Selma permitted the sheriff to use any conceivable means to block gathering of African-Americans and to hinder the training sessions with the aim of cutting off their power to help themselves.

Governor Wallace had instituted a peculiar kind of government that took upon itself the assignment of penetrating into the North and demonstrating his racist methods. As a result, an organization was formed in Baltimore called GROW (Get Rid of Wallace), that wanted to tell the truth about the principles for which this man stood. I received a letter from GROW asking me to come to Baltimore to challenge Wallace and his hate campaign.

Five rallies were held in Baltimore on Sunday, May 10, 1964. I spoke at all of them and later at Johns Hopkins University, and found the students and faculty in sympathy with the blacks of Dallas County. Many wanted to come

down and demonstrate or do whatever they could to break
the back of hate-filled segregation. Many felt that if something were not done to discourage this man, even the people
who disagreed with his approach would, through apathy,
leave the field to him and allow little Wallaces and little
Hitlers to flourish all over the country.

When I came back to Selma, I received an injunction from
Sheriff Jim Clark. I had thought he was satisfied because I
did not win the congressional seat and would let me alone
for a while, but not so. He was determined to kill whatever
encouragement the blacks might have. His letter forbade
us to congregate or have any walk-ins, sit-ins, or any other
form of demonstration. "It cannot be," I thought, and rushed
to my office, which was also that of SNCC. "Read this ridiculous injunction," I said. "I really cannot believe what I'm
reading." Several gathered around and we began to read
almost in concert:

WRIT OF INJUNCTION
IN THE CIRCUIT COURT OF DALLAS COUNTY,
STATE OF ALABAMA, IN EQUITY
COUNTY OF DALLAS
TO ANY SHERIFF OF THE STATE OF ALABAMA, GREETINGS:
You are hereby commanded, that without delay you execute
this writ, and make due return how you have executed the
same, according to the law.

Witness my hand this 11th day of July A.D. 1964
To: Martin Luther King, Jr., James Bevel, Amelia Boynton,
    Marie Foster, L.L. Anderson. . . .

We continued to read through more than twenty names
of persons and organizations, which ended with "John Doe
and Richard Roe, whose correct names are unknown to the
Complainants at this time, but who are described as persons
who have or may act in concert or participation with the
named respondents, whose correct names will be inserted
by amendment when ascertained."

After we read the list, which included some people who had nothing to do with the movement, we almost pulled the complaint apart, trying to get down to the substance of it. Buried in much legal language was the statement that the gathering of three people or more seen in any public place, including the streets of Selma or anywhere, could be considered in violation of this injunction and therefore would be subject to arrest and jailing by the sheriff of Dallas County.

We looked at each other in amazement. This meant that if the sheriff cared to arrest violators, he certainly would have to arrest the minister (the injunction included all the African-American ministers of churches in Selma and some of the rest of the county), if he had more than one person in his congregation at worship; the teacher if she had more than one pupil; and even worse, if a parent took her family to town to do some shopping, she and her brood could be arrested. We felt that this injunction must be broken and the sheriff's orders challenged.

In the face of Clark's injunction, older African-American citizens began to realize the importance of coming to mass meetings. They would go to the registrar's office and the registrar would fail to pass them. As soon as the waiting period was over, they would go back again. This process went on for several months before the nation realized the African-Americans' plight. Educators, business and professional people, lettered and unlettered, learned and unlearned African-Americans, all went to the board to be given an oral examination by a white person with not more than an eighth-grade education himself, but who happened to be white and perhaps rich.

One African-American teacher, who had earned her masters degree from a northern college, went to the board several times trying to register. A question was read which she didn't understand, and she asked the man to repeat it. He made another attempt to pronounce the big words, and the teacher said, "Those words are 'constitutionality' and 'interrogatory.' " The registrar turned red with anger, but realized she was right. He swallowed his pride and continued reading. Though she knew more about government than he would ever know, she flunked the test and was refused her registration certificate.

Another woman I knew tried to take the test many times and failed. The registrar read a half-page to her and then told her to leave the room and stand outside. She was there for more than fifteen minutes. Not knowing what to do, she was about to leave when the door opened and the man called her back. He then told her to write what he had read to her before she left the room. The frustrated woman burst into tears and ran out. So many incredible experiences have been told by the African-Americans who tried to register that if even half are true, they betray only a ridiculous fear on the part of the whites, rather than exposure of unfitness to vote on the part of the African-Americans.

Twice a month the questionnaires were changed. The registrars themselves didn't know the answers, couldn't read the questions half the time, and certainly couldn't interpret them. Applicants could not see the questions beforehand. There was no possible way for either white or black applicants to pass the test, though many whites did get the list in advance. (I was told by a white friend that she was sent a book of questions to study to prepare for registration. I also found that whites visited the courthouse on a different schedule—after hours. Of course there were not too many whites who needed to register at all, having been voters for years already.)

Even the mastermind of the questionnaire, Governor Wallace, could never pass such an examination. These and other barriers were raised to keep the African-Americans from becoming first-class citizens, and these were some of the reasons the African-Americans *had* to fight, with demonstrations, confrontations, sit-ins, stand-ins, and walk-ins, which led to the historic 50-mile march from Selma to Montgomery on March 21, 1965. But before that, two other attempts were made to march and much blood was spilled.

In December 1964, we laid plans for a mammoth mass

meeting to be held in January, with Dr. Martin Luther King, Jr. as the main speaker. This planning session of Selma and Dallas County leaders opened new avenues and gave great hope to a people which had lost the battle in their struggle to vote. Thus the curtain fell on 1964, and would rise again on a cast which had gained courage and determination. The stars were the weary and worn citizens, leaders, and Dr. King.

CHAPTER 7

The Struggle Goes On

*Nonviolence is the first article of my faith. It
is also the last article of my creed.*
                                    —Mahatma Gandhi

Having one's office across from a Southern jail for 30
years has quite an effect upon one who is in sympathy
with the downtrodden. I could hear cries and pleas of prisoners, and often the sound of straps which lashed their bare
backs. Many times I closed the door to keep from hearing
the weeping of grown men and women. Brutality and injustice we lived with, every day. The very law and order represented by the enforcement officers was such a travesty that
it was no wonder the black man was filled with fear when
he saw a white man. Day after day, there were black people
who feared meeting an officer on the street, because he
might suddenly begin beating, kicking, or clubbing him
unmercifully, seemingly without cause. This had happened
in front of my office many times, and especially because
the liquor store was in the same block.

In spite of the atrocities the African-American had to
endure, there were many, for a wonder, who had no hate
or malice in their hearts—fear and ignorance, but not hate.
They wanted only to know where to turn for help, so when
Dr. King came into the city, along with SNCC and others, to
help unshackle those in bondage, he was welcomed by all
blacks of Dallas County. Most of the prisoners and the

people who had been to jail for some slight provocation made up their minds that this time they would go for something important—their rights which had been taken away. This explains why the marches and demonstrations were so successful.

After January 2, 1965, when Dr. King came into the picture to work with us, ministers seemed to gain courage and began stepping over each other to get to the rostrum and before the audience. Cooperation improved all around, whereas previously too many were afraid of what the white citizens might think and the effect such activity might have on their credit. A few women, two of them teachers, had to bear the burden until the program mushroomed into a national movement. As the nation was made aware of the denial of civil rights, human rights, and rights of any description for the African-American in Alabama, the same problem came to light in all parts of the country.

On January 18, several hundred people, mostly African-Americans, left Brown's Chapel AME Church on Sylvan Street in Selma and, led by Dr. King, marched to the Dallas County Courthouse. En route we were advised by Safety Director Wilson Baker and his assistants to break up into small groups to keep from violating an ordinance and we took their advice. The march opened a new campaign to get the blacks to make the attempt to register and vote, even though they knew this was only a beginning and would be a dangerous undertaking. How dangerous and how much bloodshed would ensue, we did not know.

Dr. King had registered in the Albert Hotel in Selma, one of the old landmarks, built with slave labor more than 100 years before. The hotel was designed as a replica of the Doge's Palace in Venice. While there, Dr. King was kicked and punched by a white man, who was led away by his comrades.

There followed at least seven weeks of jailings, beatings, starvings, and even killings in early 1965. More than 2,000 men, women, and children were imprisoned in Selma and adjacent counties. In the county jails and prison camps the treatment was deplorable. Meals at the camp consisted of cornbread with sand and rocks in it, syrup, and coffee with salt. There were no toilets, only one open stool; the women had to form a wall around to keep from being exposed. At the time, one group was taken to the camp, there were so many people that they could not stretch out on the floor (there were no beds). The guards made the men stand in single file, each person's nose in the hair of the one before him. If anyone moved, the guard struck him in his privates with a cattle prod. The women had to sleep on a floor that was wet. Such evil treatment was similar to that ordered by Hitler.

The blacks stopped buying from downtown, and business fell off more than 50 percent. This set off a chain of resentment from the local white men, but they did not have the power to stop Sheriff Clark and his intimidations. Everyone coming into my office inquiring about him wanted to know, "What manner of man is this, that all white people in the city seem to fear him?" He typified the great power of the sheriff in the South.

One woman had told her daughter to "stay out of that mess, because my white folks told me I would lose my job if my family got involved." She had sent her daughter to the store and on the way, with no provocation, an officer arrested her. After this, the mother told me she was going to fight to the finish, and take part in every demonstration, even if it meant her job. My consolation to her was that she was in it when she was born an African-American.

Several students from Selma University were arrested for demonstrating along with hundreds of others. The president of the university bargained with Clark to let him have the students back, and promised that they would not be further involved. These students were pressured in every way by the president. This did not go so well with other students, whose parents had also been denied the right to register and vote.

A group of other students demonstrated in front of the courthouse and were joined by others of all ages. Clark proceeded to march them back past their headquarters, Brown Chapel AME Church. He told them to keep moving, and when they got out of the residential section, he sat on the hood of his car and, with a cattle prod, shocked everyone he could reach. They were driven three miles out in the country, and they tried to run. He had his driver speed up and he kept sticking them as they tried to run out of his way. Many fell to the ground, exhausted, and a few ran behind trees and under houses. After Jim Clark did all the damage he could without killing anyone, he rode back to the city and left the students to get back the best way they could.

The second and fourth Tuesdays of each month were days when those who wished to vote in coming elections could register. In addition, a solid week was set aside for registration. Hours that the books were supposed to be open at the county courthouse were 9:00 a.m. to 4:30 p.m., during most people's working hours, of course. Many African-Americans would go at 6:00 o'clock in the morning and stand in line in order to register. Sometimes they stood all day and the books would not be opened. It was obvious that all officials and other white people would do everything that they could think of to discourage blacks from becoming first-class citizens. Those were dark days for us.

Having been a voter since the 1930s, my part in the proceedings, along with several other already registered voters, was to act as a voucher. We had to know the registrant, swear before the registrar that we knew him to be who he said he was, confirm his age, his place of residence, and the length of time he had lived there. He then filled out a preliminary form with these and other statistics. After that, he had to pass both oral and written tests.

Black people, as previously mentioned, were not allowed to come through the front door and later, not even through the side door; they were told to go into the courtyard and stand. The courtyard has no seats; it was just a big open space, paved for the convenience of the whites, who had to walk from one building to the other, and for the cars of employees. It mattered not how old or crippled a potential registrant was, he had to stand and hear the abuse of Jim Clark and his deputies. I heard one say, "Damn bunch of black buzzards. I'm tired of lookin' at 'em. Who the hell they think they are? I'd close up the whole damn place and make 'em go home." Even when it was raining, instead of allowing them to go through the building to stand in the courtyard, or better still, in the hall, the deputies made them march around the block and back into the courtyard to stand in the rain.

An old gentleman asked me to vouch for him one day, and when the registrar handed him the book to sign, he began to write his name with trembling hands. The registrar watched coldly, then said, "Old man, don't you see you are crossing that line? What's wrong with you?" Trembling, the old man tried to stay on the line as he finished writing his name. The registrar then said, "You haven't finished; now write your address."

The man said, looking at me, "Mrs. Boynton will write it for me; I can't write so good."

Again the registrar raised his voice: "You can't write your address, you've failed already. You might just as well get out of the line."

At this point I opened my mouth to say something but I could never have said anything as well as the few words uttered by the prospective registrant. He stood erect, looked into the eyes of the registrar and said, very clearly and fearlessly: "Mr. Adkins, I am 65 years old, I own 100 acres of land that is paid for, I am a taxpayer and I have six children. All of them is teachin', workin' for the government, got they own business, and preachin'. If what I done ain't enough to be a registered voter wid all the tax I got to pay, then Lord have mercy on America."

I was very proud of this man, who had won his case, for the registrar then gave him the long list of professional questions to be answered (not that he or anyone else could pass the tests).

The next day I went back to wait for other prospective

voters who might need a voucher. I was in the center of the hall, and an officer told me to move. I moved back several paces, and in a few minutes another officer told me to move to the yard. Of course there was no way for a person who needed me to see me there, but I wanted to avoid any appearance of insubordination. I was in the yard only a short time when Sheriff Clark came to order me back into the hall. On the way, I told the deputy I was sent back by the sheriff, but the deputy said I was still in the way. It was nearly noon, so I went to the end of the hall and sat on one of the chairs placed there purposely for persons waiting to see the probate judge.

In another few minutes a white man walked up and said, "Git up and git the hell out of here." I told him I was there for a purpose.

In a threatening manner he said, "You aren't going to move?"

I said calmly, "No." He wheeled around as though he were going to get an officer to throw me out. I waited a few more minutes to see what he was really going to do, but he didn't come back and I went out to lunch.

After lunch, I went back and picked up a newspaper, pretending to be absorbed in it, though in reality I was watching the movements of the people in line. Pretty soon the probate judge confronted me, saying, "Amelia, get right up and move from here. You are disturbing my court."

I said, "I did not know you were having court." I had not heard conversations or seen anyone enter his office.

He only said, "I said get up and move and I mean now." I told him I was sent to this seat by the deputy and he quickly retorted, "This is my court, and I am the one to give orders here." I got up and stood until 4:30 that afternoon.

No black person successfully completed registration that day; none even got so far as the office to be processed. The next day an even larger number of blacks came, and this time I entered the hall from the front door without being stopped. There was a long line from the door of the registrar's office, down the hall, and into the alley. It was miserably cold and the sun was not shining to help warm the faithful army. Again I stood in the hall.

I had parked my car at a parking meter and when I figured the time had expired, I left by the front door to put in another dime. Coming back, I met Sheriff Clark at the front door and he said, "Where are you going?" I explained I was going to wait for those who needed a voucher. He sent me to the side door, where I encountered a wall of sheriffs with their guns drawn. I started to pass through, and one of them said, "You can't come through here." I told them I was a voucher and I was to stand just inside the door back of them. I waited in front of this human wall while one of the deputies went to the front and asked Clark about me. He came back to say, "You can go in. Go down the street around the block and come up from the back." The distance was more than a block, but I did as I was told, ending up a few feet from where I had been ordered away.

At noon, everybody left for lunch and I too left to go to my office. As I passed the front of the courthouse, I saw about 60 blacks lined up against the building with the sheriff looking down on them from the steps. This group, I later learned, had been singled out of the line in the back for talking or stepping out of line or some other insane reason, and were being disciplined. Most of them had voiced objections to having to go around the block and stand in the back alley instead of entering the front door of the courthouse. Clark had a big club in his hand and he noticed me coming down the street. He yelled to me, "Where are you going?" I said I was on my way to my office. He said, "Oh no, you aren't. You are going to get in this line." Again I told him I had to go to my office and again he told me to get into the line against the wall. Before I could gather my wits, he had left the steps and jumped behind me, grabbed me by my coat, propelled me around and started shoving me down the street.

I was stunned. I saw cameramen and newspaper reporters around and, knowing how Clark liked publicity, I said, "I hope the newspapers see you acting this role."

He said, "Dammit, I hope they do."

The African-Americans standing in line were indignant, but the only consolation they could give me was, "Go on to jail, Mrs. Boynton, you'll not be alone. We will be with you." What more consolation would one need? With a final grand push, the sheriff shoved me into a deputy's car and said, "Arrest her and put her in jail."

As I entered the county jail on the third floor of the city hall, my purse was searched and taken away from me, I was fingerprinted five different times, photographed, and given a criminal number across my chest. I was then brutally handled, pushed down the hall, and thrown into a jail cell. Later, from the cell, I heard the group, who had cheered me on at the courthouse. They had been marched the three blocks to the jail, singing, "Oh freedom, oh freedom, oh freedom over me. And before I'll be a slave, I'll be buried in my grave, and go home to my Lord and be free." This song had never sounded so sweet to me as when they stood before the barred door that led to the jail itself and began to sing again.

The jailer tried to open the door but the lock jammed. When the janitor's keys couldn't open the iron doors, the locksmith was called. He too tried and failed. Finally, he informed the jailers that he would have to go back to his office and get an acetylene torch, to burn off the hinges or locks. For nearly an hour, the African-Americans stood and sang and repeated Bible verses and interpreted scripture to those nearby. "Oh yes," said one freedom fighter, "when God closes a door no man can open it, and God closed that door." Finally the jailer gave orders to have the 60 blacks go back downstairs and come up on the elevator.

At 2:30 that afternoon, I was taken back to the courthouse for an arraignment. When we entered the courtroom there was no judge and he never did come. So back to jail I went, to remain until some sort of trial could be set and some kind of charge brought against me.

That night, another court was held and all the group was taken to the courthouse again and charged with unlawful assembly. I was the last person to be arraigned and I was charged with criminal provocation. The irony was that Sheriff Clark had done a criminal act when he arrested me and the mere fact that I was walking as a free citizen was what provoked him. But of course the court was not interested in the facts; I was "inciting" blacks to be citizens and that was crime enough. For "criminal provocation" my bond was set higher than the others.

I got home about 10:00 o'clock that night with my "diploma"—the charge of criminal provocation—and I wondered why I had not made a greater contribution to being arrested. I had missed my club meeting down the street. Although it was late, one of my friends came to the house and told me that the entire meeting was centered around the illegality of the sheriff's act and what they could do about it. All the club members were teachers, but at this arrest they lost fear of losing their jobs and made plans to call on all the teachers to demonstrate in a body against the brutal treatment and the mass arrests. Most of the teachers were not registered voters, though they had tried many times.

The next day I went to Birmingham, where my attorney filed a court order against Sheriff Clark, which would set aside his order of "unlawful assembly" of African-Americans in Dallas County. I told my attorneys that I had to get back to Selma Friday, January 22, by 2:30 in the afternoon, because the teachers were going to march on the courthouse. The lawyers laughed and said I was wasting time thinking the teachers were going to stick together.

I got back in time to join the teachers, who were led in their march by the president of the Dallas County Teachers Association, the Reverend Frederick D. Reese. Of about 135 teachers, only three were absent from the demonstration. They stood on the steps facing Sheriff Clark and a spokesman said they wanted to go to the registrar's office. The sheriff stood in front of the group with his cattle prod, and began to push the teachers off the steps. But this did not keep them from continuing to try to get through. They were repulsed each time by the line of officers. Deputies who had hardly an eighth-grade education called them filthy names and made insulting remarks. The teachers did not succeed in reaching the registrar's office, but before leaving the courthouse, they let the sheriff, the deputies, and the other whites know that they were not afraid and that they had joined the battle for freedom.

Bloody Sunday

*Nonviolence and truth are inseparable and
presuppose one another. There is no god
higher than truth.*

—Mahatma Gandhi

On February 1, 1965, Dr. King was arrested in Selma and lodged in the county jail for leading the January 18 demonstration. This aroused people in all walks of life all over the country. They began to come to Selma to offer their services in whatever way was needed. The Reverend Andrew Young, Dr. King's aide, announced at a night meeting that a group of people from Washington, D.C., including congressmen, would visit Selma unofficially.

I was to drive to the Montgomery airport and lead the group back to Selma. The congressmen would ask at city hall to see Dr. King. I was to sign his bond, and the entire group would come to my house for a meeting. I met the plane and found the fifteen congressmen, eight other friends, and a host of newsmen.

The whole group of about 50 persons tried to enter the side door of city hall, but it was locked. I thought the front door would be open, but found that locked also, so we went to the prisoners' entrance, which was open. The day was cold and dismal with a drizzle of rain. The only bright spot of the day was the spirit of the congressmen.

The hall was clear of people, except for one man, Mayor Joe Smitherman, who stood behind the entrance door with his hand on the doorknob. "Don't let them come in here," he said. He was a tall, frightened, unsteady, thin man—the mayor for one month of Selma, Alabama, a city of about 29,000. "Don't let them come in here," he said again. Although all of the group was still outside the building except Congressman John Dow of New York, who was close behind me and halfway in the door, the mayor began to recite his canned speech.

"I am the mayor of the City of Selma," he began.

I knew he meant to be heard, so I said, "Mayor, these people cannot hear you. They will have to come in if you are talking to them."

He took several steps backward, with both hands held up as though he were pushing something away from him, then said, "Well, let them come right in here" (motioning toward the small hall), "but don't let the newsmen in."

The door was open now and the congressmen began to file into the hall, so it was natural that all the others would follow. The mayor was determined to get his speech out, so he started again. "I am the mayor of Selma and we have been getting along all right until outsiders came in. We don't need any outsiders."

At this point, Congressman William Fitts Ryan of New York and others said, "We want to see Dr. King."

The mayor said, "Gentlemen, you cannot see King unless you get him out on bond."

One of the other congressmen answered, "We don't want to get him out. We just want to see him."

"Well, you just can't see him." The mayor was still nervous and did not realize that the worst was yet to come.

When all the congressmen had entered the hall and the mayor gradually backed into the larger hall, one of the congressmen asked, "Why do you bar blacks from registering and voting?" Another asked about the discriminating pattern practiced and another about the inhuman treatment of the demonstrators. The mayor, having nothing to do with these atrocities, tried very hard to answer these questions, but often found himself getting so entangled with the lawmakers of the nation that it was embarrassing.

Just then the city and county attorney came among the group and said, "Mayor, you don't have to answer their questions." But the attorney went away, leaving the mayor to continue the struggle. Later the attorney returned and took him by the elbow, as one would a child in trouble, and steered him away while he was yet talking, leaving the congressmen and the others, including newsmen, standing there amazed.

The spell was broken when Selma's safety director, Captain Wilson Baker, came and announced that Dr. King had been released. He was slipped through the front doors while the mayor was floundering with his hangups. When the group reached my house on Lapsley Street, Dr. King was there awaiting us. Included in the conference, together with some of the local black leaders and SCLC people, were the following congressmen: Jonathan B. Bingham, James H. Scheuer, Ogden R. Reid, William Fitts Ryan, and Joseph Y. Resnick, and John Dow, all of New York; Jeffery Cohelan, Kenneth W. Dyal, Augustus F. Hawkins, and Don Edwards, California; Weston E. Vivian and Charles Mathias, Maryland; and John Conyers, Jr., Michigan. The son of Adam Clayton Powell of New York was there and others who represented still other congressmen.

Dr. King, the SCLC representatives, and I answered questions about what was going on in Selma, information that the congressmen could take back to Washington. The various congressmen later scattered and visited with other people, white and black, for further details. This groundwork led to their drafting of a right-to-vote bill, ratified by Congress the following August.

But in the meantime, all was not well in Selma and surrounding counties for those who tried to register. Blacks were being beaten, jailed, and made to walk for miles in biting cold weather after being released from prison. Jimmy Lee Jackson of Marion, 30 miles from Selma, Alabama, had been shot to death by one of Governor Wallace's state troopers after a mass meeting. The officers had gone into the church and ordered the people to disperse. The people left peacefully, but they were hounded and harassed. A

trooper followed Jimmy Lee and his mother into a neigh-
boring café and began to beat the woman. Jimmy Lee, who
stayed with her, was killed in cold blood.

I can never do justice to the great feeling of amazement
and encouragement I felt when, perhaps for the first time in
American history, white citizens of a Southern state banded
together to come to Selma and show their indignation about
the injustices against the African-Americans. On March 6,
1965, 72 concerned white citizens of Alabama came to
Selma in protest. They had everything to lose, while we, the
African-Americans, who were deprived and on the bottom
rung of the salary scale, had nothing to lose and everything
to gain.

The white group included business and professional men
and women, ministers and laymen. Before they came they
asked to use one of the public buildings for assembly and
were refused. The white churches were afraid to open their
doors to them and finally they gathered in a black church,
the Reformed Presbyterian. A plan was worked out to keep
any of them from coming in bodily contact with the law.

The Reverend Joseph Ellwanger, pastor of an integrated
Lutheran congregation in Birmingham, was the group's
spokesman. (He was the son of Dr. Walter H. Ellwanger of
Selma, president of the Alabama Lutheran Academy and
College for twenty years). Two by two these people marched
to the courthouse. As they assembled, other people were
already gathered, the whites to jeer and the blacks to cheer.
While the Concerned White Citizens of Alabama (CWCA)
sang "My Country, 'Tis of Thee," a group of white hecklers
began to scream, yell, and whistle. Even when the minister
offered prayers, they showed all kinds of disrespect. The
CWCA ignored their irreverence and prayed for them.

During Pastor Ellwanger's reading of the "Purpose of the
Concerned Citizens," a gang of white men raced down the
street in an old car with no exhaust pipe. The noise was
horrendous. Suddenly, the car stopped in front of the minister and the gang yelled at him. One of the men held up the
hood of the car from which came some type of chemical,

which made a smoke screen and gave off a repellent odor. The sheriff, who with his deputies was surrounding the CWCA, paid no attention to them, but neither did the CWCA people. The annoying group finally left.

With all our conferences, pleadings, confrontations, and demonstrations, the registration board and the Black Belt officials were determined to beat the African-Americans down physically and mentally. Every time the African-Americans came back up, fighting nonviolently.

We knew that the crux of the trouble in Alabama lay in our governor, George Wallace, and we decided to march the 50 miles to the state capital and hand our grievances to him. The march would begin the next day, Sunday, March 7, 1965.

The city knew of our plans for the march, but did not know how to stop it. Meetings were held day and night to map out strategy by which we could appeal to the conscience of the diehards. People had begun to come in from all over the country to lend assistance in the registration and voting drive. The country board of registrars refused to permit African-Americans to vote, the county officials kicked them about for asking to register, the governor of the state gave them mountains of legal questions that were impossible to answer, and the Congress in Washington was still filibustering and allowing the Southern bigots to twist their arms. We were left no alternative but to walk 50 miles to the capital, not to ask, not to plead, but to demand the right to register and vote.

The night before the march, we gathered at the church and talked with the citizens, asking them to walk with us regardless of the cost, even if it meant "your life." I was afraid of being killed and I said to myself, "I cannot pay the supreme price, because I have given too much already." But I also then thought, "Other mothers have given their lives for less in this struggle and I am determined to go through with it even if it does cost my life." At that moment, a heavy burden fell from my mind and I was ready to suffer if need be.

The next morning I rose early, cooked breakfast, and fed the fifteen guests staying with me. I went to Brown's Chapel to offer my assistance before the march. Little did I know that that day would mark one of the greatest struggles for freedom in modern times. Little did I visualize what would really take place, and what effect it would have on the nation at large. That day I met such people as the former governor of Florida, LeRoy Collins; Walter Reuther, labor leader; and other dignitaries, and I began to understand more deeply than before that we were not alone.

As we passed a line of well-wishers and little tots who wished they could join the group, a woman said to me, "Honey, I can't walk but I sure will pray for you all." Another said, "Thank God he done sent his disciples to help us." Still another said, "I prayed so hard for you all. It might be stormy but God will bring you through!" All of these sayings I kept in my heart and I too uttered a prayer to be saved from the evil to come.

As we left the church, we saw scores of officers of the city, and county and state troopers huddled in groups, smiling and looking somewhat human. I did not have a hat but was otherwise prepared for the cold weather. My friend Margaret Moore said, "Here is my raincap, put it on. You'll be needing it." Then Marie Foster and I fell in line third from the front.

We marched from Brown's Chapel AME Church in the black section toward town. The officers had us close ranks and walk faster and by larger groups. This was different from previous marches, where we had to walk two by two and ten feet apart, regardless of our large numbers.

The marchers were accompanied by portable latrines, first-aid buses, water, and food. Like the children of Israel leaving Egypt, we marched toward the Red Sea and we were on our way, not knowing what was before us.

As we approached the Edmund Pettus Bridge, which spans the Alabama River, we saw the sheriff, his posse, deputies, and men plucked out of the fields and stills to help "keep the niggers in their place." As we crossed the bridge, I saw in front of us a solid wall of state troopers, standing shoulder to shoulder. I said to Marie, "Those men are standing so close together an ant would get mashed to death if it crawled between them. They are as lifeless as wooden soldiers." Marie pointed to the troopers on the sides of our marching lines and said, "It doesn't take all of them to escort us." But a second look convinced us that trouble was brewing for the nearly 1,000 marchers.

Each officer was equipped with cans of gas, guns, sticks, or cattle prods, as well as his regular paraphernalia. Beyond them, men on horses sat at attention. I remembered the words of a little girl, who wanted to go with us because she wanted to be free, and prayers that were being offered on our behalf, and the old lady who said she would stay on her knees while we were away. I knew we would need all those prayers as I looked on the faces of these men, who were just waiting for a chance to shed human blood.

Part of the line being across the bridge, we found ourselves less than 50 yards from the human wall. The commander of the troops, on a sound truck, spoke through a bullhorn and commanded us to "stop where you are." Hosea Williams of SCLC and Cong. John Lewis and all the line behind them halted. Hosea said, "May I say something?"

Major Cloud retorted, "No, you may not. Charge on them, men."

The troopers, with their gas masks on and gas guns drawn, then began to shoot gas on us and the troopers in front jumped off the trucks. Those standing at attention began to club us. The horses were brought on the scene and were more humane than the troopers; they stepped over the fallen victims.

As I stepped aside from the trooper's club, I felt a blow on my arm that could have injured me permanently had it been on my head. Another blow by a trooper as I was gasping for breath knocked me to the ground and there I lay unconscious. Others told me that my attacker had called to another that he had the "damn leader." One of them shot tear gas all over me. The plastic rain cap that Margaret

Moore gave me may have saved my life; it had slipped down over my face and protected my nose somewhat from the worst of the fumes. Pictures in the paper and those in the possession of the Justice Department show the trooper standing over me with a club. Some of the marchers said to the trooper, "She is dead." And they were told to drag me to the side of the road.

There were screams, cries, groans, and moans as the people were brutally beaten from the front of the line all the way back to the church—a distance of more than a mile. State troopers and the sheriff and his men beat and clubbed to the ground almost everyone on the march. The cry went out for ambulances to come over the bridge and pick up the wounded and those thought to be dead, but Sheriff Clark dared one of them to cross the bridge. At last a white minister and a black citizen told him, "If you don't let the ambulance over the bridge, these people are going to retaliate by killing some of you and you may be the first one." The ambulance was then permitted to pick us up. I also heard that I was taken to the church after being given first aid on the way, but when I did not respond, I was taken to the Good Samaritan Hospital.

When I regained consciousness I wondered where I was, but then I remembered the voice through the bullhorn, the gas being shot, and the men with gas masks. From the looks of the other patients around me, Highway 80 across Edmund Pettus Bridge must have had a bloodbath.

Many months after this march, I went to a specialist for throat problems. I was told that my esophagus was permanently seared and scarred by the teargas. One result, besides continuing throat problems, is that it changed my voice from lyric-soprano to mezzo-soprano.

Though it was months before I recovered from the experience, my spirit soared as I realized what it meant to sing and really feel, "Oh freedom, over me; and before I'll be a slave, I'll be buried in my grave, and go home to my Lord and be free."

CHAPTER 9

Friends Pour into Selma

*There is only one good, knowledge, and one
evil, ignorance.*

—Socrates

Throughout the country, citizens were rising up in indignation over the treatment of human beings in Selma on
March 7. Mayor Jerome Cavanaugh of Detroit and Michigan's Governor George Romney led a protest march of
10,000 people. Demonstrators blocked traffic for hours in
Chicago. Cities in Georgia, North Carolina, California, New
York, and other states saw huge demonstrations, which
protested against the Selma atrocities. The Concerned
White Citizens of Alabama issued a statement interpreting
further its March 6 declaration.

All news media carried the story of Bloody Sunday.
Friends of the movement began to pour into the city from
the West, East, North, and South by trains, planes, buses,
and cars. The young, old, white, black, rich, and poor all
came with the expectation that we would march again, and
with a common purpose: to help attain justice and human
dignity for all Americans.

Dr. King was in Selma again and had called a meeting of
SNCC and the SCLC people of Selma and Dallas County. He
said he was very much disturbed and in a dilemma, because
the President of the United States was saying, "Don't march,
don't march to Montgomery, don't attempt to go the 50

miles," while people had come from throughout the United States and from abroad because they wanted to help in whatever way they could. Dr. King did not want to defy federal regulations and the request of the President, nor did he want to disappoint the thousands of people who had come to march with him.

Along with others, I suggested that we should march anyway, even if we did not go very far. The people assembled at Brown's Chapel Church for instructions and to hear Dr. King's decision. "All morning," he said, "I have been agonizing and I've made my choice. I have decided that it is better to die on the highway than to make a butchery of my conscience."

Although I was still feeling the effects of the gas and the blows of Bloody Sunday, I was determined to march again. We were to leave the church at 3:00 p.m., March 9. Leaders informed the people that later on there would be another march, this time all the way to Montgomery, which of course raised a cheer from the crowd.

Our destination was the other side of the Pettus Bridge, and no one was talking about what might happen once we crossed the bridge. There was optimism that the state troopers on the highway would not again attack, although it was known that they were there with clubs and rifles. At 2:25 p.m. there was a great rustle in the crowd, heads were turning, and applause spread from front to back—Dr. Martin Luther King, Jr., had come to lead the march. It was a warm day, quite sunny. Some of the marchers hoisted signs which said, "Police intimidation enslaves us at all times." Another said, "Silence is no longer golden." Dr. King led off, with the other civil rights leaders immediately behind. Among the train which followed were many prominent people from all over the country—clergy, actors, scientists, and celebrities from all the professions. We passed a portion of the George Washington Carver Homes, a black housing project, and marched through the rest of the African-American section and into the business section of Selma. Crowds stood on the sidewalks, both black and white. Some of the whites were mumbling filthy words and saying, "Go back where you came from—we don't need you." But the marchers were dignified and paid them no heed.

A traffic officer glowered at us, but stopped traffic to let us through as we turned onto Broad Street and headed for the bridge. We crossed the bridge, then halted at the point where we had been attacked the previous Sunday. Stanley Fountain, chief deputy marshal of the Southern District of Alabama, read a court order forbidding us to proceed further.

Hundreds of state troopers were lined up on each side and formed a solid wall in front, but they seemed to have a different facial expression and a different attitude from the last time we encountered them. After we had knelt in prayer, we turned around and marched back to the church.

Selma African-Americans had scored a technical victory and saved face by staging the march. We were happy that there had been no violence—a victory in itself in this state. There was another cause for rejoicing—the marches meant more to the African-Americans and whites alike in Selma and in the whole state, for that matter, than anyone will ever be able to evaluate. It made the African-Americans realize that people cared and thousands or perhaps millions of white people in the upper class financially had meek and humble hearts. They were willing to come and share in the struggles of people in the poorest circumstances. For this, I am most grateful. I met great and noble spirits, who typified the rich life of ministering to those in need and who were unselfish enough to respect the humanity of "the least of these, my brethren."

Among these great men was the Reverend James Reeb, a white Unitarian minister from Boston, who gave his life.

About 7:30 that evening, after the march was over, Reverend Reeb and the Reverend Clark Olsen, minister of the Beverly Fellowship of Unitarians, and the Reverend Orloff Miller went to the black section, Washington Street, to have supper in a white café. They noticed the staring eyes of some whites and decided to go back to Walker's black café.

Later, as they left Walker's café and started down the street, a group of four or five white men came toward them. Mr. Reeb was on the sidewalk nearest the street. One of the white men swung a lead pipe or club violently against his head, and Mr. Reeb dropped to the ground. Another man attacked Mr. Miller, who also fell. While they were down, they were kicked by their attackers, who continued to beat them brutally for some time, then departed, leaving them on the ground.

Mr. Olsen tried to help the other two up, but Mr. Reeb was so badly injured that he could not walk and was incoherent. His friends helped him along and somehow got him to my office, two blocks away. Many of the workers were still there when the trio appeared. We went next door and asked the director of the funeral home to get an ambulance. Dr. William H. Dinkins came and accompanied Mr. Reeb to Burwell, the only African-American-owned and operated hospital in the area, but because of his serious condition he soon ordered him transferred to Birmingham for more specialized help.

After several delays Mr. Reeb finally reached Birmingham and the University Hospital, where he lay unconscious for several days. Then, the announcement was made that he would not live.

Word came that Mr. Reeb had died while we were holding a civil rights meeting in Brown's Chapel on March 14. African-Americans outside the church became very confused and went in to find out what they could do, to demonstrate and let the world know that they protested against the killing of one who had come to help. We held a memorial service then and there. Demonstrators standing in the street reported that carloads of whites were seen driving up and down the street in the African-American section. The public safety director said that the police had stopped three carloads of armed white men, some from as far away as St. Augustine, Florida.

President Johnson met for more than three hours with Governor Wallace and then told newsmen that he had respectfully suggested that Mr. Wallace do the following: First, publicly declare his support for universal suffrage in the State of Alabama and the United States of America; second, assure that the right of peaceful assembly be guaranteed in Alabama as long as law and order were maintained; third, call a bi-racial meeting to seek greater cooperation and to ask for greater unity among Alabama citizens of both races. Governor Wallace said he would give careful consideration to the President's suggestions, but he reserved further comment until he would appear on *Face the Nation,* a Sunday TV program. (On that occasion he said, among other things, that he "couldn't understand why people were calling him a racist.")

The President said he had made clear, whether the governor agreed or not, that the right of peaceable assembly would be preserved. The Senate and administration leaders tried to reach an agreement that new voting rights legislation should provide a simple, relatively quick method of assuring African-Americans the right to register and vote, as well as the right to demonstrate. The registrars should be federal officials, probably appointed temporarily to sign up prospective voters in areas where it had been determined that local registrars were not doing the job properly. President Johnson took the rallying cry of African-Americans into Congress by pledging that "we shall overcome" what he called "a crippling legacy of bigotry and injustice." He demanded immediate action on legislation designed to remove every barrier of discrimination against citizens trying to register and vote. This round of the battle seemed to be won, but the reforms were far from being put into effect.

Each time we protested against an illegal move by the officers, something happened that was even worse. We asked white ministers who were visiting the city to call on the mayor, and 80 of them went to the mayor's home and knelt to pray on the lawn. City police then arrested them, and demonstrators with them, and took them to jail, where they were held in protective custody (so Mr. Baker said) for about three hours. When released, the ministers at first refused to go, and some of them said (in the tradition of St. Paul), "We will stay until the mayor issues an apology for taking us into custody for merely exercising our constitutional rights." However, this was soon seen as a vain hope, and they left.

As for Mr. Reeb's attackers, they were identified as Namon O'Neal Hoggie, his brother William, Elmer L. Cook, and R.B. Kelley. Their ages were from 30 to 42—they were not juveniles. They were arrested for assault and battery and later arraigned before the U.S. Commissioner for murder and released on $5,000 bond. They were charged under an 1870 conspiracy law that carries a maximum penalty of ten years in prison and a $5,000 fine.

I sat in the Selma courthouse and was disgusted, though not surprised, to see that there were no black people on the jury. Some of the jurors were friends of the murderers, and I was told that one was an in-law of one of them. The defendants were very much at ease during the trial. Of course the jury's verdict was "not guilty," and the state freed the men. Then there was much congratulating, back-slapping, and handshaking. This was justice in Selma.

The following letter to me (excerpted here) from civil rights leader Marius J. Anderson, now deceased, gives a vivid sense of the horrors and injustices that we encountered in this struggle to win our rights as full American citizens:

". . . I was with you the night of horror in Marion. It was you and I who concealed Reverend C.T. Vivian from a white mob threatening to kill him. Do you remember me breaking through a human barrier at the entrance of the Pettus Bridge by ambulance to evacuate *you* and others, the day of Bloody Sunday? Do you remember me picking up Reverend James Reeb off the street the night of his slaying? He was carried to Burwell Infirmary and later transferred to University Hospital, Birmingham. I, along with Dr. Dinkins and Charles Williams, met with much hostility getting to Birmingham. I made the call also to pick up Viola Liuzzo, but I was told very hostilely that nothing had happened, and the State Troopers gave me an ultimatum of three minutes to evacuate the area. She was later picked up by a white funeral director of Montgomery. Yet I could see her bowed down over the steering wheel of her car flooded with blood. One of the doors was open, and that allowed the courtesy lights in the car to remain on, in spite of the loss of control after the contact of the bullet."

CHAPTER 10

The Great March to Montgomery

*Resist not evil: but whosoever shall smite
thee on thy right cheek, turn to him the
other also.*   —Matthew 5:39

On March 20, I spent a couple of hours at Brown's Chapel Church, where instructions were being given to marchers, then went to my office, where SCLC officials were busy getting out last-minute notices for the greatest march on earth. We all waited for the green light from President Johnson to begin again the 50-mile march to Montgomery that had started March 7. Our aim was to lay a petition for African-Americans' rights before Governor Wallace.

An SCLC official came in jubilantly and read from a paper: "President Johnson assured adequate protection for civil rights pilgrimage from Selma to Montgomery, saying he would call out the Alabama National Guard if Governor George C. Wallace was unable or unwilling to do so." This was the signal we were waiting for. Dr. King said the long-planned and twice-blocked trek would be the most massive march ever staged on a state capital in the South. He had called on friends and well-wishers to meet him in Selma, and preparations were made for 3,000 people to start out the next morning, Sunday, March 21. The route would take us through the downtown section, across the Edmund Pettus Bridge again, down Highway 80 to Montgomery. The first overnight stop would be about ten miles from Selma on a farm. The second stop, Monday night, would be on the Steele plantation in Lowndes County, owned by a black family. The next night would be spent on the Gardner farm in Lowndes County, and Wednesday, the last night of the march, we would camp on the grounds of the St. Jude Catholic school in Montgomery.

As we worked on the last-minute plans, a deputy stepped into my office and handed me a summons. I waited on several people in the office, and then, because I didn't want to be interrupted again, I got into my car and drove a short distance out of town. As I began to read, I said to myself, "Wow! What a suit!"

When the Dallas County Voters League and the SCLC began to have their demonstrations, we had to have some way of carrying people back and forth, so the DCVL had bought three minibuses to convey them. The parties mentioned in the summons were to appear in the circuit court and "plead, answer, or demur within 30 days . . . to the complaint of Selma Bus Lines, Incorporated, a corporation." It looked as though the plaintiff did not realize that the buses had stopped running long before December 30, 1964 (which was when we started running our little buses). Such complaint was a sign of the jitters of the city and the economic pinch that was being felt. My first thought was how stubborn these creatures were. They prefer to hold the African-American in servitude and starve him rather than put their prejudices away and reason together with their black brother.

I headed back to the office and no sooner had I arrived than I was faced again by the same deputy sheriff, who gave me another summons. This was also from the Selma Bus Lines and its accusation was the same thing. I said, "This is getting to be funny." The minute I said it, here came the sheriff again with another complaint, which he threw on my desk. His attitude, which had been accompanied before by a grin, had become belligerent and I thought it best not to say anything to him. The contents of the paper were ridiculous, but I was used to that. This time it was an injunction of another nature. It was the first barrier for the marchers, and forbade us to camp on the Minter plantation (the farm near Selma which was leased by a black farmer from a white owner). We had anticipated such setbacks and were prepared to use substitute places for the campsites.

Sunday morning, I arose early to fix breakfast for a houseful of guests, then placed the key where anybody who wanted to could go in the house, and we all went down to Brown's Chapel. There hundreds had gathered and soon there were thousands milling around in and out of the church. There was not room for everyone inside, so Dr. King, who was preaching, and all the congregation came outside to worship. Then we lined up.

It was a beautiful scene. Black and white and backed by the armed might of the United States, 3,200 persons marched out of Selma on the first leg of an historic venture in nonviolent protest. Hundreds of army and federalized state troops stood guard in Selma and lined the highway out of the city to protect us. The troops were authorized by President Johnson, after Governor Wallace said that Alabama could not afford the expense of protecting the marchers. With federalized troops on each side, helicopters over our heads, and being led by Almighty God through our leader Dr. King, I felt that no harm could befall us now.

The Sunday night camp and all the others were well guarded by the troops. SCLC and SNCC also had men on duty around the clock. The skies foretold rain, perhaps the next day. There were conveyances to take the older people and the lame ones. From Selma well into the rural sections there were groups of white rabblerousers carrying the Confederate flag, waving and cursing, and many saying, "Go back to Africa where you belong, you black jigaboos!" One youngster retaliated, "I can't go back to Africa, you white folks took it away from us, just like you took America from the Indians!" He was told not to say any more and he was obedient.

As we trudged along in the rain and mud on the narrow

highway the following day, Jim Leatherer, a white man who had only one leg, was falling back in the crowd. Ambulances and cars taxied up and down the road to pick up the weary, so I said, "Why don't you ride, Jim? Aren't you tired?"

"Tired?" he said. "Robert Moore was not tired." He referred to the postman from Washington, D.C., who was killed by snipers in the northern part of Alabama while en route to Mississippi.

My friend Marie Foster vowed that she would walk every step of the way, though she, like others, was getting stiff from the unaccustomed long hours on her feet. She insisted walking was a pleasure, even in the rain and cold.

As far as the marchers were concerned everything went off smoothly, but the troopers and organized marshals were kept busy beating the bushes for possible snipers. They found men in the woods of Big Swamp with sticks of dynamite, possibly to be used to blow up the brick abutment near the creek that the marchers had to cross (and more ominous, the marchers themselves). They also found a truck driven by a white farmer with ammunition in it, possibly to supply the snipers. A light plane flew over us and dropped leaflets, which called on black citizens to join "Operation Ban." This was a scheme to turn African-Americans against other African-Americans and cause them to fight among themselves.

The teenagers were a great inspiration on the march, keeping us in high spirits with their wit and their songs. Many walked barefoot all the way to Montgomery. I was much impressed with a fifteen-year-old Selma boy, Louis Moton. His face beamed with pride as he carried the American flag. We watched his great physique and the manner in which he bore the flag, and every now and then he would burst into song and we would join him often in singing the "Star Spangled Banner."

When we reached the Lowndes County halfway point in the 50-mile journey, a minister said Lowndes County was worse than hell. I could share that sentiment; it was there in 1958, after I had testified before the Civil Rights Commission in Montgomery, that a local Uncle Tom had warned me not to come back or I would be killed. Lowndes County has an 80 percent African-American population. In March 1965 not one African-American was a registered voter. Almost all the African-Americans in the county are either school teachers or sharecroppers, "which means that the whites have strings on them all, one way or the other," was the comment of Andy Young, Dr. King's executive assistant.

We reached Montgomery Wednesday evening and camped at St. Jude. The large athletic field was literally covered with human beings from all over the world and included newsmen and cameramen, walkie-talkies, and loudspeakers. The sea of cars parked in every nook and cranny made one know that the humble and the proud were as one. They had come by plane, bus, train, Cadillac and jalopy, as well as on foot. We looked forward to the great entertainment which would take place at 8:30 p.m. A huge platform and lights had been installed. Many people took their seats near the stage as early as 4:00 in the afternoon to have a good view.

During the day stage and screen stars flew in, among them Sammy Davis, Jr., Harry Belafonte, Tony Perkins, comedian Nipsey Russell, comedienne Elaine May, actor and playwright Ossie Davis, the folk singer Chad Mitchell, Tony Bennett, and Dick Gregory. Thousands of others, many of them poor, and of varied colors, came to be with the marchers. The next morning, March 25, the crowd on the campus grew so large that the overflow had to go to the black high school across the highway.

After breakfast, the place was cleaned up and the people were asked to form lines of eight abreast and prepare to go to the state capitol building. The sun went behind the clouds and a light rain began to fall. Nevertheless, the last lap of the march began.

As we walked through the ghettoes of Montgomery, the visitors had first-hand information from some of the residents who walked with us and a glimpse of the shacks in which many poor blacks lived. The looks of the community

told the common story: low salaries, little food and milk for
the children, parents who had to leave their children to take
care of themselves while they did domestic work for white
employers, many of whom hated African-Americans.

On and on we marched, out of the ghettoes and into a
better community where higher salaried blacks lived, and
into the business section where American Jews, Italians,
Greeks, and others had dingy stores. From there we walked
over cobblestones out of the black community into the
white residential section and the downtown business
section.

White hecklers, together with secret sympathizers and
well-wishers were among those who watched us. Some of
the hecklers had to be restrained by the police and SCLC
security groups. A young white woman, very pretty and
intelligent looking, stood in the doorway of an office building. Seeing the integrated group passing seemed to enrage
her and she screamed vile things. To be sure we saw her
contempt: She held her nose, turned her back to the street,
and hoisted her dress. Not one comment was made by those
around me.

We moved down Dexter Avenue toward the capitol and
passed stores that were practically deserted. We saw the
many state buildings where there were more than 10,000
employees, hardly any of them blacks, except in menial
jobs. Finally, we came to the platform and Dexter Avenue
Baptist Church, the only piece of property owned by blacks
near the capitol. Dr. King had been pastor there during the
Montgomery bus boycott in 1955.

We saw the state capitol, with its Confederate flag and
state flag proudly flying above. Alabamians are not supposed to forget that Montgomery was "the cradle of the
Confederacy." One of the Yale professors asked me where
the American flag was and I told him he could see it if he
walked on the other side of the building, where it flew below
the level of the other flags, and below the height of the
capitol. This was almost unbelievable to him.

Andy Young touched me on the shoulder and asked me

to take a seat on the platform. From there we could see a beautiful sight—at least 50,000 people marching down the wide street. Ten minutes, 30 minutes, an hour or longer, the people continued to pour in, though all the seats were long taken.

Andy Young came back to me and handed me the petition to be read to the governor. This was indeed an honor, but I would much rather have faced him while reading it. We knew that the governor was too small to attend this meeting, which had such dynamic and moving speakers as Martin Luther King, Walter Reuther, Roy Wilkins, Ralph Bunche, Whitney Young, Bayard Rustin, and other powerful figures, but we hoped he was at least in the capitol, which was just a few feet from the platform.

After the meeting, a committee of eight was to present the petition to Governor Wallace in person. As we approached the steps of the capitol, we encountered state troopers standing shoulder to shoulder in a solid line and a second row of city officers a few feet from them. With riot guns and bayonets, the city officers moved toward us in formation, and someone asked, "What do you want?" We told them we wanted to see the governor and were told that he was not in. This was only minutes after our spokesman, SCLC secretary Reverend J.E. Lowery of Birmingham, had been told by Governor Wallace's personal secretary that the governor was in his office.

We went back to the Dexter Avenue Church to plan a different kind of strategy. Then we walked back to the capitol and this time we were approached by the captain of the rank as we neared the officers. We said we had a message for the governor and he asked us to follow him. We went through the solid line of city police, then the state troopers, up the beautiful marble steps of the capitol and into the rotunda, where we were met by Cecil Jackson, Governor Wallace's secretary. He said the governor would not see us because "it was after business hours." Reverend Lowery then asked for a definite date on which we could call upon him, but Mr. Jackson (who was from Selma) said the governor would not see the entire committee of eight, but would select whom he would talk with from the committee. We decided at once that we would not permit him to choose a spokesman, and spent the rest of the afternoon saying goodbye to the many people who came to our rescue and helped us in our struggle.

It was after 6:00 o'clock that night when, with my friend Marie Foster, I drove toward Selma on Highway 80. We paid little attention to the passing cars and the dangers that our car, with only women in it, could encounter. As we drove through Lowndesboro I noticed an unusual number of cars headed toward Selma, including one with blinking red lights. We thought there might be a wreck up front.

We kept going and soon saw a light car against the fence and two officers keeping the traffic moving. We turned the radio on a few minutes later to hear that we had just passed the car in which Mrs. Viola Liuzzo had been killed. She had been using her car to shuttle marchers from Montgomery back to Selma, and had with her a young African-American boy. He said a car had followed them for several miles and finally had pulled up beside them. One of the occupants fired a single shot at Mrs. Liuzzo's head. The boy tried to steady the car but it stopped at a cattle fence. He then jumped out of the car, eluded the attackers, and hitchhiked to Selma to report the murder to the police. Mrs. Liuzzo was 38 years old and was a white woman from Detroit, Michigan, where she had a husband and children.

The march from Selma to Montgomery afforded a great chance for America to get her house in order and implement the laws which spelled out the rights of all her citizens. It was a wonderful opportunity for Alabama to stop fighting the Civil War and begin to live in the twentieth century before it fades into the twenty-first. It was a time for the entire South to become a part of the Union in action as well as words.

The march to Montgomery was born fully matured, but not until people were jailed, beaten, cattle-prodded, and gassed, and had lost their homes and jobs by the thousands in the city of Selma and in Dallas County. It was not born until the streets and highways flowed with human blood and the very lives of black and white Americans had been sacrificed. The march was for the right of every American citizen of 21 years and over (the voting age at that time) with sound mind, to register and vote.

There was an education in the struggle. In our suffering, we learned that many people do care and that thousands of white people of all classes were willing either to come to Selma and help us or to change their hearts and sympathize with us in our struggle for human rights.

CHAPTER 11

The Unsung Heroes

*Love your enemies, bless them that curse
you, do good to them that hate you, and
pray for them which despitefully use you,
and persecute you.*   —Matthew 5:44

Looking back at this inhuman treatment and thankful
that I am still alive to tell the story in my own words as
it really was, I thank God for having saved me, when so
many of my friends, those with whom I worked in Alabama,
Georgia, and Mississippi, have made their contribution and
gone on to a greater reward, out of reach of the Jim Clarks,
the George Wallaces, the Orville Farbuses, the Lester Mad-
doxes, and the hate groups. In addition to Martin Luther
King himself, who was assassinated in 1968, while leading
a march of striking sanitation workers in Memphis, Tennessee, many died immediately at the hand of the KKK. Others,
like C.J. Adams, Samuel W. Boynton, and Fannie Lue
Haimer, died because of prior beatings or harassment,
which first caused physical impairment, then death.

Then there are those, like me, who are living to look
back, evaluate the accomplishments from the struggle and
set a timetable for the distance we still have to go. This
time we can enlarge our circle and, by reenactment of our
struggle and the nonviolent accomplishment, this one little-
known spot, Selma, Alabama, can be the candle of hope
that will shine all over the world as the light of justice,
compassion, and love is exchanged for cattle prods, tear
gas, billy clubs, and attack dogs.

Selma is not a heaven and the struggle still goes on. Through its struggle, Selma's African-American citizens have deprogrammed themselves from the brainwashing of more than 200 years, the robbing of their culture and heritage, and are fighting and gaining their rightful places in the city and county. There still is much to accomplish.

The year 1965 was a turning point for America. It is hard to enumerate the many contributions African-Americans gave to this land, during the struggle for civil rights. They will never be given their rightful recognition, as scientists, engineers, inventors, navigators, and industrialists, to name just a few of their professions, unless we demand it.

Though there will remain many unsung heroes, here are a few of the names we do know, and of whom we should be very proud.

• Special tribute is due to Bruce Carver Boynton, who in 1958, en route from Howard University to Selma, was arrested for asking to buy a sandwich, was thrown into jail, causing his case to go to the U.S. Supreme Court, which outlawed segregation in interstate travel. This opened the way for the first freedom riders and lunch counter sit-ins.

Special tribute is also due to:

• CORE, NAACP, SNCC
• Daisy Bates, who integrated Little Rock public schools
• W.C. Patton, who encouraged me to invite SNCC and SCLC to come to Selma
• Attorneys Hall and Billingsley, who in 1954 accepted S.W. Boynton's invitation to defend William Earl Fikes, accused of dozens of attempted rapes, including some committed after he was incarcerated
• Reverend Fred Shuttlesworth
• Dr. John Cashin, who organized the National Democratic Party of Alabama, on whose ticket I ran for U.S. Congress in 1964, and many candidates won election
• Emory O. Jackson
• James Orange
• Ben Chavis
• Marie Foster, voter registrar

▪ Reverend Hunter, pastor of AME Zion Church on Lawrence Street in Selma, who was the first in Selma to open his church to the civil rights movement

▪ Reverend M.C. Cleveland, pastor of First Baptist Church, who was the second to open his church

▪ Reverend L.L. Anderson, pastor of First Baptist Church, where the first mass meeting was held on May 13, 1963

▪ Reverend Bernard Lafayette, the first SNCC activist to come to Selma (in the fall of 1962)

▪ The Fourth Congressional District for Registration and Voting, comprised of eight counties, of which my husband was president and I was secretary

▪ The Daughters of the Elks and the Elks. For eight years my husband and I were chairmen of the Civil Liberties Department, and registration and voting were its priorities

▪ The Sultan Moore family, forced to leave the county because their sons sat in at lunch counters

▪ The Washington family, forced to leave Selma because Mr. Washington made attempts to register his children at the white school in the 1950s

▪ E.D. Nixon, who in the 1920s worked for voter registration and civil rights until stopped by failing health

▪ C.J. Adams, who in the 1920s was founder of Dallas County Voters League and worked tirelessly in civil rights causes until he was forced by racists to leave Selma

▪ Charlene and Rachel West, Germaine and Sharon Platts, and all the children who ran from Jim Clark and the many Jim Clarks across the country, were cattle-prodded, beaten to the ground, thrown in jails, gassed, bitten by dogs, and *molested* by the very men who threw them in jail and those who guarded them

This was the pattern throughout the country. They are the youth, who did not expect laurels, but only asked for a pat on the back or a smile of recognition.

In the many books I have read, few if any tell it like it really is. In most cases, the book's information is centered around a popular figure and camouflaged with untruth, in order to sell the book. I know, because I was there.

CHAPTER 12

Keeping the Dream Alive

There is no grievance that is a fit object of redress by mob law. —Abraham Lincoln

We must remember that behind every good man there is an inspiring and forceful woman, who cooperates with his programs, giving to him of her strength and wisdom to carry on. In Martin Luther King, Jr.'s life, this person is Coretta Scott King, Dr. King's inspiration, Dr. King's wife.

After his death, Mrs. Coretta Scott King decided that she would strive to make her husband's dream a living memorial. It took great courage, after hearing of the death of her husband on April 4, 1968, to go to Memphis, Tennessee to lead the sanitation workers' march in the place of her husband, who had just been assassinated by James Earl Ray. Like a Joan of Arc, she led the march to victory. Returning home, she made preparation for his burial. After the funeral, she turned her attention to making his dream a reality.

As a strong, courageous, and determined woman, Coretta was determined to carry out the plan, discussed with her husband Martin during his life, of some kind of school to teach nonviolence, not only to the people on the street, but to everyone who would stop at the center, look at the literature, and listen to those who live by the nonviolent method. I'm sure Martin himself did not visualize his wife's dual role as a mother of four children, organizing and campaigning for funds, that resulted in a $10 million complex. It took the cooperation of the King family, friends, and well-wishers, led by a woman with courage and determination, fighting through obstacles, discouragements, and mountains of thistles and thorny roadblocks. In spite of it all, she came through with flying colors. Today, we have Dr. Martin Luther King's living dream.

Mrs. King was born in Marion, Alabama in a home that was not wealthy by measure of money, but enriched with cooperation in the family, respect for each other, loving, sharing, and caring. After meeting her parents, one departs feeling benefitted by the conversation in a home where love is extended to all who enter their door.

Mrs. Scott (Coretta's mother) is a charming person, whose experience and wisdom cannot be easily forgotten when she speaks. Because of the struggle during the Depression days, Coretta's parents did not have access to economic opportunities, but her mother would always economically produce the necessities for her family. She said to her daughter, "I'd be happy to own just one dress, if I could get an education in exchange." She felt education was the preparation for life. It was a struggle to make ends meet, Coretta told me, "but I got an education. Yet the best education was learned at home. There, I learned the lesson of love. I understood what it was to care, to help, to support. I learned givingness."

Coretta also spoke of her father and the impression he made upon her, which has been lasting. "I was taught to have pride and dignity, to be an independent thinker," she said. "Somebodiness has to do with self-control. It's not having anybody tell you how to think or what to do. There was no financial security in my family, but I was emotionally secure. I felt a richness of spirit and that made me feel rich.

"My father, a barber, taught me to be non-judgmental. Martin was so much like my father. People liked to hang around my father. People liked to hang around Martin. My father had confidence and worked hard; my husband was like that exactly.

"Yes, my faith has been tested. When Martin was assassinated, I prayed for strength. I prayed that my strength could be transmitted to those around me. Still there were times I was weak, times I wondered if I could withstand the pain. I've been physically exhausted, too. But I've never stopped.

"What sustains me is that God has transforming powers. God is synonymous with Good. Individuals have to be creative forces for good, instruments of peace and justice. My life is a pilgrimage, but I grew into the pilgrimage. I didn't ask for it, but I've always wanted to do the right thing.

"Martin Luther King, Jr. was thought of as the conscience of the nation. My best role is to be there as a conscience force, or simply a conscience. I would rather take a position that is morally correct than politically expedient. Somebody has to speak of ideals."

Not only did Coretta Scott King take up leadership of the sanitation workers' strike in Tennessee after her husband's assassination; she also spearheaded the effort to fulfill Martin's dream of a Poor People's March on Washington.

The Martin Luther King Center for Nonviolent Social Change is a living testimony to Coretta's will power and determination to complete the first phase of her husband's dream.

The Center is located at 449 Auburn Ave., N.E., Atlanta, Ga. 30312. Some 500,000 people, including college and high school students, down to primary school classes, visit the center each year. Classes are conducted in the principles, philosophy, and methods of King's nonviolence. Located there are a learning center, recreation center, bookstore, nursery school, day care center, playground, library, large auditorium, offices, Dr. King's crypt, Dr. King's birthplace, the Freedom Hall meeting facilities, and the Ebenezer Baptist Church. The center has a $3.2 million annual budget and 63 employees.

It has been quite a pleasure for me to have been associated with Mrs. King for many years, especially as a board member of the Martin Luther King, Jr. Center for Nonviolent Social Change since its infancy. I have seen great strides made toward the goal and I have met many people throughout the country who have been benefitted by the center's work.

CHAPTER 13

The Civil Rights Monument

If you would not be forgotten,
As soon as you are dead and rotten,
Either write things worth the reading,
Or do things worth the writing.
                              —Ben Franklin

On November 5, 1989, the Civil Rights Education Center, under the auspices of the Southern Poverty Law Center, 400 Washington St., Montgomery, Alabama, unveiled a monument in memory of those who were killed during the struggle for civil rights.

There were many people whose names or families could not be located and there is an untold number of deaths that occurred because of pure harassment, pressure, and stress, brought on because they worked for freedom and justice for the poor and underprivileged. Of special note on that monument are the names of my late husband Samuel W. Boynton; C.J. Adams of Selma; A.A. Hicks, formerly of Thomasville, Alabama; Fannie Lue Haimer, Ruleville, Mississippi, and many more, who were forced to leave their homes and establish themselves elsewhere.

It is worth a trip to Montgomery to see this monument. This monument to those who died during the civil rights struggle was designed by Maya Lin, an Oriental, who designed the Vietnam Veterans Memorial in Washington, D.C. The Civil Rights Memorial includes a black granite table, engraved with names of those giving their lives, most of them killed by members of the KKK.

On that table, which stands about three and a half feet high, a sheet of water constantly flows, which glistens with light and reflects the image of the viewer. Opposite it is a much larger semicircle extended from the patio to the ground. It too is of granite and flowing waters over Dr. King's most famous biblical saying: "Let righteousness roll down like waters and justice like a mighty stream."

Hate
by my sister Ann

Hate is a heavy cross to bear
It touches people everywhere,
It stiffens, cripples, makes men small,
It hinders growth in growing tall.
It causes grief and anguish, too,
It hurts, it harms, and so, would you
Retard your growth and tempt your fate,
By stooping to this thing called hate?

It creepeth like a poisoned vine
Into the heart and brain and mind,
The *hater* it destroyeth first
And not the *hated*, in reverse.
The poison seeps into the soul
Of his director—leaves him cold
And cruel, half but never whole.

CHAPTER 14

Portrait of a Heroine

*Out of the mouth of babes and sucklings
hast thou ordained strength, because of
thine enemies; that thou mightest still the
enemy and the avenger.* —Psalms 8:2-3

I thought it would be appropriate to close this section of the book with this essay, written by my niece, Germaine Bowser, for a college class she took last year, after starting her own family. Germaine lived with me during the fight for justice in Selma. I believe it gives the reader a sense of the impression that this whole period had upon the youth who lived through it. This fight will never be forgotten.

Portrait of a Heroine
A Expository essay by *Germaine Bowser*,
English 101, Sec. 47
Feb. 20, 1989

During the early days of movie-making, Joan Crawford, Betty Davis, and Marlene Dietrich were all portrayed as incredible women. But my Aunt Amelia was not unlike any of these women. Whenever she entered a room, her presence was known. She was a tall, beautiful, statuesque woman with prevalent, ancestral, Indian features. Even though she was in her fifties, Aunt Amelia's hair remained jet black in a close crop. The polyester suit and run-down pumps were worn with dignity. If one had the opportunity to hear her quiet but firm words of wisdom, or watched her hold strong to a principled issue, one knew that he was in the company of an heroic woman.

Aunt Amelia showed remarkable courage during the terrible year her husband suddenly had a stroke. Aunt Amelia had an employment agency, but when her husband became incapacitated, she was faced with his real estate agency, a son in college and two teen-aged girls. Her own agency required that she sometimes drive from 60 to 80 miles a day in order to pick up rural area girls interested in going to New York for employment. Many of these girls lived in one-room shacks with outside toilets. Therefore, Aunt Amelia would keep them in our home for proper training before they could be sent to New York as domestic workers.

Along with this responsibility, she took full control of her husband's real estate agency. Once again, she was forced to drive many miles to appraise, buy, or sell property. Because some of this property involved many acres of land, Aunt Amelia walked long distances, putting a good bit of red clay and wear on a pair of high-heeled shoes. I also remember how she sat until two or three o'clock in the morning, preparing income tax statements for a great deal of Selma's residents. Never a day did she miss spending quality time with her husband, when he was confined to the hospital. Aunt Amelia would come home at nights, totally exhausted. When her husband died, she continued to control both agencies, because she needed the money to pay for hospital bills, college bills, and hired companions for my sister and me.

Aunt Amelia was also self-sacrificing. When a family was without food, she would ramble through the kitchen for food to give away. If a disaster found one without clothes, "God forbid," Aunt Amelia would hunt all through the house for unused clothing. Once I was especially attached to a dress I had outgrown. I protested against giving the dress away. Aunt Amelia understandably said, "Honey, you must make room for new dresses." "Making room" for others was her specialty.

Once while gathering young ladies for employment, she found a woman named Laurian. It was obvious to us all that Laurian was not a fast learner. Seeing that Laurian was not a candidate for New York, Aunt Amelia decided to employ Laurian in our home with the knowledge that this woman was more child than adult. For years, my sister and I would become hysterical with laughter at the impossible situations Laurian could get into. Many times Laurian infuriated my aunt, who did not have a big sense of humor. Nevertheless, Aunt Amelia regretfully tolerated Laurian until she married and restored peace into our home by moving out.

Above all, Aunt Amelia was legendary. In spite of her busy schedule, she always had one ear tuned towards my sister and me. Being young and impressionable, we had begun to emulate our aunt's air of importance. We decided to join the SNCC. This was a civil rights organization, founded by Dr. Martin Luther King, for the youth. At first Aunt Amelia had reservations about the amount of time my sister and I spent with the organization, but she attended a meeting with us one evening and Selma, Alabama was never the same again. When she realized the importance of the organization, Aunt Amelia began to register voters wherever she could, during her travels throughout the rural areas. Some of her influential friends shied away from her, while some joined Aunt Amelia in her crusade for civil rights.

One night, the Ku Klux Klan startled us from sleep, by shattering our picture window with a brick. Aunt Amelia took the note off the brick, read it, and amusingly said, "They are afraid of us." Then the Ku Klux Klan began to phone us with terroristic threats, and made a return visit to our home. This time they shot through the window. Even though Aunt Amelia remained calm and showed no fear, deep down inside this lady did fear, but not for herself, so much as us. She sent my sister and me 90 miles from Selma, to a private boarding school. My sister and I feared for her life.

On the day the march from Selma to Montgomery was scheduled, the entire student body, including my sister and me, gathered around the television. There in plain sight, was Aunt Amelia linking arms with heaven knows who, singing "We Shall Overcome." Then, a scuffle broke out, and we helplessly watched as my dear Aunt Amelia was beaten to the ground and made unconscious by a police-man's club. Afterwards, she spent a few days in the hospital, wore the scar and continued in the crusade.

Once again we gathered around the television set to witness the second attempt to march from Selma to Mont-gomery. This time she was with Martin Luther King and the National Guard. However, my sister and I did not breathe any easier, until she reached the capitol of Montgomery's steps. I still had my doubts but it was slowly replaced with pride as my aunt made her speech.

I do not know what the world saw in her that day, but I saw on that television set a portrait of a heroine.

PART V

The Decades After Selma

*I have a dream that one day
on the red hills of Georgia the
sons of former slaves and
the sons of former slaveowners
will be able to sit down together
at the table of brotherhood.*
—Dr. Martin Luther King, Jr.

CHAPTER 1

Building Resurrection City
May to June, 1968

He who has done his best for his own time
has lived for all times.   —Friedrich Schiller

We all realize the great improvement we made during the time we marched and demonstrated for the right to vote and for the Civil Rights Bill. It's all on paper, just as the Constitution of the United States is on paper.

Yet, there were many things that we needed to do to bring to the attention of the entire world, that in this United States of America, the land of the free, the home of the brave, there were millions of people who were hungry; there were people who were tilling hundreds of acres, and yet not able to give food to those who were suffering, emaciated with malnutrition, and even dying, because of the lack of food, proper attention, medicine, and decent living conditions.

In 1968, after demonstrations and after the Right to Vote Bill and the Civil Rights Bill were enacted, Dr. King and his associates realized that there were many, many other fields to cover, to realize what the bills stood for. It was immediately after the bills were passed that Dr. Martin Luther King, Jr. and his associates decided that we would have people of all races, colors, and creeds come to Washington, to cry out against the atrocities and injustices that were perpetrated against people of color. These plans and programs were made, and I believe that this was the final nail driven in Dr. King's coffin, because this country's establishment has never wanted people to be together, has never wanted communication between races of people.

Dr. King and his associates got together and decided that they were going to have a Poor People's Campaign. The objective was to bring people together of all races, colors, creeds, denominations, conditions of employment, and birth. The plan that was made and carried out, was to use the park across from the Abraham Lincoln Memorial and the Reflecting Pool, to build a new, temporary city for poor people from around the nation, as a base from which to put pressure on Congress for legislation to end poverty in America. Word of mouth, notices by letter, newspaper, radio, and television announced that there would be a city built in Washington, D.C. beside the reflecting pool and in front of the Lincoln Memorial. This is one of the many places still left since the 1920s, where Washington's white buildings sparkle against the sun and there is a park within a block or two of every federal building, with underground restrooms in many.

We didn't realize, however, the hostility that we would encounter from the federal government, because the objective of this campaign—of Resurrection City, as we called it after we got there—was to call to the attention of the senators, the congressmen, the President, and all those who have charge of this country, the plight of poor people throughout this nation—the blacks, the whites, the Indians, the Chicanos, the Mexicans, and all of the others who were in want of the decencies of life.

All Americans were invited, including students, unemployed, mothers, fathers, sisters, brothers, blacks, whites, reds, browns, yellows, poor, and the abused. Those who were sick, aged, some with missing limbs, some with babies, some with unborn babies, all were invited, and all of them came to Resurrection City, because they were in quest of decency, and a good, honest, clean place to live.

Unfortunately, Dr. King himself never lived to see Resurrection City built. He was gunned down by an assassin's bullet on April 4, 1968 in Memphis, Tennessee.

At the memorial service for Dr. King in Memphis, Tennessee, where the Poor People's Campaign March to Washington began on May 2, 1968, Dr. Ralph Abernathy gave the following words of invocation:

". . .The dreamer is slain. Who will make his dreams come true?

"The Southern Christian Leadership Conference, now led by Dr. Ralph D. Abernathy, is carrying on Dr. King's last campaign. Thousands of poor people have come to Washington determined to stay until definite and positive action is taken by the government to provide decent jobs and adequate income for the poor. The response of the citizens of America will decide the success of the campaign and the fulfillment of Dr. King's dreams. . . .

"Our goal is a decent job for everyone who can and should work and a guaranteed minimum income for those whose job does not pay enough to support their families or who cannot and should not work.

" 'Resurrection City,' designed by a professor of architecture at the University of Maryland, has been constructed just south of the Lincoln Memorial. From here and from churches in and around Washington, thousands of marchers trained in nonviolent methods are calling on congressmen and government officials and staging demonstrations."

In May of 1968, we were given the opportunity by Congress to occupy a piece of property, and of course we chose the Lincoln Memorial, because it was President Lincoln who had freed the slaves. This is also the place where Dr. King gave his most inspiring speech—"I Have a Dream." However, it is interesting to know that while at Resurrection City, many people saw the Lincoln Memorial for the first time.

As the word went out that there would be an establishment of Resurrection City around Abe Lincoln's Memorial and the reflecting pool, there were many questions asked by people from all walks of life, particularly affluent people. Some of the questions were: Is poverty *my* problem? Why don't these people get jobs? Isn't there enough legislation already, instead of disturbing legislators for more? What does the Poor People's Campaign want? What will these programs cost us? How will they run the campaign? Do they have the right to do this? Is it wise at this particular time? Realistically, what can be achieved by having Resurrection City and poor people coming to Washington? Who runs the campaign? What about these large demonstrations that are going on from time to time? Does the campaign need my support? These and many other questions were asked before we went to Washington to establish Resurrection City.

The questions were answered before the federal government closed it down. They gave us from the first part of May until June 16 for our experiment. Within that length of time, it was almost impossible, we thought, to build the shacks, or A-frame houses, but within two weeks, the A-frame buildings were built out of plywood and encased on the inside with plastic. There were many people, many industries, who sent the things that we needed. We were given plywood and plastic. Food was brought in by large trucks, and within two weeks, we had nearly 100 A-frame houses put up. Also, we had a city hall and several other buildings, where we could get together and listen to the speeches.

I decided to go to Resurrection City and to give my services wherever I could. The marches and demonstrations in the South were over, I thought, and everybody had been intelligently informed where and how to vote. The Civil Rights Bill had been passed and other barriers had been brought down through the shedding of blood, sweat, and tears.

I boarded the first bus from Alabama en route to Washington, D.C. and Resurrection City in May 1968. Hosea Williams and his committee were very diplomatic in handling the busloads of people from all walks of life. Members of the caravan were constantly reminded that they were representing our slain leaders nonviolently and all were told to bring their weapons and place them on the table. There was no fear of being insulted, disrespected, mistreated, or victimized by violence of any kind. It seems that the have-nots were glad to be recognized and respected. Many of them were given responsibilities to work in some way with those who were entering the caravan, as we passed through other states.

From Alabama we passed through Georgia, South Carolina, North Carolina, and Virginia, then into Washington, D.C. This was a first-time trip for many, and an education that most will never forget, I am sure. Happiness, contentment that they were in the care and protection of our nation's government, trust and eagerness to work for a more just system through the organization beamed from the faces of many caravan riders, who lived in roach- and rat-infested, broken-down shacks. Some of these poor people came through all kinds of adversities and setbacks with flying colors, and pushed to a higher level of life, in spite of the biased and discriminatory practices they encountered from government representatives. The method of divide-and-conquer—trying to keep the races apart and giving plush offices to militant leaders—didn't always work.

Reaching Washington, D.C., we first paid tribute to the grave of President John F. Kennedy, then marched on to the Lincoln Memorial and its surrounding territory, where the A-frame houses and other buildings were being built.

It was really astounding to see the cooperation of various people. There were gangs, who had had nothing to do but beat up each other, or to cut, shoot, or whatever they felt they wanted to do in violation of the rights of others. As some of these people came to Resurrection City, we found that they had wonderful potentials. People who had been told, "You're no good, you'll never be anything, you're just a shame, a disgrace to your community," came to Resurrection City, and we used them as marshals, and it was the most interesting thing to see how many of them brightened up, and felt as though they were somebody, because they were recognized.

They made some of the best marshals that could be found anywhere. They kept down any type of uprising that might have occurred in Resurrection City. They saw to it that people who would come in for the purpose of discouraging others or to start something, were kept out of Resurrection City. They also saw to it that when it was time for curfew, which was 9:00 p.m., those people who came into Resurrection City just to see what was going on, were escorted out.

They were glad to have something to do. This is something that America should take note of. We should employ this principle, instead of just giving people a handout, while not seeing that they have a decent place to stay, making it almost impossible to have a job, taking away their dignity and their self-respect—to do that reduces a person to feeling less than a human being.

Even after Resurrection City was destroyed by the federal government, and the poor people went their own way, many of them went back to school, and received degrees and training in fields they wanted to follow in life. And we were very happy to know that, if Resurrection City did nothing else, it gave so many young people something to hold onto—the determination to be somebody and to do something.

From the beginning of the work on Resurrection City, there were many curiosity seekers from Washington's center city; there were also people wondering where they would stay. Many of them realized that if they were permitted to stay there, they would have a place where they would not have to pay exorbitant rent, and they would not have to live with the rats, the roaches, and the mice. Among them were elderly people, who had no place to stay, and wanted a place of their own.

The city was quite an interesting place to me. It reminded me very much of the Indian reservations, where I had seen houses very much like that—teepees, as they were called. These houses, built on some of the reservations out West, were made of what is known as sticky dirt. I remember this very well because my grandmother had her chimney built with sticks and dirt, and yet no rain, wind, storm, or hail destroyed it.

These houses were put up in the form of an A, and they were quite liveable. They even had electricity. The water system existed only in certain specific places in Resurrection City. The toilets were latrines, and they were few in number. There was a place for women to go out and wash and another for the men. Many of the poor people visiting Resurrection City were invited by those who lived in the city to come in and take a shower.

We had a machine there to dig ditches for sewage removal. Unfortunately, the machine broke down. Residents of Resurrection City took over and, with spades or what not, they made an attempt to do what the machine would have done. They were able to dig several trenches, and tried to find the old sanitary system underground.

Food was no problem. Beyond what SCLC could afford to buy, there were many, many companies who sent all the food, canned and otherwise, that was needed. We had a dining room, which would seat a large number of people, and they served from 7:00 in the morning until 9:00 at night.

Unfortunately, a company sent a truckload of hams, and instead of the hams being delivered to Resurrection City, the truck never reached that city. I'm quite sure that there were other things that were sent and, for one reason or another, the trucks went on their merry way, never reaching the city.

We had no rules as to who would be allowed in Resurrection City. It was called the Poor People's Campaign, because its objective was to open the eyes of those people who lived in ivory towers to the fact that people were in poverty at their doorstep.

The supporting organizations cooperated beautifully, as the people came in, for we knew not how many were coming to Resurrection City. Consequently, the houses went up as the people came in. We have to give credit to more than one group, for volunteers came from all over Washington, who aimed to do what they could. All Souls Unitarian Church housed 100 marchers, furnished the food, supplied the SCLC in their gymnasium, and opened their doors for meetings. A committee of 100 volunteers from the congregation served meals to the people. A group of nuns from

Trinity College came in and served sandwiches to people. The Columbia Heights church made beds, cooked, and served meals, and tried to keep track of people, as the first contingent of the Poor People's Campaign arrived in the City.

I was one of the first to get to Resurrection City. My objective was to go and offer my services wherever I could. While the men were going down to the federal buildings to demonstrate and to plead for the things that the poor people needed, it was my job to gather the people left in Resurrection City and give them something to do.

The plan that we had, and it was carried out until Resurrection City was destroyed, was to have the Indians teach beading, the Mexicans teach ceramics, and the blacks and whites teach clothing and food preparation. And we had a beautiful thing going.

After finding so much enthusiasm for having the different races of people teach the things that everybody needed, I contacted the International Ladies Garment Workers Union and then asked that we be given a building for a sewing factory. This idea came to me because my sister had a sewing factory in the basement of her house. We were even told that someone would come from the International Ladies Garment Workers Union and teach people how to use the high-powered machines. That was a blessing. That meant that everybody in Resurrection City could find something to do. I was given a check for $500, in order to get the necessary things, including a kiln for ceramics. But when the city was destroyed, the check was destroyed with it.

It happened that the very day that I received the money and went out to get the material needed to build the building, which would house the sewing machines, was the day that Resurrection City died. It was destroyed by our government, who feared the consequences of poor people getting together.

CHAPTER 2

The Hungry Children

If by the mere force of numbers a majority
should deprive a minority of any clearly
written constitutional right, it might, in a
moral point of view, justify revolution—
certainly would if such a right were a vital
one.   —Abraham Lincoln

This was the correct time to challenge the federal government. During the first days of Resurrection City, Reverend Abernathy and his associates spent hours talking with legislators. Questions were asked about the discrimination which led to malnutrition and even the death of so many people.

After having gone into several congressional offices, to see the congressmen, senators and their aides, we went to the Agriculture Department, because we felt that, if you at least feed people, you give them a mind to do something. As long as their bodies were emaciated and they were starving, there was nothing they could do.

As a result of our meeting that day in the Department of Agriculture, the children of Selma were finally given a decent lunch at school. If Resurrection City accomplished nothing else, at least it succeeded in staving off starvation among some of the children of Selma and other poor Southern cities, which, until Resurrection City, were entirely neglected by the U.S. government.

Hunger, like a vulture ready to descend, shows on the faces of the children in Selma and the county. I told our lawmakers about half-starving young ones in school, who

297

sat at the table in lunchrooms, saw dinners brought to those whose parents could afford a 35¢ meal for them, smelled the aroma of prepared, hot meals, but could not taste or touch them. The report was so incredible that one of the Department of Agriculture officials, in a most diplomatic way, challenged me.

I was asked to go to the office of Mr. William Seabron, Assistant to the Secretary of Agriculture, who said he would like to visit Selma and the surrounding counties. Mr. Seabron's job was to give orders to the regional, state, and county officials, to read reports of how the money was distributed, and to receive the records marked "satisfactory." Like nearly all Washington officials, he thought the job had been done, the less fortunate had been fed, and there were no hungry stomachs in America. I was pleased to know of his interest and gave him my address.

When I returned to Selma, after Resurrection City was part of history, Mr. Seabron followed up that initial contact. He came to visit Selma in May of 1969, with Attorney Orzell Billingsley of Birmingham, and together we were to visit the schools. We entered the lunchrooms of the East End segregated school just as the first graders were filing in for lunch.

Side by side the children sat, some of them with lunch boxes containing jelly or peanutbutter sandwiches, some with crackers, and occasionally one with a meat sandwich. They bought only a 5¢ carton of milk. Others bought hot meals for 35¢.These were the few who perhaps came from families with only one or two children in school. But there were also dozens of black boys and girls with absolutely nothing to eat. Their tiny arms and legs told of their lack of decent food at home. They turned and twisted in their chairs and placed their fingers in their mouths and watched their classmates' every move, from the first forkful to the cleaning of the plate. It was the order of the board of education that every child must go to the lunchroom and be seated at the table.

Many of the kids with food felt sorry for those who had

nothing and occasionally a child took a piece of bread or a sandwich and passed it under the table to her classmate, who had enough pride not to want to be seen accepting the handout. If a child did not want her lunch or a portion of it, it was readily devoured by a child nearby.

Mr. Seabron walked toward the table of the tots and asked, "Why aren't you eating lunch, little boy?"

The boy looked down at the floor as he answered, "I ain't got nothing."

"Why?" he was asked again, and this time he said, "'cause I don't have no money."

"Didn't your mother give you money?"

"She ain't got none 'cause she ain't working," was the answer.

Mr. Seabron left the child with a sad look on his face and moved to the next hungry child. "Why aren't you eating?" he asked. The child gave a similar answer.

"What did you have for breakfast?"

The answer: "I ain't had no breakfast."

Mr. Seabron continued to question several others asking, "When did you eat last?" As he went on, he found many who had not eaten since supper the previous night and most meals consisted of corn bread, buttermilk, and greens. This was the meal cooked after the mother returned from working all day, serving and training the white children and cleaning the white family's house.

With tears in his eyes and an incredulous look on his face, Mr. Seabron ordered lunches for all the hungry mouths. This reduced his pocketbook quite a bit, but convinced him that there are starving Americans in this land of plenty.

As we walked out, I asked him if he wanted to see some of the other classes coming in for lunch or would he rather go to some of the other schools. His reply was, "No, what happens at this school, I'm sure is true at others." He then said, "Mrs. Boynton, when you made that report in Washington I knew it couldn't be true. I could not conceive of such a thing."

I said, "The half has never been told, Mr. Seabron. I'd like to take you into the country, where conditions are worse and families are larger."

He asked that I report to him about the lunch program the following year. The principal was disconcerted because of Mr. Seabron's visit, and charged all teachers never to let another visitor in without his consent. All poor children are now getting at least a peanut butter sandwich at lunch.

The officials in Washington need to move in more freely and more often among those who have charge of the federal programs in the states. As long as segregationists have charge of the issuing of federal funds, the poor people, especially the blacks, will never get their fair share.

I am reminded of a recent conversation I had with Sheila Jones, Schiller Institute Board member and candidate for mayor of Chicago, with reference to her having brought to public attention an African-American opera singer who was discovered living in the city's flea market, because this country refused to respect and accept his talent, though he sang with many symphony orchestras in Europe. This was the discovery of a diamond in the junkyard.

How many bushel baskets full of diamonds has this country thrown in the junk pile because of prejudice, discrimination, and racism?

In this scientific world, education is a must, if one is to be successful. One cannot reach one's potential unless one is given a fair chance to compete. The fear of permitting slaves to read and write before emancipation still remains a hangover today, but instead of being confined to the Southern plantations, it is being done throughout the nation.

In Selma, Alabama many years ago, I went to the only school bookstore to get my son's tenth grade books. Approaching the section clearly marked "tenth grade," I pointed to the books I needed—political science, history, etc. I was told that those books were not for the Negro school; those books were located in another place. Though education in Alabama was rated next to the bottom in the nation (Mississippi was the lowest), the African-Americans were lower than that, because their books were of inferior standard.

Have things changed that much since slavery? According to an article appearing in the *New York Times* on May 8, 1990, "At Emory University in Atlanta, last March, a black woman found racial epithets scrawled in her dormitory room and her stuffed animals ripped apart. At Trinity College in Hartford, billiard balls were thrown through a window of a black cultural center. Incidents range from racist graffiti and hate notes to the formation of white supremacy groups and allegation of racially motivated brutality by campus police. . . ."

It is almost unbelievable that such schools as the University of Michigan, Amherst College, Brown University, Smith College and many others known to be the meccas of education are becoming spawning grounds for violence and hate toward black students, who are the most influential and brilliant products of their communities. Because these black students are competitive in classrooms and on the athletic field, the racists are demonstrating their envy and jealousy. When such racists gain political power, it results in the kind of struggle we see in Selma today.

CHAPTER 3

Government Sabotages the City

As I would not be a slave, so I would not be a master. This expresses my idea of democracy. Whatever differs from this, to the extent of the difference, is no democracy.

—Abraham Lincoln

There was no time before Resurrection City that any black person had ever been in control of a city. It was not perfect, but the main good thing about it was the communication between people, and the understanding. In light of that, it's almost unbelievable to think how conniving our governmental officials were, to destroy something that they did not like, which was going to be successful.

One day, one of the A-frame buildings burned to the ground. The next morning, I went to the young man who had been living in this house, and I asked what had happened. In the course of the conversation, I seem to have gotten his confidence, and he told me that he was paid by one of the federal officials to burn the place down.

I had the opportunity to talk to some of the others, and it soon became clear to me, that many of them were working with people on the outside, that is, with those in the federal government who were trying to destroy the buildings, to destroy the entire Resurrection City.

Another thing that struck me as quite unusual, was that every day we would have downpours. I often would get in a car and go just on the other side of the Washington

Monument, and there wouldn't be a drop of rain, while it was pouring over Resurrection City.

There was a very lovely lady who lived in McLean, Virginia who came by and asked me if I would like to go to her home and have dinner and take a bath, or just sit and talk. Her son worked in the Agriculture Department and he said to me, "Have you ever heard of seeding the clouds?" I said yes. He said, "Have you noticed that the rain goes no farther than Resurrection City?" I said yes. He said, "Well, you can use your own judgment."

After he had gone, the mother said, "I was talking to my son, and he spoke several times about how much mud the citizens of Resurrection City have to live in." He told her that he is going to compare how much of the chemicals that are used to make rain were used during the life-span of Resurrection City, compared to similar short periods in the past five years.

It seems unreal, that our government would do a thing like that. But, we had so much rain that we were bogging down, and many people could not get out of the A-frame houses even to go to the city hall, or go to their meals.

What made me realize that there was a possibility that it was true, was when two people deliberately started a feud with each other, to set off a reaction by the police. Our policy was not to allow the police into Resurrection City, though they would be around the reflecting pool and in front of Resurrection City on the street. It was not long after the feud was started, that the police on the outside used tear gas, and gassed every one of those A-frame houses. All along the way, bordering the street, tear gas was used. We had to leave Resurrection City, and go as far as the Washington Monument, until the gas was cleared out.

Those are some of the things that make you think that there is no limit to what our governing bodies will do to have everything as they would like to have it. On June 15, when Resurrection City was supposed to have closed, and we asked to be given a little while longer, so that we could

clear out and get all our things together, the saddest thing
in the world was to see the officers coming into Resurrection
City, setting fire to the A-frame houses, bulldozing them,
pushing them down. Then we were told to carry our things
to city hall, but it wasn't long before the city hall was
destroyed, and with it, all our belongings. And the people
were crying, because the few little things that they had
gathered were destroyed. They said, "This is worse than
living on the plantation, because at least there they don't
tear the houses down."

After the Washington, D.C. Resurrection City was looted,
burned, and destroyed, a thick cloud of tear gas was discharged by riot squad officers with tear gas helmets. With
others, I stood on the furthest part of the Washington Monument, avoiding the tear gas while real tears flowed from my
eyes for those who had nowhere to go.

CHAPTER 4

Living in the Ghetto

Where justice is denied, where poverty is enforced, where ignorance prevails, and where any one class is made to feel that society is in an organized conspiracy to oppress, rob, and degrade them, neither persons nor property will be safe.
— Frederick Douglass

The destruction of Resurrection City left me with a deep sadness about this country. I knew then that those who had responsibility for helping poor people would go to any length to avoid making necessary changes.

With the destruction of Resurrection City, there were many people who had nowhere to go. Before going to Resurrection City, they had not been able to pay their rent. They had nothing when they went there. They were able to accumulate some clothes while there, but those went up in smoke with the fire. I asked one fellow whose acquaintance I had made, what he and his family were going to do. He was standing with about 40 other homeless people and said, "I just don't know. Look at these people, they have nowhere to go."

They left there, as everybody else did, because the tractor came in and leveled the buildings to the ground. I heard that they went to a church, and this is a story that was told to me by Ray Robinson, who was one of the most vocal and most interesting fellows in Resurrection City.

I was making preparation then to find a place to live in the ghetto, in the low income section of the capital, to continue to work on the first edition of this book. So I said

goodbye to Ray Robinson and the others and went house-
hunting. It happened that I was able to get a place on
Fairmont Street, where the houses, at least on the outside,
looked nice.

Having made myself acquainted with the person who
lived in this house, I accepted the flat in the basement,
because I thought it would be quiet there. It was not very
long before I heard quite a bit of noise on the outside in the
back. I looked out of the window and I saw rats as big as
cats, fighting over something that they had gotten out of the
garbage can. That was the first time I had ever seen a rat.
I had seen mice, but not rats. I turned my back and went
back to my work, because there was nothing that I could
do, but I feared that they would come into the house.

I went upstairs where the lady who lived in the house
was, and I noticed the door had a large brick behind it. I
asked what was the reason for that brick. She said, "that is
just one brick in the daytime, but at night, I put three bricks
up there."

I asked why, and she said, "Because if I don't, the rats
will come in. They will come in between the door and the
casing of the door. Therefore, I have to put something heavy
enough to keep them from coming in."

The lady didn't have anything to eat, and I went to the
store to get whatever I thought she could eat. She was quite
an elderly woman. In many cases, I stayed there a whole
week, and there were days that she was not able to cook
for herself.

The next day, I heard a great noise in the front. When I
looked out, I saw men who had nothing to do, but to stand
by the lamppost, talking to themselves about what they
wanted to do, and that they had no jobs. The next day, I
saw some kids playing around that same post. They were
playing the same games that they had seen the adults on
the street playing. They were cursing and one said, "Let's
fight," and the other one said, "No, let's play soldiers," and
then, "I'll take my gun [they had sticks], and I'll shoot you

dead before you shoot me dead." This was all that they knew to do, to play little games of destruction and horror.

I was thoroughly amazed at what one might find in the ghetto. I have a strong belief that a man can live in the ghetto but the ghetto need not live in him. Those kids' faces were too bright and intelligent to remain in such living conditions. I wished I could have found a better place for them to live.

CHAPTER 5

We Try a New Resurrection City

We make a ladder of our vices, if we trample those same vices underfoot.
— St. Augustine

One afternoon shortly after I had arrived there, somebody came to the door, and the lady of the house said, "there's someone to see you." I wondered who in the world knew I was down there, since I did not tell anybody where I was going, because I didn't know myself. As I came to the door, I saw Ray Robinson and two or three other people. He seemed to be so jubilant, and I wondered why. But when he opened his mouth, I realized that he had a reason to be happy. So he thought, and so I thought.

He said, "Mrs. Boynton, I want you to come and see where we are going to live."

I asked, "Where are you going to live?"

He said, "We have a place now, and the owner is going to let us buy it. Do you know, when we left Resurrection City, we went to a school, and they said to us, you can stay here for the night, but you can't stay any longer. We spent the night there, and the next day we had to leave. Then when we left, we didn't know where we were going, but there was a church, where they said, 'we'll let you stay here a couple of nights, but you must leave after that.'"

There were about 30 people at that time—40 of them had started out together. They went to the church, stayed there, were fed, and given a chance to take baths, but when the time came for them to leave, they were told they had to go. But they protested, "We don't have anywhere to go." And, as Ray Robinson told me, the head of the church said, "I'm sorry, you *must* leave."

They had nothing—no clothes or anything else, because the clothes that they had had been destroyed in Resurrection City. They said, "We have nowhere to go, we don't know anybody, and we'll just have to stay outside." So they stayed on the lawn that night—it happened to be a warm night in June—and they slept out on the lawn.

While they were there, several fellows came on motorcycles. They said that they were the Hell's Angels. Somebody had told them that these people were there on the lawn with nowhere to go. So the Hell's Angels went to the store, bought food, brought it back to them, and helped them to leave there and go to Alexandria, where they camped under a large tree in a pasturelike place.

They found the owner of the place, who was a black man, and he said to them, "I'm going to let you stay here, and those who can work, will work, and I'm going to charge you toward buying this farm." There were five acres on this farm, which they were to buy for approximately $60,000. Ray replied, "Oh yes, we can do it, we can buy this place. We're going to pitch tents, we're going to stay under the tree until we can pitch tents, and then we're going to work and we're going to buy it and it will be ours."

The very next day, this black man came back and said, "You have to leave. You can't stay there."

Ray countered, "But you said that we could buy the place."

He said, "Yes, but the white people downtown told me that if I let you have this place, then I'll find myself dead or in the Potomac River. You cannot stay here. You are just going to have to leave."

So, they had nothing else to do. It happened that the people in the community were coming back and forth, and helping them during the two or three days that they were there. There was one fellow who said, "You can come and stay with us. I don't have much room, but there are trees there, and you can stay under the trees." I happened to be there during this transition time and I rejoiced with them. This Good Samaritan who offered his backyard had only a half acre, most of it in brambles, and he was out on parole. The gesture of giving a part of the little he had was far better than any professed church or Christian they met.

So Ray and the little group went down to this man's house, and stayed in the arbor. The thickness of the branches and the trees and shrubbery was such that it made an overhead cover for them.

When I went there, I said to them, "If you were in Selma, I'd give you ten acres of land."

Ray said, "Is it true, would you really give us ten acres of land?"

I said yes. And I meant it. I had decided that it would be a good cause, and it would carry out the idea that my husband had had, before he passed, to give a portion of the plot of land that we had in the countryside, to some organization or some people, and it seemed to me at the time that this was more worthy than any other organization I knew. Perhaps this could become another Resurrection City, I thought.

When I said they could have the ten acres, I had no idea that the group would even think of coming to Alabama. But around the first part of December, I received a letter and then a call from Ray Robinson, saying, "We are coming down. You promised to let us have the land and we are coming." Well, I thought it was great, and I went to the community where the land is—it's in the country—and I told a number of the people there, that these people were coming down, and I was going to give them this land. They were very receptive; all they wanted to know was, how many of them are coming. I said, "I don't know."

Forty of them started out, and each day some of them left, because they found some other way to live or to exist. But on one of the coldest nights, Ray Robinson and sixteen people arrived. I took them immediately to the country, where people were waiting for them. They fed and housed them until the next morning. Then we went to the farm, where there was a vacant house. I told them, "You can have this land with this house on it, and, of course, you can do the repairs that would need to be done."

They got together and were very happy. We made some stipulations: there would be no drugs; if anybody came there who had been using drugs, they must be rehabilitated; there must be a daycare center and a laundry; they must plant food and take care of themselves.

Well, they began doing that, and I was very pleased. Quite often, I would take people out there to see the progress that they had made. Then there was a confrontation in Minnesota, at Wounded Knee, where the Indians were having trouble with the federal government. Ray Robinson decided that he would give his service at Wounded Knee to help the Indians. Ray Robinson has never been heard from since.

The ten acres were managed by his wife Sheryl, who had other plans. She was able to retain a piece of property on a public road about one and a half miles from the new Resurrection City, and raised money to build a clinic in the name of the Poor People's Campaign. Money was raised throughout the country, but not enough to build the ultra-modern clinic demanded by the racists who were determined to stop it. For example, the health department gave the legal description of the septic tank for the medical center. When this was done, another representative of the health department condemned it and had her remove it. The same thing was true about the wiring, and every little discrepancy from the regulations—from the growing of the grass to the kinds of flowers planted—was criticized.

Finally, Sheryl left the county and went back to her home somewhere in the Northwest, but not before (without my consent) she placed a man and woman in the house who refused to keep the house repaired. Thus, portions of the house became unliveable. It took a court order in 1985 to have them evicted and reclaim the land, that could have been like an oasis in the desert.

This is the story in part of Resurrection City, its citizens, and in what terrible need were the people who came to Resurrection City. I only wish it had been possible that the land that I gave to those who had nowhere to go, could have been developed into a new Resurrection City, which would be able to help those who were unable to help themselves. I only wish that it would have been there, that we could have had a clinic, a washeteria, a school for the youth, a rehabilitation center, a place that they could be proud to look at and say that this came out of Resurrection City.

The few weeks that Resurrection City survived and the many people whose lives were touched by it mean more in giving to the unwanted and castaway a new lease on life, the will to give, and to know they are loved, needed, and recognized, than any legislation could give. I thank God that I was able to make a contribution to this.

CHAPTER 6

Robert W. Billups

Greater love hath no man than this, that a
man lay down his life for his friends.
                                        —John 15:13

In 1969, a year after Resurrection City and nearly eight years after my husband Bill passed, I decided to marry again. The 27 years of a very good and loving marriage made me somewhat skeptical, because I didn't believe that there would be another person as cooperative and compatible as my first husband.

On December 30, 1969, I met a gentleman from New York, who had come to Selma to bury his wife. His wife's sister owned the hospital where my late husband Bill was often hospitalized.

On December 26, 1970 we were married. Bob Billups played with the big bands during the Depression, with Duke Ellington and Father Hines, and even wrote music for some of the bands. After the bands declined, Bob went back to school and became an electronics technician.

Bob was among the best in whatever he did, but most of all he was a warm, affectionate, appreciative person. He had a coop apartment paid for in New York, and property in Texas and California, which meant as a retiree he was free of obligations.

We lived in New York for a short time and then returned to Selma. Though we were in a most beautiful apartment in

New York, we decided to sell the apartment and move back to Selma where Bob had made many friends. The four years we spent together were a very happy time for me, both personally and politically.

On March 13, 1975, our friend Gloria, who had a program on one of the local radio stations, had gone to Daufuskie near Savannah, Georgia, and wanted to make another visit for her program. We decided to accompany her, together with Margaret Moore, a good friend, spending the night before the trip in Savannah.

The plans for the boat to take us about eighteen miles had fallen through, but plans were made to have a resident of Daufuskie take us over, with assurance he traveled the Right River daily.

We passed the island where the waving girl lived for 90 years and the pass which steamers used going to the ocean. A large pleasure boat from Hilton Head Island, S.C., making a trip to Savannah to pick up some dignitaries, disregarded the small craft we were in and the waves from the large boat turned ours over. We were swept overboard. I saw the owner of the boat floating face downward. Only the stillness of his lifejacket made me aware that he was dead, perhaps, I thought, from a heart attack. Our lifejackets were no protection against the high waves, as they were old and rotten and the fasteners were unstable.

Though the sun was shining on this crisp March morning, it was still cool, and the river was 42 degrees. It was 40 feet deep, and said to be over 100 feet wide. As the four of us— Gloria, Margaret, my husband and I—clung to the overturned boat, wave after wave made us weaker and more frightened, but all except Margaret kept from panicking. Finally, a large wave, like a giant, separated Margaret and me from the boat.

If you have never heard the death screams from a person asking you please not to let her drown, you're lucky. Not being a good swimmer myself, I endured the voice of one who could not swim at all, calling on God and me to "Please, don't let me drown." I knew not to touch a drowning person unless you know how (by the top of their hair). I asked God to give me the strength to save my friend. Being frantic, she would keep her mouth open screaming, thus taking in an unusual amount of water. My husband continued to call to me, "Honey, are you alright?" The last two times I heard him calling to me, as Margaret and I drifted continuously farther from the boat to which he and Gloria were still clinging, his voice was very calm. Still, he continued to call out calmly, "Baby, are you alright? Please keep the faith." Then silence. I knew they had the boat to cling to.

I continued to try to keep Margaret from sinking as I talked to God, believing firmly in his miracles, saying, "O dear God, I can't drown, I just can't drown. I have too much to do." I continued to say, "Father, I can't drown, I've too much to do." What did I have to do that I would talk to God like that? Frankly, I had nothing specific nor in general on my mind that I had to do.

Bob, being the kind, selfless person he was, though he acknowledged to me several times that he could not swim, thought about our friend Gloria. He tried to console her, probably thinking she was as exhausted as he was. Finally, a small gas tank holding about five gallons and no doubt kept in the boat for emergency fuel, floated past him, and he had the strength to get it to him. Knowing he and Gloria were in a life and death struggle, his kindness would not permit him to hold to the tank when she had nothing. He handed her the tank, saying, "Here, hold this, it will keep you afloat for awhile." Within minutes the boat sank and he went down with it. Gloria survived because Bob gave her the tank. I survived because I believed God had something for me to do. We both (the only two survivors) survived because of God's will.

It was estimated that we were in the water twenty minutes before rescue came, by accident. A boat with about twelve children between the ages of eight and fifteen were on an ecology field trip, when one of them remarked that there was a lot of trash in the river. Someone else noticed movements and the adults on the boat were alerted. They found

Gloria and me, Margaret, who did not survive, and Mr. Bryant, the owner of the boat, who had been the first to die.

After being taken into the boat, I asked, "Where is my husband?" The answer was that his body had not been found; it was recovered seven days later.

My minister, Reverend Cleveland of First Baptist Church of Selma, asked that I have the unopened casket brought to the church, for he would like to preach the funeral. I consented because, though Bob was not a regular churchgoer, to the residents of Selma he had exhibited Christianity wherever he went during the four years we were married.

The church was filled and the minister took his text from the Biblical saying, "Greater love hath no man than this, that a man lay down his life for his friends." A more beautiful charge to the living I've never heard, for it took away all of the grief I might have had and gave me the courage and the will to find all of the things I told God I had to do.

CHAPTER 7

Running for Office Again

The God who gave us life, gave us liberty at
the same time.   —Thomas Jefferson

While Bob and I were married, I had decided to run for office again. In all of my campaigning for political office, I never ran with the intention of winning, but to prove to my people that they had the opportunity to run and win. This is their inalienable right.

Thanks to the involvement of African-Americans in politics, there are now African-Americans in every political department in Selma. My son, attorney Bruce Carver Boynton, is the attorney for the county commissioners, and saved the county over $1 million in road equipment costs the first year of his employment.

In the county, the probate judge is elected for six years. In each case, the deciding factor of a vote is white, and it means programs are mostly in their favor. I knew that the probate judge played a big part in keeping blacks from registering to vote and I also knew, from some of the sources working closely around him, that Probate Judge Bernard Reynolds was far from being a judge who was fair in his dealings to all citizens alike.

Judge Bernard Reynolds had been probate judge of Dallas County for more than 25 years. Under him, progress had become stagnant and blacks were mistreated. When blacks were going down to the courthouse by the thousands to register, the probate judge's attitude was less than human.

In 1973, being a member and officer of the National Democratic Party of Alabama, a black party within the Democratic Party, and with fragments of the Student Nonviolent Coordinating Committee still in the city and many of the Selma citizens still being charged by the electrifying and overwhelming success in the political field, I felt that I would have a lot of help in running for Bernard Reynolds's office, as Dallas County's probate judge.

Though I didn't win the race, I felt that my running for these political positions encouraged my people to run for office, too, and many of them won.

In 1974, I ran for Alabama State Senate from District 29. I ran with a slate of candidates of the National Democratic Party of Alabama (NDPA) and my platform had six points: 1. Lower taxes for the average person. 2. Quality education for everyone. 3. More jobs and industries in this district. 4. Better health care for all. 5. Decent housing for all citizens. 6. Registration offices for voting in each community.

In the *Selma Times Journal* of October 19, 1974, Associate Editor Nikki Davis Maute gave an account of the underhanded method used to remove the names of the NDPA candidates from the November general election ballot, in an article titled "NDPA Candidates Taken Off Ballot."

"Dallas County Probate Judge Bernard Reynolds said . . . five candidates failed to comply with the Alabama Corrupt Practices Act." Named among the five was Amelia Billups, Senate District 29. "These candidates with the exception of Mrs. Billups and Schwenn failed to file a declaration of appointment or selection of a campaign finance committee as required by the Corrupt Practices Act or failed to file within the time allowed by law, which is within five days after qualifying for office with the probate judge."

After we protested this unfair action, a federal judge ordered the probate judge to place our names on the ballot. Again, while we didn't win, we won a substantial number of votes and set a positive example for African-Americans.

CHAPTER 8

James Robinson

The best portion of a man's life has little,
nameless, unremembered acts of kindness
and of love.   —William Wordsworth

Shortly after the death of my second husband, I received a call from Tuskegee offering whatever assistance the caller might give. This man's voice was familiar but I could not recognize it until he told me he was James Robinson, who had been in school with me at Tuskegee. That voice seemed to haunt me day and night. I asked God to please take this man off my mind.

About 45 years before Bob Billups's death, James Robinson and I were schoolmates. Both of us sang in the famous Tuskegee Institute choir. Since the choir practice was almost a block from the entrance to the chapel, most girls were escorted to the front door by a male choir member. Often, although we had shown no specific interest in each other, James was the one who would escort me to the front door. Later, I found that my college sweetheart was his roommate.

Through the years, he had married and become a physical therapist, and was employed for many years by the U.S. Veterans Administration. He also had an interior decorating business, in which he employed at least eight people.

He was asked by a mutual friend to bring an electronics technician to Selma to evaluate the expensive equipment that Bob had left. When we began to correspond, I felt he was such a nice fellow, that when I needed an escort I would call on him. So it was not long before we married, with my expectation to stay in Selma. One of the Alabama colleges wanted him to head the interior decoration department, but he refused because he didn't want to close his business in Tuskegee.

There are some things that are stranger than fiction and destiny works where we least expect. My husband was a beautiful combination of the morals of both previous husbands, and we were very compatible. He was not in the very best of health, and three years after we were married he became ill, and was in and out of the hospital until his death August 17, 1988. During those years I never became tired, exhausted, or ruffled waiting on him, and my mind reflected back to the river, telling God I could not drown because I had too much to do. James said he saved me for him, for I lengthened his life with the kindness and care I took of him. If this is the work God had for me, I certainly thank him for preparing me physically and mentally to make my husband happy.

Since James's background is such an historical one, I feel it would be of interest to recount some of the highlights here, if only for history's sake.

In the 1890s Charlie Robinson, James's father, lived in Charleston, South Carolina, tilling the soil for the barest of existences. He talked with his wife and they decided to go to Kansas City, to seek a better life.

Charlie equipped his wagon for the trip to Kansas, taking all of the necessary equipment for the long cross-country journey. From the beginning of the trip, he encountered jeers and all sorts of obstacles and hurdles from the white farmers, merchants, and some of his own people, who feared for his life.

Early one spring morning, he, his wife Elizabeth, and their one child left in a covered wagon en route to Kansas—the West. For many days they traveled, forging streams and crossing deep forests, following other covered wagons and, sometimes, Indian trails. Once they caught up with a caravan, whose leader told them to go back, or they would take their wagon and leave them on the side of the road. They turned back but it was not long before another caravan came along, whose leader he told that he had gotten lost. They were kinder and accepted the Robinsons, if Charlie would agree to be a lookout man for the Indians.

These were cold nights and hot days. They encountered snakes, coyotes, mountain lions, and many creeping things. Soon the caravan turned off the trail, leaving Charlie to continue his journey to Kansas alone. While they were en route and alone, Indians on horses stopped the wagon. He had little protection and, not being a violent man, he depended upon his wits to help solve his problems. The Indians began a friendly conversation in signs, as neither could understand the other, and helped them through the woods.

Finally, they reached Kansas City, tired and frightened. Charlie did not like the city and city work. He heard about the territory in Oklahoma, where the government was giving 40 acres to a family for staking out a claim. With his few clothes on a stick over his shoulder, he set out early one morning to stake out a claim. At the end of many days, he was miles away from the place, and there were no highways, roads, or houses along the way—only Indian trails. At night he would make a fire to keep away the mountain lions, wolves, and reptiles, sleeping the best he could. Nearing the territory where the claims could be made, he saw some men traveling on a buck-board. They permitted him to ride with them, since all were headed to the same place.

Charlie staked out his claim and made a brush-harbor for himself. There was no way to communicate with his family, so he worked to build a shelter for them. He first built the brush-harbor, and then, after clearing the land, he built a log house.

After his family joined him, Charlie built another house, as his family began to grow. Before he passed away, he became the road overseer for the new town, the rural tele-

phone president, and worked in the animal husbandry department of Langston University. He accumulated 900 acres
of land, eighteen head of mule, untold numbers of cattle,
hogs, and poultry of all kinds, as well as oil wells, and was
the father of ten children, of which my husband was the
seventh.

Having been born in the wild, James had a profound love
for the Wild West, fearing nothing and loving everything that
was a part of nature. He would bring wounded animals
home and doctor them when he was a child, but his greatest
love was for horses. There were many wild horses in that
territory and people would come to him for a horse or to
have a young one broken. This was a source of income that
helped him to attend Tuskegee.

A packing house in Chicago employed him to buy cattle.
As the first black cattle buyer for a national packing house,
he was not allowed to go into dust storm shelters in some
places, while in other shelters he was protected by what he
called "rootin'-tootin', gun-slinging cowboys." Thousands
of cattle were shipped to the packing house.

James liked to talk about the many incidents that occurred in the Wild West. One was of two famous outlaws,
known as the Dalton brothers. Once they rode by James's
house and asked for a drink of water. While he was getting
the water, one of them went into the house, took the pan of
bread off the stove, threw him $10, and rode away.

Finally the Dalton brothers, who were in the same cate-
gory of criminal as Jesse James and Pretty Boy Floyd, were
caught and jailed. James said the brothers had a hiding
place on his family's property, where they had dug a cave
on the Cimmarron River, a place where James used to play.
He had an uncle by the name of James Jenkins and the
Dalton brothers had a brother by the same name. They
wrote a letter to their brother from the jail, and addressed
it to James Jenkins, Corley, Oklahoma. It read, "Dear
Brother, we are here in jail and plan to break out. Don't
know how soon but we hid three bags of money under. . . ."
They named the tree and the direction to go to find it.

It happened that the letter was placed in James's mail box and his uncle James Jenkins opened it. There was a map. That evening he got two other men with shovels and hoes and headed to the Daltons's hideout. They dug according to the map, keeping one fellow as lookout man. Three days they dug in that section but never found the money. James's father said he appreciated at least their making the soil easier to plant.

Later, the Dalton brothers escaped from jail and went on a rampage, which ended in the death of both brothers.

Cowboy James McKinley Robinson made enough money to attend Tuskegee Institute, majoring in agriculture, which caused him to be in direct contact with Dr. George Washington Carver. Later, he settled in Tuskegee and, having a small farm, he furnished milk daily to Dr. Carver for more than a year.

CHAPTER 9

Volunteer Work in Tuskegee and Selma

It is not work that kills men. It is worry.
Work is healthy. You can hardly put more
upon a man than he can bear. Worry is rust
upon the blade. It is not the revolution that
destroys the machinery, but the friction. Fear
secretes acid, but love and trust are sweet
juices. —Henry Ward Beecher

I have sought throughout my life to find avenues where I could put my energy to work, to help bring about a better world. When the civil rights movement was not as active after the death of Dr. Martin Luther King, Jr., I looked around for organizations that I could work with, to achieve the same goals as we strived for with Dr. King and the movement. On the local level, I have involved myself in the struggle for fundamental needs of our citizens, in Selma and then, after 1976, in Tuskegee. On the national and international level, I have worked with the Schiller Institute since 1984—but we will leave that for the final chapter.

In 1975, Selma was so badly in need of a senior citizens' home, the Dallas County Senior Citizens organization, working with an attorney, spent thousands of dollars to get approval from the Farmers Home Administration (FmHA) to build one. We were sure that the project would be approved, as a housing expert had helped to bring the proposal, the blueprints, and the location to standard.

The final day for approval was announced by the FmHA representative from Washington, who congratulated us for the perfection of the plan and said he was sending a man from Washington to bring the approval to Selma directly.

The FmHA representative met the attorney and the committee on the land set aside for the project, which happened
to be almost adjacent to a low-income project.

Before asking any questions about the dimensions or
the organization, he said, "I'm not going to approve that
project."

"Why?" I asked. "It has been approved by Washington."

He replied, "Because I said so. It's too close to the city
line."

I then asked him where the guidelines were and who
makes them, since the officials from Washington had been
down and approved it. His answer was, "I make the guidelines." Later I found out that this man was from the Montgomery FmHA office and had no intention of approving a
black project.

In 1985, the Macon County Senior Citizens organization
toured Washington, D.C., and one of the focal points was
to meet our congressman, Bill Nichols. He took us around
the Rotunda and, to his surprise and discomfort, I began to
ask questions. I asked him, "With all of these statues in the
nation's Capitol, and the many political contributions we
have made since slavery, where are the statues of African-
Americans?" (This was before the statue of Dr. King was
erected.) His answer was, "You see, the states sent these
statues in, and they have never sent a black man's statue."
This, of course, was not satisfactory to me. "I'm sure you
know of Benjamin Banneker, don't you?" I asked. Silence
fell over the group. "He was the black man who took over
the planning and laying out of our nation's capital, the
District of Columbia, in 1791 when the French architect left,
not to return. As such, he was the first black presidential
appointee in America, appointed by President George
Washington. He was also the man who made the first almanac, and the first American clock. I am sure you know of
Dorie Miller, too, who was the first to shed blood for this
country in World War II. Where are their statues?"

Being a little embarrassed and a lot ignorant, he resorted
to the old Southern method of throwing blacks off their

mental tracks. He said to the 35 of us, "Come, come follow me."

He took us to a very small room, just large enough for a half-dozen people, and said: "Now this is where we congressmen come every morning before going to Congress. This is our prayer room, where we always ask God's guidance through the day. Ah, will one of you good Christians lead us in prayer?" It would not do to tell what I thought of this false camouflage mask.

We were quickly taken out of the Capitol. Reaching the steps, someone asked that we pose for a picture. One of the official photographers was also taking pictures. I said to the congressman, "Since we receive your briefings each month, please see that this picture is placed in it."

Needless to say, it never was.

I live today in the city of Tuskegee, where I went to college. Tuskegee University, founded by Dr. Booker T. Washington, is a key institution in the history of African-Americans, as well as in my personal life.

Having lived in Selma from 1929 to 1976, I surprised myself by deciding to leave. My decision to leave Selma was something I had not planned on doing, but, like a child who grows up and is able to take care of himself, I realized that I had trained many people to fill my shoes in all sorts of tasks. In 1976, my son and his family moved into the same house I had occupied for 40 years. Knowing that the house was well taken care of eased my anxiety, because I knew my son could direct things. I also knew that coming back to my alma mater, I would meet friends and classmates who still lived in Tuskegee.

When I moved back to Tuskegee, one of the very outstanding early Tuskegee graduates came to see me and took me to a meeting of the Tuskegee Institute Women's Club. This is the oldest, still active club in the state and perhaps the country. It was founded by Mrs. Booker T. Washington. She had discovered so many homeless children in the area, that she decided to organize the club, as well as clubs all over the state. The combined efforts of these clubs resulted in the purchase of 150 acres or more of land, which enabled the Women's Club to establish a boys' reform school and later, a portion of that land was set aside for girls. Many years afterward in 1979, I became the president of the Women's Club, and remained so for ten years, resigning in 1989.

There are chapters or branches of organizations in Selma of which I am now a member in Tuskegee, including the Red Cross (board member), State Association of Women's Clubs, Delta Sigma Theta Sorority, and the Tuskegee Alumni Association. I also transferred my church membership from First Baptist Selma to Greenwood Missionary Baptist Church.

I was also introduced to a Mrs. Sadie Edwards, who is supervisor of the Retired Senior Volunteer Persons (RSVP). I found this lady to be one of the few hard-working, sincere, dedicated persons who knows no night. I fell in love with her program and have been giving her a part of my time or working with others through her.

The telethon program with RSVP is of great service to the elderly, who accept our courtesies. We go to the police department and call each person on our list, all of whom live alone, to see that they are alright. If they don't answer their phone, we have the name of a friend or neighbor whom we ask to contact them. In the event we reach neither, there is an officer who goes out to see if help is needed. Often people are sent out to give medicine or find out the condition of the elderly person and report it to their doctor.

Another program I work with, which is dear to my heart, is the youth group under the supervision of Mrs. Teague, who has saved many girls and boys and given them guidelines by which to live. It has been quite successful. Working with this program makes me realize how much young people want to know that they are needed.

Working with them and writing short plays, skits, and games for them, is a delight to me as well as an inspiration for them. Trying to play my part in these and other activities enables me to keep my balance, physically and mentally.

CHAPTER 10

How I Became a Member of the Schiller Institute

*I refuse to accept the idea that the "isness"
of man's present nature makes him morally
incapable of reaching up for the "oughtness"
that forever confronts him.*
—Dr. Martin Luther King, Jr.

After the final march from Selma to Montgomery and the passage of the Civil Rights Act, I had even more of a reason to fight for life, liberty, and the pursuit of happiness. I had a desire to tell the whole world of the struggle, because men and women, white and black, had come from throughout the world to help us.

After Resurrection City, I began to affiliate with peace groups, including the Women's Strike for Peace, Women's International League for Peace and Freedom, the National Negro Women's Clubs, and other long-standing organizations. However, this did not seem to satisfy my desire to reach out to others.

Attending a meeting in Washington, D.C. in 1983, I met a young man named Dennis Speed, who approached me and started a conversation. At first I was somewhat apprehensive, but being a good listener, I learned that he was with an organization known as the Club of Life. As he spoke about the Club of Life's struggle against drugs and its concern about starvation in Africa and other parts of the world, I immediately knew that I wanted to help wherever I could.

Later, Dennis invited me to New York, where he was

sponsoring a meeting in the heart of the ghetto with many people in attendance. As there was a good deal of dissension against our appearance, I knew how sick these people were and how much help they really needed. Could this organization be the answer, I wondered?

At that time, Reverend Bernard Lafayette, who was the first from the Southern Christian Leadership Conference to come to Selma to work with me in 1962, was living in St. Louis, Missouri. He was bringing two busloads of young people on a tour down South and wanted to stop in Tuskegee. I invited Dennis Speed to come to Tuskegee and address the group, which he did.

Shortly thereafter, in 1984, Dennis invited me to a meeting in Virginia. The information I received there about the world situation from Lyndon LaRouche, the keynote speaker, has been proven correct to this day. In 1984, he discussed the impact that the closing of factories, capping oil wells, and foreclosing on farmers would have on America and the world—and he was right.

Later that year, the Schiller Institute, an international organization, was born, and I was asked to be on the advisory board, which I gladly accepted. Today I am a member of the board of directors. Helga Zepp-LaRouche is the chairman of the Schiller Institute both here and in Germany.

While working with this organization I have become more enlightened about the structure and functioning of the government, the wheeling and dealing as well as the real manner in which it operates. I have learned to use my own judgment and to dig deeply in history and the Constitution, which sits on the shelf while biased judges and ignorant juries defy all reason and justice.

One of my colleagues on the Schiller Institute Board is Mrs. Sheila Anne Jones. Sheila Jones, an African-American, is well known in Illinois as one of the state's most courageous and outspoken political leaders, and the leading Midwest spokesman for the Schiller Institute's movement for the inalienable rights of man.

As part of this effort, in 1984 Mrs. Jones accompanied

me and the former Borough President of Manhattan, Mr.
Hulan E. Jack, who was also a board member of the Schiller
Institute before his death, on a fact-finding mission and tour
of West Berlin on behalf of the Schiller Institute. We called,
prophetically, for the reunification of the two Germanys and
the toppling of the Berlin Wall, which occurred five years
later.

In August of 1987, Mrs. Jones toured the nation of India,
bringing the message to thousands of Indian citizens, that
Lyndon and Helga LaRouche's international movement for
the inalienable rights of man is the continuation of the
legacy of both Dr. Martin Luther King and Mahatma Gandhi.

I asked Sheila to write about how she went from an
eighteen-year-old Milwaukee student leader in Dr. King's
movement to a leader of the Schiller Institute. These are her
words.

Have we learned the lessons of Dr. King?

In 1978, I met a man, a woman, and a movement, who
have opened up answers and solutions to the many questions I have held hidden since the murder of Dr. King—
questions which I, as an eighteen-year-old girl asked twice:
while standing in the vestibule of St. Boniface's Church in
Milwaukee, when we were told that Dr. King had been
assassinated, and while standing under a magnolia tree in
Atlanta, Georgia, at the funeral service for Dr. King. Who
were the man and woman? Lyndon and Helga LaRouche.
The movement? The Inalienable Rights of Man Movement.

Aware that the miseries befalling mankind were in no
way limited to just blacks in the United States, but in fact,
were being levied out to millions across this globe in Africa,
India, Ibero-America, Southeast Asia, as well as in Western
Europe and behind the Iron Curtain, Mr. and Mrs. LaRouche
built a movement, taking up where Dr. King had left off.
They realized that the United States was the first republic
born in modern history, and that, because of the international, conscious conspiracy by the Founding Fathers, together with the Marquis de Lafayette, Baron von Steuben,

Friedrich List, the networks of Amadeus Mozart, Ludwig van Beethoven, Friedrich Schiller, and others, there must be an universal image of mankind, which transcends all racial differences and barriers.

The basis for their elaboration on the theme initiated by Dr. King was manifested in Mr. LaRouche's own personal contribution to the field of economic science. By fighting for the marriage of theology, philosophy, and economic science, Mr. and Mrs. LaRouche have courageously waged the most aggressively loving fight to bring mankind to the highest level of thinking, in order to ensure the defeat of the banality of appealing to any form of "blood-and-soil" common denominator of thinking.

Seeing the horrendous plight of the world's population as a result of leaders' sinking to the "lowest common denominator" in the contemplation of solutions for the survival of mankind, Mr. and Mrs. LaRouche realized that there must be not only a renewal of the spirit of Dr. Martin Luther King, linked to the American Revolution, but an elevation of the substance of that movement, in order for that movement to continue to reach new heights of achievement for the entire human species, beyond its own physical existence.

In the LaRouches' endeavors to achieve their goals, they have dauntlessly faced the opponents of justice, naming the names of the perpetrators of the mass-genocide being meted out, which has resulted in crimes *100 times worse* than Adolf Hitler. The building of international alliances—of Africans and Ibero-Americans, black city dwellers with rural agriculture producers, Christians with Jews, Eastern Europeans with Southeast Asians, budding classical artists with retired concert prima donnas—has set into motion an unstoppable force.

Mr. and Mrs. LaRouche have been concerned with the future of our children, because, as they have stated over and over again, the future of our children requires inspiring the hearts and minds of the downtrodden of this world. They have shown that we must achieve grand enterprises, so that the citizens of this world remember the great wealth of scientific and industrial breakthroughs, which brought children in the 1960s to the realization that man could walk on the Moon and beyond.

The Schiller Institute and the numerous institutions founded by the LaRouches have insisted that we must establish for our children what is important in our living, and having lived. I can think of no better criterion for that, than teaching our children that we must contribute to human progress, not go back to days fraught with backwardness. The question to be raised is: "How can we teach our children whether the results of our generation's work will be ultimately good?" I am convinced, because of my collaboration with the LaRouches, that if we assert as our fundamental goal the enrichment of the moral character, and the science-oriented, intellectual development of the coming generations, we shall rarely go wrong.

A wise nation lays the foundation for what will be bequeathed materially to its posterity, 50 years or so ahead, Mr. LaRouche has written in his grand design for the colonization of the Moon and Mars. This means that the citizenry is inspired to see that plan achieved, beyond the individual's own lifetime.

So, with Mr. LaRouche and his international movement fighting to overturn the destruction of the beautiful ideas which this nation has produced, he has been in a head-to-head confrontation with the likes of Henry Kissinger, David Rockefeller, the International Monetary Fund and the World Bank, the gangsters in the Anti-Defamation League of B'nai B'rith, and the Soviet Union's KGB. As Mr. and Mrs. LaRouche have understood that there comes a time, when, as Schiller said, you must be willing to lose your life in order to save your life, they are now viewed as the true "standard-bearers of the legacy of Dr. King."

Through the work of the Schiller Institute, which was created by Helga Zepp-LaRouche and Amelia Boynton Robinson, together with former Manhattan Borough President Hulan E. Jack, I, as an active participant, see that Dr. King's efforts are being observed and learned by forces and individuals who were never in his physical presence. When I journeyed to India, on behalf of the cause of the LaRouche movement, as a guest of the All-India Lawyers Association, I met Indian parliamentarians, congressmen, lawyers, teachers, students, and scientists, who knew of the work of Dr. King, and felt this to be one of the greatest pearls in post-American Revolution history. Having read the works of Mr. and Mrs. LaRouche on economic development, and the crucial questions of energy, culture, and the moral questions facing civilization, they were in unanimous agreement that the life work of Lyndon LaRouche was a direct continuation of Dr. King's movement.

Looking at Mr. LaRouche's works, I can say to all, that though forces associated with Henry Kissinger wish Mr. LaRouche dead, and this is the reason that he has been unjustly imprisoned, "An idea can not be killed . . . it cannot be expunged from the memory of humanity, if but a handful still carry it in their hearts!"

Courtesy Frank H. Lee

(Above) Amelia Boynton Robinson with Dr. King's widow, Coretta Scott King. Mrs. King was the featured speaker at a 1984 fundraising program at Tuskegee University. Also pictured are the president of the student council (far left) and Tuskegee Mayor Johnny Ford.

(Below) The Martin Luther King Center for Nonviolent Social Change. Amelia Boynton Robinson serves on the board of this center, devoted to realizing the dream of the slain civil rights leader.

(Above) At Resurrection City in 1968, Mrs. Boynton prepares to build the sewing center—a building that never was.

(Below) Handing the contract to Ray Robinson for ten acres of land near Selma to build a new Resurrection City.

ELECT
Amelia Boynton
BILLUPS

29th SENATORIAL DISTRICT
November 5, 1974
A VOTE FOR ME IS A VOTE FOR
HONEST PROGRESSIVE, FEARLESS
COURTEOUS AND FORWARD REPRESENTATION.

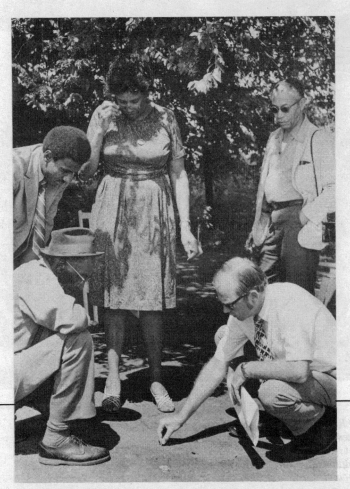

In 1974, her hat in the ring again, this time for the State Senate, Amelia Boynton Billups discusses plans for a housing project in Selma with a representative of HUD.

(Counter-clockwise from top) An oil painting of the home James Robinson built in Oklahoma; Amelia Boynton with Senator Hubert Humphrey in 1965; Amelia Robinson with civil rights leader Hosea Williams in 1987 on Martin Luther King's birthday in Atlanta

Stuart Lewis

Stuart Lewis

(Above) In November, 1984, Amelia Robinson addressed the Schiller Institute's Rally for the Inalienable Rights of Man in Washington, D.C.

(Below) Shaking hands with the Hon. Hulan E. Jack, former Manhattan Borough President, at the Schiller Institute's Fourth International Conference in 1985. Mr. Jack was a board member of Schiller Institute until his untimely death in 1986.

Stuart Lewis

On April 30, 1987, Mrs. Robinson joined a press conference at the National Press Club to expose the violations of civil rights and human rights against Lyndon H. LaRouche and his associates in the U.S. government's illegal raid and bankruptcy actions.

Michael Vitt

A Tribute to...

Mrs. Amelia Boynton Robinson
A Champion of Human Rights
February 26, 1991

Mistress of Ceremony, Chenee Johnson, 11-01

Posting of Colors	JROTC
Pledge of Allegiance	Audience
"Lift Ev'ry Voice and Sing"	Audience
Purpose	Chenee Johnson
Musical Selection	Choir
Poetry Reading	Jason Hines, 9-07
Introduction of Guest	Merrell Waters, 10-01

Guest Speaker's Address...

Mrs. Amelia Boynton Robinson
Author and Human Rights Activist

Musical Selection	Jazz Band
Acknowledgments	Leonecia Perry, 9-08
Musical Postlude — "We Shall Overcome"	Audience
Closing Remarks and Dismissal	Mrs. Jean B. Owens, Principal

Lift Ev'ry Voice and Sing

Lift ev'ry voice and sing,
Till earth and heaven ring,
Ring with the harmony of liberty;
Let our rejoicing rise
High as the listening skies,
Let it resound loud as the rolling sea.
Sing a song full of the faith that the dark past has taught us,
Sing a song full of the faith that the present has brought us,
Facing the rising sun of our new day begun,
Let us march on till victory is won.

In an East German city during her April 1990 tour.

On February 26, 1991, Frederick Douglass High School in Baltimore, the second oldest black high school in the United States, held an extraordinary tribute to Amelia Boynton Robinson. She addressed the school's students in the high school auditorium, where a huge banner read "Welcome Amelia Boynton Robinson, Civil Rights Leader and Champion of Human Rights." During her address, she told the students that they must "seize the opportunity to contribute to humanity." This is the program for the event.

Mrs. Robinson leads a group of East German youth in the traditional singing of "We Shall Overcome." Her April 1990 trip brought the message of Dr. Martin Luther King and the Schiller Institute to thousands of newly liberated East Germans.

PART VI

From Civil Rights to Human Rights

Unearned suffering is redemptive.
—Dr. Martin Luther King, Jr.

CHAPTER 1

Whence America Today?

World history is the world's court.
—Friedrich Schiller

After the civil rights marches and demonstrations, which taught the race-haters and others that their hatred did more harm to the hater than the hated, some of them began to realize that we were all created by God, as of one flesh. There were many cases of communication that opened doors of unity and understanding. The unfair jailings, the beatings, the murders, the disrespect for human beings, brought to the attention of the world that it is necessary for a bridge of communication to be built.

But in spite of the sympathy and the physical, mental, and monetary help Dr. King received, the cause for which he fought seems to be going backward. We are widening the gap of misunderstanding and communication. Little wars in foreign countries are still wars, and people are suffering the same fate, including murder, starvation, greed, and abuse.

We cry out for peace, but there is no peace, when lawmakers are our greatest lawbreakers, in many cases sanctioning the lawbreakers, or playing God and pardoning their every sin. They get off free while others, black and white, have deliberately been denied due process of the law. Such vile misrepresentations of the law inspired me to pick up my pen and write. We can have a better world if we have as our motto, "Let there be peace on earth, and let it begin with me."

It is not slavery before emancipation that disturbs me; it is slavery of the present time. The worst slavery is now, with blacks living in substandard housing, with no jobs to feed their families, living on the streets in big cities, eating from garbage cans, their children not able to attend school because they have no address to give. Shelters may be furnished, but only for a short time; at 7:00 a.m., they must get out and hit the streets. No one is to be found out there to speak a kind word except the drug dealers, who offer our children jobs as drug pushers, or make them addicts, so they can forget their pitiful condition.

Blacks and other "minorities" (this is just a word, because the "minorities" are a majority in this country if one knows who is white and who is black or ethnic) are being mistreated. Housing is awfully hard to find and harder to rent. Many years ago, I went to Harlem, New York. The housing condition was excellent. People of all races and nationalities lived in peace and harmony. But, because of the lack of jobs, people had to move out, many returning to the South. Inflation, high rents, no jobs—the once-lovely homes were abandoned. Squatters took over, though there was no electricity, heat, or water and in many cases no toilet facilities. The mafia took over, it is alleged, and encouraged the destruction of the inner structure, then bought the buildings, repaired them, and raised the rent. Where are the squatters going?

As former U.S. Attorney General Ramsey Clark, now a defense lawyer for Lyndon LaRouche, told the third conference on Human Rights Violations at the Conference on Security and Cooperation in Europe (CSCE) in June 1990, we have 2,300 people on death row in America, most of them minorities. Some 850,000 homeless are on the streets as well, he said. That's where the squatters have gone.

It is very unfortunate that America, controlling many parts of the world, is still practicing, as it nears the 21st century, the same methods it used nearly 300 years ago, when the white man brought the first group of black slaves to become beasts of burden. The disgrace of this country is that it is still using the same racism, frame-ups, discrimination, mind-control, low income, and (a modern version of the poll tax) diluting the voting strength through redistricting, to prevent African-Americans from gaining high political office.

Washington, D.C. attorney Mary Cox, long associated with human and civil rights issues, told the Schiller Institute's Martin Luther King Tribunal on June 2, in a stunning indictment of the Department of Justice, that 43 percent of the more than 6,700 black elected officials in the U.S.A. today are either currently under investigation or indictment, or have been. The pattern has been followed since the end of Reconstruction, when one by one, either because of false accusation, coercion, or entrapment, black legislators have been disgraced and driven from office, leaving African-American voters to regard the leaders of their race as political failures, and unworthy to hold such offices, thereby also mentally degrading themselves.

Even more frightening, Mrs. Cox referred to the FBI's *Fruhmenschen* policy, under which, according to testimony of FBI agents read into the *Congressional Record* on January 27, 1988 by Congressman Mervyn Dymally, the FBI has been consistently targeting black elected officials for legal harassment. *Fruhmenschen* is German for "early man." The assumption behind this "unofficial" policy, according to FBI testimony, was that "black officials are intellectually and socially incapable of governing major governmental organizations and institutions."

The Reed case (see below) and cases like it all over the United States have given many people grave reservations with regard to what progress African-Americans have gleaned from the Civil Rights Act. Like the U.S. Constitution, the Civil Rights Act is a great piece of legislation, which has long been a part of the Constitution, which has typed in bold print, "All men are created equal." It depends on us to make that equality real.

We have made some progress, through consistent struggle, though retrogression has been ever-present. Twenty-five years later, at the beginning of the last decade before the 21st century, we can list some of the accomplishments in Selma of those 25 years. Perhaps the most progress has been made in the Selma school struggle, still ongoing at the writing of this chapter. There are, however, other signs of progress to point to:

• Where there were no appointed or elected black officials in 1965, African-Americans today number one judge, one county board attorney, five on the board of education, four on the city council, and three county commissioners (the only ruling body in Selma where blacks are in the majority, though blacks are the majority in the population of Selma). When tie votes are to be broken on the commission, it always goes in favor of the white officials, because the chairman is white and can vote to break a tie.

• There is an African-American president of George Wallace College, where once a person of color was not allowed on the grounds.

• The Welfare Department (pensions, Social Security), unemployment office, and Post Office are all run by African-Americans, though some were appointed by the federal and state governments.

But at the same time that these gains have been won, lawsuits had to be brought against realtors for discrimination before we were given the right to live where we choose. Though the Black Belt counties have more African-Americans as residents than any other, their accomplishments were attained only by their inner strength to withstand the cliques, set-ups, traps, and lies spread about those who fought for liberty. Certainly it hurt and was humiliating, but they came out with flying colors, winning control for African-Americans in Green, Perry, Wilcox, Lowndes, and Sumpter counties.

CHAPTER 2

The Reed Case

*Look beneath the surface for the true
meaning of justice.*

A very famous case took place in Tuskegee while James
and I were living there, and the fight around it continues to this day. The case of State Representative Thomas
Reed, from Alabama's 82nd district, bears heavily on the
future of black political leadership in America today. It
demonstrates that there has been no slowing down in the
determination to disgrace, humiliate, and discredit African-
American leaders. Representative Reed is still in prison
today, serving a four-year term.

In 1978, Rep. Thomas Reed, an African-American resident of Tuskegee, and the first black man to be elected to
the Alabama State Legislature since 1872, was tried *five*
times (with no new evidence introduced), for having attempted to bribe a state senator, whom he ran against and
defeated. Senator Dudley Perry, a white man, accused Reed
of having tried to make a deal with him, to vote for a bill in
the state senate for a dog-racing track to be built in Macon
County, to bring in needed revenue.

The Alabama State Attorney General, Bill Baxley, with
whom I met to demand that he drop the trumped-up charges
against Representative Reed, told us that he knew Reed was

guilty. Later, he said that he would try Reed again and again until he was convicted.

Reed had two strikes against him as far as the racists were concerned. First, he was the president of the Alabama State chapter of the National Association for the Advancement of Colored People and second, he was in a position to and did open many doors for blacks. Some of his contributions as a legislator included the following: He introduced more bills to help African-Americans economically than any other representative; he filed charges against the state troopers' department, forcing Alabama to hire black state troopers; he caused the first investigation to be made of the Alabama prison system; he led the fight against bringing back the use of capital punishment (the electric chair) in Alabama; he forced the State of Alabama to enact an affirmative action plan to hire blacks in all state jobs. Reed also caused much revenue to come into Tuskegee and throughout the state. Tuskegee Institute alone received over $12 million through his efforts.

Dudley Perry was determined to put this black lawmaker in jail, to send a message to all blacks: This is what will happen to you (to militants daring to run for office) if you invade this political field.

The trials began on December 6, 1976, and ended February 22, 1978. The trial ended each time without a verdict: twice through a mistrial, once through a deadlocked jury, and twice a judge said he had no jurisdiction over the case.

Though the trials cost Reed more than $70,000 and stripped him down to a man of poverty, he still held his head high and vowed that his spirit and struggle for justice for all men would *never* be broken.

So why is Thomas Reed behind bars today? According to his family, he was finally convicted on trumped-up charges. As a senior representative in the state legislature, Reed acted as a mediator between the state and prisoners, presenting prisoners' cases before the parole board. There was a case with a parolee whose nephew had a long sentence (both are white) and it was alleged that the parolee paid

Reed $10,000 and gave him some furniture for his restaurant—all of which was allegedly unreported. The ensuing investigation found no evidence of any additional furniture in Reed's place of business nor of any deposits of money unreported in bank accounts. Then why did Reed become a target again?

In 1987 the African-American state lawmakers in Alabama decided to do something about the Confederate flag flying over the capitol building in Montgomery, and made complaints to the appropriate offices. This symbol of racism once hung above the U.S. flag, until many citizens of both races complained and the U.S. flag was given top position.

The Confederate flag stands as a grim reminder of black people being treated as chattel, deprived of all rights as human beings. It still flies today over Alabama and several other Southern state capitols. While some states realize the Civil War is over and have removed it, others proudly keep it as a reminder for their offspring, as part of the brainwashing that the color of their skin is what matters, and not their ability to contribute to the nation and the world.

After waiting several months following their complaint and receiving no reply, Representative Reed again asked the authorities to take the Confederate flag down in Montgomery and place it instead on the side of the building, where flags of other nations fly. This request was refused. Another request, then another was made. Still there was refusal.

After a joint meeting of senators and representatives, Representative Reed announced that if the flag were not down by January 5, 1988, he would personally climb the poll and take it down. That deadline passed, and the Confederate flag still waved with Old Glory.

I went to Montgomery to witness this historic occasion. It was a dismal day, with overcast skies and cool temperatures. The capitol being under repair, there was a high wire fence surrounding it and all the gates were locked.

Several hundred people gathered outside the fence, white and black, to witness the confrontation. The lawmakers of

color, headed by Representative Reed, made an attempt to
climb the fence. The guards inside the fence pushed Reed's
hands back, using a stick resembling a billy club, as he
attempted to make it over the fence. He made several other
attempts, each of which was repelled. Rep. Alvin Holmes
then tried, with the same result. One lawmaker after another
tried and each time was pushed back. Attempts were made
for more than an hour without success.

The crowd was mixed. The whites were there to cheer if
the flag remained, the African-Americans to cheer if it came
down. It was easy to hear conversations among groups.
Standing beside a man with two boys aged about nine and
twelve, I heard him say to them, "See that Confederate flag
up thar boys? That means always keep your foot on da
nigger's back." Only self-restraint kept me from responding,
because I didn't know how to respond. I couldn't get that
statement out of my mind, because I know that the Confederate flag is symbolic of the bigots' ongoing fight for white
supremacy.

I remember the many years since 1932, as we went to the
polls to vote, I had to vote in all state and city elections
under the symbol of a rooster proudly strutting in a white
ribbon inscribed "white supremacy." When the rooster vanished, the Confederate flag became the accepted symbol of
white supremacy.

What became of the African-American lawmakers? They
were all carted off to jail, charged with unlawful assembly
and given a small fine.

Not too long after this episode, Thomas Reed was
charged with accepting a bribe in the parole case mentioned
above. Reed's trial was moved from Montgomery to Mobile
because of the widespread publicity surrounding his attempts to remove the Confederate flag from the capitol. On
October 11, 1989 the final verdict of guilty was declared.

Reed's appeal was unanimously rejected by a three-judge
panel, though the judges noted that a prosecutor improperly
referred to Reed's role in the Confederate flag controversy.

Reed's request for a retrial, due to the testimony of a new

alibi witness, was also denied. A spokesman for Reed told the press, following this action, "The flag has been a major issue in Reed's case. If he had not called for the removal of the state Confederate flag from atop the capitol building, he [Reed] would be in the state legislature today."

In my view, this case should be of great interest to all people concerned with civil rights. One only has to look at the continued flying of the Confederate flag in Alabama to this day, to see the injustice of the South symbolized there.

Rep. Alvin Holmes, one of those who tried with Reed to remove the flag, was quoted on June 13, 1990 on WSFA-TV in Alabama, declaring that he will not vote against the burning of the U.S. flag until the Confederate flag ceases to fly over the State of Alabama, which is a humiliation to its African-American citizens.

CHAPTER 3

Targeting of Black
Political Leaders

Don't throw stones at your neighbors',
if your own windows are glass.
— Benjamin Franklin

New York State Senator Andrew Jenkins, who is chairman of the Committee to End the Harassment of Black Elected Officials of the National Council of Black Legislators, gave an important speech at the January 1989 Martin Luther King Tribunal, sponsored by the Schiller Institute, on the subject of the ongoing targeting of black elected officials in the United States. I want to include a portion of his remarks here, because this targeting and assault must be stopped now.

"There was a young man who, prior to his coming to America, believed very much in the advancement of our people, and worked very hard for it. And he was the forerunner, in the forefront of what we would like to have seen develop in America—that is, a sharing of power, that if you proved to be good at your job, then you had a right to ascend to the highest seats in the land. If you worked yourself to death, and produced for your constituencies, then you too could be governor, or lieutenant governor, or U.S. senator, or congressman, or President of the United States.

"But America's not about that. And there developed a very fast hatred of the black elected official, and anyone in the minority community who would look to uplift or organize—especially to organize—be he black or white, in the minority communities. During Reconstruction, we elected seventeen blacks to Congress, and once the Reconstruction period was over, it only took eleven years to flush them out of office. So, by 1890 we had seventeen. By 1901 we had none. And then the long road back began.

"Marcus Garvey was the first to realize that we were a people in need of organization, and perhaps America would not work. 'These are the times that try men's souls,' are they not? And so he organized, and began to tell people that it was time to go home.

"We were wrested from the bosom of Mother Africa, and brought to various shores and various rocks in the islands and the ocean, and told that 'This is where you will now live. . . . Don't worry—you won't be paid. Have all the children you want. Oh, don't worry, you'll never see them grow old. Work in the sun all the day long, and sing songs at night.'

"And so Garvey said, let's go back and see if we can't reclaim that which was ours. And so, they decided that they didn't need him around! They put him in jail. That was the last time he saw his supporters, or his wife—a good wife! She worked very hard and very diligently for him. . . .

"The National Conference of Black Lawyers formed an organization to bring to light the FBI's harassment of black elected officials, and lesser blacks. The FBI and the federal government did not always prosecute the cases they investigated. Some they gave to local officials; but they sought out, brought out all of the information, and then presented the case to whomever was going to try it, and they did the dissemination of information—the disinformation—concerning the black elected officials; and they worked very closely with the press.

"We, in the National Conference of Black Lawyers, were barred from bringing to the attention of the judges, the FBI's true intentions! The bureau ran an organized disinformation campaign, that focused on the federal, state, and local levels, and it was called—I'll spell the acronym for you: Cointelpro!

"The first target was Martin Luther King. Why? Because he attacked J. Edgar Hoover. J. Edgar Hoover quickly retaliated, [with a multimillion-dollar budget to do it.]

"It is up to us, those who recognize the problem, to change this. Those who do not recognize the problem are part of the problem. But it is up to us, those who recognize the problem, to stop this.

"This is a great country, built on great and sound principles, but it demands the participation of its citizenry. It's as honest as we make it; it is up to us to make it honest. And we must remember, as Martin Luther King said, 'None of us is free as long as one remains in chains.' "

CHAPTER 4

The 1990 Selma
School Battle

There is no substitute for self-respect.

Anyone who was alive in the 1950s and 1960s has an indelible picture in his mind of the marches and bus burnings, the firehoses and vicious dogs turned on unarmed citizens in Selma, which resulted in permanent damage and even death. Another generation (mostly unborn at that time) is now fighting nonviolently for the same goals: equal justice and the inalienable rights of man.

Since the supposed integration of schools in Selma, the policies from segregation days were carried over into the segregation-camouflaged-as-integration era. All students enter the same doors of the school in an integrated manner, but once inside, segregation begins with the leveling or tracking system. African-American students in many cases are encouraged or coerced into taking courses leading to trades, while white students take advanced courses preparing them for law, medicine, and other professional tracks. During commencement exercises, many students of color receive certificates, while the whites receive high school diplomas.

In what appeared to be a real step in the direction of improving these conditions, Dr. Norward Roussell was hired as the first African-American superintendent of the Selma schools by the Selma City Board of Education in 1987, with a three-year contract to expire in June 1990. A few months into the school year, parents of both races saw the improvements in their children's education and praised the superintendent for lifting the educational standard. Much of this was achieved simply by retiring and replacing some ineffective teachers, and enforcing stricter guidelines for teachers and students.

In 1987, a group of African-American parents formed a support group known as BEST (Better Educational Support Team), having as its primary goal to assist in dismantling the tracking/leveling system and providing parental support for improving education in Selma.

It is widely believed that Dr. Roussell's attempt to eliminate the leveling system is what led to his firing. In addition, his push for a new school in East Selma—where students cannot attend school when it rains because of the mudhole it is built on—did not find favor with white society in Selma. (This is the same school I brought Mr. Seabron to visit following Resurrection City.)

The five African-American Selma school board members discovered in December 1989, that the six white board members had been secretly meeting with Mayor Smitherman (the same man who has been mayor since the 1960s), to strategize the termination of Dr. Roussell's contract. On December 21, 1989, in the middle of the week, in the middle of the month, and near the middle of his contract, Superintendent Roussell was fired. The white board members, who comprise a majority, voted to fire the superintendent and the African-American school board members walked out in protest.

Parents, teachers, and students attending the board meeting requested a renewal of Dr. Roussell's contract, but their request was not granted. Then BEST asked parents to keep their children out of school, despite Mayor Smitherman's threat to fine each parent $500 or face six months to one year in jail. The students followed with a sit-in at Selma High School.

   Their demands were the following: keep the superintendent with at least a three-year contract; no action against
teachers or students involved in the protest, regardless of
race; an elected board of education; resignation of the six
white elitist school board members; reinstatement of the
five black board members; employment of more black
teachers (as the student ratio is 70 percent/30 percent black/
white); giving the Selma school superintendent authority
equal to that of the white school superintendents in Alabama; and that no board member's children shall attend a
private, segregated school. These are the demands read to
the board by Mrs. Alice Boynton, wife of my son, attorney
Bruce Boynton, and president of BEST.
   Because of the pressure which BEST brought to bear, Dr.
Roussell was temporarily reinstated, but was told that his
contract would be terminated in June 1990, with no consideration for renewal.
   While the attempted firing of Dr. Roussell was occurring,
Mayor Smitherman had appointed Rev. F.D. Reese, the
black Selma High School principal, to co-chair the 25th
anniversary celebration of Bloody Sunday, to be held March
4, 1990. Reverend Reese claims to have walked to Montgomery three times with Dr. King, to have brought Dr. King to
Selma, chaired or organized the Voters League, managed
many of the marches and demonstrations, and to be in the
midst of BEST and Century 21 organizations in cooperation
with Congressman John Lewis. He permitted himself to
be coopted as a co-chairman, together with white banker
Mothland, both having been appointed by Mayor Smitherman. This was after many meetings with white and African-
American citizens where the foundation was already laid
for the celebration of the 25th anniversary of Bloody Sunday.
   In fact, Reverend Reese was not present on March 7, 1965
at Bloody Sunday. But he did not want to give up this
co-chairmanship. So the citizens forced him to make a
statement that he would work with the original organizers
of the commemoration. Mayor Smitherman then abandoned
his attempted takeover of the event.

On December 22, 1989 in record cold weather, two banks
were picketed because of their part in the firing of Dr.
Roussell. Peoples Bank and First Alabama Bank both had
connections through associates or family to the white members of the school board. Bank accounts were then with-
drawn on a specially designated bank account withdrawal
day, directed by the BEST organization. Students boycotted
the schools. Over the next few weeks, all-night vigils were
held at Selma High School, supervised by parents. Demonstrations, boycotts, sit-ins, and stand-ins were continuous,
because the white officials refused to show anything but
bad faith in their negotiations.

On February 4, 1990, when the all-white school board
met and in a fifteen-minute meeting announced that Rev.
F.D. Reese would take over as superintendent, in addition
to his principalship of the city's only high school (and of
course pastoring his church), a group of twenty parents
called on Mayor Smitherman in his office to discuss the
school situation. Four persons—C. Williams, M. Brock, P.
Varner, and attorney Rose Sanders—were arrested. Varner
and Williams remained in jail in lieu of signature bonds and
attorney Sanders, who had led the March 4, 1990 reenactment of Bloody Sunday, was assaulted, injured, and hospitalized.

On Wednesday, February 7, hundreds of protesters (no
whites) marched to city hall and formed a human chain
around the school board building, while attorney Sanders
(whose husband is also an attorney and a state senator)
held a press conference from her hospital bed. About 200
students took over Selma High, refusing to leave, pending
the reinstatement of Superintendent Roussell and the positive resolution of Rose Sanders's case.

A third group visited the mayor's office, demanding that
officer Rushing, who man-handled attorney Sanders, be
suspended and Magistrate Calloway, who slapped another
woman during the arrest, also be suspended. They were
told that the magistrate had already resigned and that officer

Rushing would be assigned to off-street duty (i.e., kicked to a higher-up position).

On February 13, when Rose Sanders left the hospital, the students were so happy they began to sing in the lunchroom. Eighty-six of them were suspended.

Attorney Hank Sanders, Rose Sanders's husband, drew up a bill for a referendum calling for an elected city school board.

A large demonstration of several thousand was held on March 3, coinciding with the 25th anniversary re-enactment of Bloody Sunday.

In early April, two people chained themselves to the bell in the city hall entrance, while other protesters gathered in the hall and outside with signs. Many people were jailed, in an action reminiscent of the days of Bull Connor and Jim Clark.

The protesters were told not to come inside city hall or to be on the streets outside, but the demonstrations continued. In a mass meeting in mid-April, those who were in sympathy with the cause for justice and human rights were asked to toot their car horns as they passed city hall. On April 20, four more people were arrested for this sympathy action.

After the arrests, the police demanded that people clear the sidewalk around city hall (the jail is on the top floor), and that nobody sit on the veranda or porch. The next day, April 21, demonstrators brought lawn chairs and sat on the sidewalk. Police came out and picked up the lawn chairs, while the demonstrators obeyed nonviolently. Three people were arrested for contempt of court, because the previous week, the judge had banned any gatherings on the steps or lawn of city hall. As of the end of June 1990, two of these people were still in jail.

After the picketers were made to clear the front of city hall, they complied as demanded. However, a retarded teenager, who was standing on the steps, spotted a marking pen on the step of the building and returned to retrieve it.

He was grabbed by twenty police, who scooped him up like a piece of dirt and put him in a jail cell. A demonstrator who had just been released from jail protested the arrest and because of her protest, she was rearrested and jailed.

Several men were fined as much as $500 and sentenced to five days at hard labor. The city attorney attempted to get the judge to issue an injunction against these men being able to walk by city hall, but the judge refused this motion. The judge also refused the motion of defendants' attorney J.L. Chestnut, Jr., to stop the arrests of people walking in front of city hall.

BEST has sued in the U.S. District Court for the Southern District of Alabama, Northern Division for a declaratory judgment against the conspiracy to maintain white control over the Selma School Board. Specifically, the complaint asks that the laws and actions adopted by the Alabama State Legislature, the Selma City Council, and the Selma City School Board, whereby an eleven-member school board was created with a permanent white majority, be nullified; that the illegal actions which resulted in the termination of Dr. Roussell's contract be nullified; and that restitution be made to Selma's African-American students, who have gravely suffered from discrimination in their education as a result of race prejudice.

In June 1990, attorneys Bruce Carver Boynton (my son) of Selma and John R. Donn of the Civil Rights Division of the U.S. Justice Department, argued a related case, opposing the attempt by the white members of the school board to cut the terms of the black members to two years from the current four years. They won the suit and the term of all members remains four years.

As of January 1991, a compromise has also been reached on the question of the school board chairmanship. Each year, the chairmanship will rotate between a black person and a white person.

CHAPTER 5

A Tour of the Two Germanies

I would rather die on the highway than to make a butchery of my conscience.
—Dr. Martin Luther King, Jr.

In March and April of 1990, in the middle of the Selma school battle, I toured East and West Germany for the Schiller Institute, meeting with thousands of citizens of the two states, and telling them about the struggle in America for civil rights from the 1930s to the present. The purpose of the tour was to conduct a living dialogue with citizens of the two Germanies, who had been using the methods of Dr. Martin Luther King, Jr. to conduct a peaceful revolution against the tyranny of communism. They were most interested to hear from someone who had worked with Dr. King, and to discuss the method of nonviolent resistance as it applied in America and Germany today.

Though I had been to Europe seven times before, this was the most meaningful trip I have ever taken. Why? Because during the four weeks I lived in East Germany, I was repeatedly reminded of the Biblical children of Israel and the African-Americans who were brought to the New World, stripped of their right to communicate with their families, to use their own minds, and to think for themselves.

Lectures to the East Germans came easily for me, because it was simply a question of comparing my experience with theirs. I found the people very kind and friendly. East Germany having been separated from the outside world for more than two generations, and most East Germans having never seen an African-American before, I was surprised to see the dignity and respect shown me, compared to our culture in America and its disrespect for human beings, particularly those of color.

As I entered East Germany, or the German Democratic Republic (GDR), I found many anxious faces, eager and willing to hear about America and how we in the civil rights movements attained freedom (such as it is). One could see the strain of hard work in the faces of these people, young and old, and anxiety as to how to better their condition.

The cities behind the Berlin Wall are old, though once beautiful, telling the story of kings, queens, and noblemen, who lived in splendor. The castles and cathedrals are among the oldest in Europe. But in many cases, we found only the shells of what *was*.

For over 45 years and two generations a country has been mentally handicapped and, now that the Wall has come down, not having experienced freedom, they don't know what to do with it. Doesn't this remind you of emancipation of the slaves in America?

Some of their handicaps were:

1. Not being able to think for themselves.

2. Not being able to travel on the other side of the Wall to visit relatives.

3. Food shortages.

4. Fifteen-year wait for a car. All cars are two-passenger with a 40-kilometer (27 mile) speed limit.

5. Informers in all communities, who reported every move to the state dictators, and who were planted even in the homes.

6. Only the children of informers and Russian employees could get into college.

7. Of the wonderful farm and factory produce, the best went to Russia, the second best was sold to West Germany, and the leftovers were sold to the East Germans, who had

money given them each month (like welfare) but nowhere to spend it.

There are many migrant workers in the fields and factories from such places as Korea, China, Africa, and Poland. All of them are living in ghettos. They cannot marry, mix, or mingle. They live in dormitories three to a room. This of course is a continuation of discrimination and segregation. It is typical of "the oppressed becoming the oppressor."

When I told my family and friends that I was leaving for Germany and would be gone for several weeks, they asked many questions: Why are you going? Who do you know there? Aren't you afraid of getting lost or thrown in jail?

First I informed them that I had no fear, and that I was going to communicate with a people who have gone through the same mental slavery as the African-Americans in the United States. I told them that I have a family over there, a big family known as the Schiller Institute, headed by its beloved founder (now my adopted daughter), Mrs. Helga Zepp-LaRouche, whom I admire and love for her wisdom, sympathy, caring, and sharing for the unfortunate. I am never alone when I reach foreign soil. The family is always beside me to see that the best is always within my reach. I will never be adequately able to show my appreciation to my new family.

Those who know my affiliation with Dr. Martin Luther King, Jr., my sacrifice in Selma, including the mental pressure, the beating and gassing on Bloody Sunday, and the sympathy and appreciation shown by Schiller Institute here in the United States, realize that I am always among friends (actually my first adopted family) when I am with them.

I began my tour in the week before East Germany voted in a new, noncommunist government, and was there to celebrate the coming reunification of Germany, for which the Schiller Institute has been campaigning since its inception in 1984. I spoke with thousands of Germans from both sides of the former Berlin Wall, in churches and meeting halls in dozens of cities and villages, and everywhere I went,

I found intense interest in what I had to say about fighting
for freedom.

Following my trip to Germany, I spent three weeks in
May touring the Eastern seaboard of the United States and
Canada on behalf of the Schiller Institute. I had the opportunity to report to hundreds of Americans and Canadians on
the conditions in East Germany and the fight for freedom
as I intersected it there.

The Coalition for Human Rights

Silence is no longer golden.

Following the European tour and my report-back meetings in the United States and Canada, on June 2, 1990, I gave a keynote address at the Schiller Institute's Martin Luther King Tribunal in Silver Spring, Maryland. This was a most significant gathering of civil rights and human rights fighters from around the world, who came together to found a new Coalition for Human Rights. Speakers at the tribunal spanned the globe. Freedom fighters were there from the Soviet Union, China, Vietnam, Cambodia, Romania, Afghanistan, Armenia, and Panama. From the U.S.A., my old friend Rev. James Bevel, who worked so closely with me and Dr. King in the Selma struggle, was there to help launch the new coalition. Attorney Mary Cox of Washington, D.C., gave a stirring account of Mayor Marion Barry's struggle against judicial tyranny in his case. There were American Indians and Mexican-Americans.

In my speech, I addressed what has become the most critical issue facing not only minorities but humanity as a whole today—AIDS. I want to conclude this new version of *Bridge Across Jordan* with the text of this speech, because it goes to the heart of the struggle we must face and win today. The new Coalition for Human Rights has committed itself to this fight, and I hope that my readers will do so, too. If we don't win this war, there will be no survivors to clean up after us. This is a battle for *all humanity*—for Western civilization as we have known it for nearly 2,000 years.

AIDS stands for Acquired Immune Deficiency Syndrome, perhaps the greatest medical threat ever faced by the human race. In the magazine *21st Century Science and Technology* of June and July 1989, it states: "We face a worldwide epidemic of a lethal, incurable disease. It has no respect of race; however, ignorance, unsanitary conditions, unbalanced diets, lack of medical check-ups, poverty, and drugs are hastening the genocidal destruction of the entire population. The rich, the poor, the high and the low are included."

The chairman of the National Council of Public Auditors, Samuel Evans, has called for an investigation of allegations that the AIDS virus was developed as part of a biological warfare weapon to reduce the number of black or other nonwhite people.

What we do know for certain is that AIDS is the first known appearance of a killer form of a slow-virus epidemic in mankind, similar to a group of such slow viruses found to be transmittable among monkeys and apes.

It is possible that the infection of the T-cells carries the infection over the entire body, affecting the nerve and brain tissue.

The incubation stage can be five or ten years, each carrier infecting hundreds and thousands of others. There is no doubt that it is the deadliest disease known to man and one of the most horrible in terms of suffering.

Tens of millions of Africans are going to die over the next decade. Most of them are already infected. Unless drastic action is taken, the entire continent will be depopulated.

Believe it or not, many welcome the AIDS or HIV plagues killing off the black and the poor because they believe there are too many people on the earth. If Africa dies, along with poor people the world over, many insane oligarchs believe that they can go into Africa, and possess its riches. They do not realize that *they* are next in line.

Unfortunately, much of the virus is found among African-Americans and Hispanics living in the slums of rich America, due of course to substandard living conditions. Don't let anyone fool you: there are many ways to get and transmit AIDS besides through dirty needles, homosexuals, and blood transfusions.

How can you recognize it? There is no way you can always recognize it for sure. One's immune system becomes infected and can counter none of the viruses or diseases that infect the very air we breathe, the water we drink, and the food we eat. In some parts of Africa, it often takes the form of slim disease, with chronic diarrhea and a wasting syndrome, leaving its victim like one in a concentration camp, developing skin disease, often eaten alive by fungus, bacteria, and parasites.

Dr. Bernhard Godot, author of "The AIDS Disaster: Negligence or Mass Murder," a review of evidence published in October 1989, demonstrates that insufficient measures have been taken to research or slow down the AIDS virus.

The free world, during the Jimmy Carter presidency, pegged the population level of 1980 as the ideal world population for the year 2000. This was incorporated in the Council on Foreign Relations' treatise *Project 1980s.*

In his 1941 book *Impact of Science on Society*, Bertrand Russell writes, "I do not pretend that birth control is the only way in which population can be kept from increasing . . . but perhaps bacteriological war may prove effective."

There is little doubt that an artificial origin of AIDS is a scientific possibility, at least in the sense that the AIDS virus might have arisen accidentally—or on purpose. If some powerful people are capable of deliberately allowing a deadly virus to spread unchecked for the purpose of population reduction, then we must be prepared to fight.

Hitler's vicious, murderous mind is not dead. Satanic organizations like Hitler's are growing by leaps and bounds from the White House to the poorest villages, for the sole purpose of getting rid of the poor, the old, the blacks, Jews, the uneducated, unemployed, the hungry, and many others. That's why there are ghettos with poor plumbing, rat- and roach-infested quarters, dope peddling, legalized needles and condoms, and God knows what. It is time for people of color to work with others to demand a stop to this genocide of African-Americans and others throughout the world.

One of the first, and by far most famous, attempts to call attention to this crisis was California's Proposition 64, on the ballot in 1986. Lyndon LaRouche, announcing his 1988 presidential candidacy in 1985 on this issue, fought through all kinds of opposition to lead an effort to inform citizens through a legislative resolution, including the following text, which was placed on the 1986 California ballot:

"The purpose of this act is to:

"A: Enforce and confirm the declaration of the California legislation set forth in Health and Safety Code Section 195, that AIDS is serious and life-threatening to men and women from all segments of society. That AIDS is usually lethal and is caused by an infectious agent with a high concentration of cases in California. . . ."

Because of LaRouche's concern about the destruction of the poor and the helpless, he became a target of harassment. Every conceivable means was used to keep Proposition 64 off the ballot. Officials of other states took side with the opposition. They denied the civil rights of those who initiated Proposition 64, which was finally placed on the ballot and received 34 percent of the vote. One of those who petitioned for Proposition 64 was attacked on the street by a homosexual who had AIDS. He was bitten several times. The state's attorney systematically blocked all attempts to prosecute the attacker for attempted murder.

Bank accounts were seized; offices were looted, several supporters of the proposition were summoned and some were arrested. (Eventually, all charges were dropped.)

Why? Like Martin Luther King, Jr., Lyndon LaRouche is working for humanity—the poor and the helpless. He's giving his life to see that love and understanding, the greatest weapons in the world, be used to protect, not destroy, to bring peace, not war, to use our Constitution as our guideline for human justice.

The Schiller Institute and its leaders are determined to work toward the time when "righteousness shall roll down like water and justice like a mighty stream"—to quote Dr. King.

We all want to live. Now is the time for all of us to become concerned and let it be known.

There will be an international coalition to address this issue and human rights in general, beginning right here. All persons and organizations, including ministers, doctors, lawyers, churches, fraternities, sororities, housewives, business people, professionals, and just people of all walks of life: Be prepared to join the war against AIDS! Remember: Divide and conquer cannot be used in this war. The next victim might be you.

The following Call for a Coalition in Defense of Human Rights, was passed by voice vote at the June 2, 1990 meeting of the Martin Luther King Tribunal. I believe that it sums up the philosophy of the new global humanist movement, which is continuing the work of Dr. Martin Luther King, Jr. and the civil rights movement of the 1960s.

Call to Build a Coalition for the Defense of Human Rights In the Image of the Living God

The essence of all proper law, inclusive of relations among states and peoples, is the fact that mankind is distinguished by a principle not possessed by any beast, and which is common to all the so-called races of humanity. This principle sets mankind and the individual human being apart from, and above, all other creatures and things. This principle is manifest as the creative power of reason. We recognize the creative power of reason, most simply, by reference to valid, fundamental discoveries in physical science; that is, discoveries which pertain to principles of nature, to universal laws of nature.

Only man can discover these principles, or can conceptualize them among all creatures. More important, mankind can, having generated such a discovery, transmit it throughout the human population, and mankind can assimilate such discoveries to the effect that these discoveries enter into practice, change practice, and improve practice.

There is a direct relationship between the discovery of a less imperfect notion of a law of nature, and an improvement in the productive powers of labor. This improvement occurs through society's investment in using the new scientific discoveries to increase man's productive powers. This improvement occurs, in modern times, through what's called energy-intensive, capital-intensive, investment. There is no other way in which society can avoid destruction than through technological and scientific progress, used to increase the productive powers of labor by no other means generally, than capital-intensive, energy-intensive investments in production of physical and related things.

This power of reason exists as a potentiality within the individual, and, as to the degree it is developed, it is a *sovereign* power of the individual.

All creative discoveries, even though such discoveries are influenced by social processes, and depend upon social processes for the development of these powers in the individual, yet the discoveries themselves, each individual discovery, is made within a single, individual human mind. So, therefore, this process is sovereign.

Since these discoveries by individuals, and the transmission of these discoveries by individuals, and the assimilation of these discoveries by individuals, are essential to the continued existence of mankind, and are also the very nature of mankind, this casts mankind in the image of the living God, or, as it is said in Latin, *imago viva Dei*.

Only man has this power of creative reason. This is the true definition of the word reason. Science is the application of this power of creative reason, possessed only by man, and possessed by man in the form of a potential which is sovereign within each individual.

Thus, it's not only man *imago viva Dei,* the individual in the living image of God; but this quality lying with individuals, which renders all individual human life sacred.

In this set of considerations lies the essence of natural law, and the essence of human rights.

Creative reason is also the essence of all of those forms of art which we call classical. For example, the principle of art understood by Plato in his "Dialogues"; the principles of art understood by Leonardo da Vinci or Raphael. Or, also, Johannes Kepler, insofar as he refers to this as a central part of his own work; or by the great musicians. The classical, well-tempered polyphony typified by Bach, by Beethoven, by Mozart, by Schubert, by Chopin, by Brahms, by Schumann, and so forth. This kind of music is classical music, with certain known roots, and it is the only form of music which corresponds to the same principles as scientific discovery.

All classical art, because the classical principle employs a rigorous form of artistic composition, in which innovation comes only through application of the creative principle, is a reflection, celebration and strengthening of the principle of creative reason within the individual. Thus, science so defined, classical art so defined, are in the image of the living God, and reflect that aspect of humanity which is sacred.

The process of valid discoveries is associated with a very specific quality of emotion; an emotion which comes from sources above the belt, not below. This emotion is called, in the Greek New Testament, *agapē;* it's called in Latin *caritas;* in the King James Bible it's called *charity.* It is the kind of love which is expressed between a parent and a child and the child and the parent. It is the kind of love which the parent experiences in seeing a child engaged, as in block play, in simple, but nonetheless creative, discovery of new rules of the universe. The child is ecstatic; he's found a way to pile blocks in a way he couldn't before: Discovery

of a principle. And the child is happy. This is the emotion
we feel with great classical art. This is the highest emotion
which is shared between husband and wife, where there is
a good, well-developed marriage.

The principle of reason, as is associated with creative
science; the principle of reason as is associated with classical art; and the principle of reason as expressed by this
quality of love to which St. John and St. Paul referred, in
their respective gospels and epistles, all go together. That
is the essence of man; that is the essence of the law. The
form of human society must always become consistent with
this sacredness of the individual, and consistent with the
development and furtherance and celebration of that principle of creative reason which sets mankind apart from, and
above the beasts. Under this principle, there are no races.

In the case of human beings, among all the so-called
human races, all individuals, in our experience, have exactly the same kind of potential; and within the racial group,
so-called, the same potentials, the same height of potential,
exists; there is no difference among human beings in respect to that which makes them in the image of the living
God; and that is also a principle of natural law.

These principles of natural law are higher than any government; they are higher than any constitutions; they are
higher than any treaty agreement; they are higher than any
law passed by any court, any legislature, or any other body
within a nation. Those who violate the natural law, even
with the backing of the positive law of the state, of treaties,
of courts and so forth, those are criminals. They have violated the law.

For example, the Declaration of Independence asserts
the right of the United States to exist independent of its
oppressor, Britain (King George III), in spite of, and by
virtue of a law superior to, all existing treaty agreements, all
existing statutes, all existing court decisions. The United
States is a state which was constituted as an independent
nation on the authority of nothing less than God's natural
law. And there is no law which can modify or oppose God's

natural law. Thus, those things which pertain to natural law, are properly called human rights: A regard for the condition of the individual, for the opportunity for the development of the individual, for the opportunity of the useful expression for the good of the potentials of that individual: These are matters of human right. And that is what we must defend.

PART VII

Thoughts on African-American History

*I have a dream that my four
little children will one day
live in a nation where they
will not be judged by the color
of their skin, but by the
content of their character.*

—Dr. Martin Luther King, Jr.

CHAPTER 1

On Being African-American

*The Negro was willing to risk martyrdom in
order to move and stir the social conscience
of his community and the nation.*
—Dr. Martin Luther King, Jr.

Many years ago, African-Americans celebrated Negro
History Week. Just about the time the history began,
the week ended, for most African-Americans leaving many
questions about their backgrounds unanswered.

Later, a bill was introduced into Congress, extending the
time to one month and designating February Black History
Month. Why a week or a month or a certain year? Does the
Italian-, French- or Greek-American have a designated time
to discover himself?

Setting aside a specific time for me to discover myself,
and all of the other nationalities to be discovered by me in
the eleven other months is a violation of *my* human rights.

African-Americans have made hundreds of thousands of
contributions to America in all fields, which were and are
freely given to help make this nation great. And what do
we get for it? The shortest month in the year to discover
ourselves! That is just as wrong as giving us five years. The
Voter Registration Board once opened for only two days per
month and only four hours each day, before the right to vote
expired and Congress spent more time and money to extend
it. That's wrong!

We are Americans and are entitled to *all* of the rights and privileges of all citizens. I am proud of being an African-American and of the contribution of my ancestors and other African-Americans, but I choose not to have any prefix to my being an American. In filling out applications, when asked my "race," I always say "the human race." When all people in this country have to write a prefix to their nationality, such as Italian-American, German-American, or Indian-American, then I will be comfortable in saying, I am an "African-Indian-French-German-American."

In this concluding section, I want to give some examples of the real achievements of African-Americans. Many of these heroes were in books when I was a child. These stories are to be found in many other books as well, but I think it is important to include them here, because they tell the truth about African-Americans better than almost anything else.

CHAPTER 2

Dr. Drew and
Blood Plasma

*Cleanliness is next to godliness. Present
your body, a living sacrifice.* —My mother

D r. Charles Drew was born in 1904 and died in 1950. He was a world-renowned surgeon, a medical scientist, educator, and authority on the preservation of blood. He was a pioneer in blood plasma preservation, leaving mankind an important legacy—the blood bank.

Born in 1904 in Washington, D.C., he was the eldest of five children born to Charles and Nora Drew. He was an outstanding athlete, graduating from Dunbar High School in 1922. He excelled in football, basketball, swimming ,and track, with much acclaim. At Amherst College in Massachusetts, he was an achiever in both sports and academics, graduating in 1926 with high honors. He went on to become an instructor of biology and chemistry and director of athletics at Morgan State College in Baltimore, Maryland.

Charles Drew loved sports and was a tough competitor. He could have become a professional athlete, or perhaps an athletic coach, but his desire to become a doctor was stronger. In 1928, Drew entered McGill University Medical School in Montreal, Canada, and won membership in its Medical Honor Society. It was at McGill that he became interested in blood research.

He received his masters degree in surgery and became

an M.D. in 1933. After internship at the Royal Victoria Hospital and the Montreal General Hospital in Canada, he taught at Howard University's medical school. Later, at Columbia Presbyterian Hospital in New York City, he researched a process for blood preservation.

During his two years at Columbia, he developed a technique for the long-term preserving of blood plasma. He earned a Ph.D. in science and medicine in 1940 with his dissertation on banked blood.

In World War II, England suffered heavy casualties and called upon Dr. Drew to initiate its military blood bank program. There, he introduced the use of preserved blood plasma on the battlefield. This system worked so well, that the British asked him to organize the world's first mass blood bank project. Dr. Drew also became the first director of the American Red Cross blood bank.

Also during the 1940s, Dr. Drew received scores of awards and honors, and was recognized as one of the world's leading physicians. In 1941, Dr. Drew resigned his position with the American Red Cross blood bank, after the War Department sent out a directive stating that blood taken from white donors should not be mixed with that of black donors. This issue caused widespread controversy. Drew called the order a stupid blunder. He further stated that the blood of individual human beings may differ by blood groupings, but there is absolutely no scientific basis to indicate any difference in human blood from race to race. He returned to Howard University to teach surgery at its medical school.

This man, who gave so much to the world, got so little from it. The irony of his death should be a lesson to us all.

At Tuskegee Institute, we had what was known as Medical Week. Physicians from all over the world came to the medical meetings that the institute sponsored. Top doctors in every field gave demonstrations on how to use the best instruments to get the best results.

As one of the world's greatest physicians, Dr. Drew attended the clinic annually, demonstrating the life-giving fluid, blood plasma, which he gave to the world.

While on his way to the Tuskegee meeting in 1950, Dr. Drew was in an automobile accident in Alabama. The irony of his death is that his life might have been saved if he had received immediate medical attention following the accident. But he was taken to the nearest hospital, and it happened to be a white hospital. When his comrades told the hospital officials who he was, that he had had an accident and needed blood, the hospital officials looked at him, saw he was a black man, and turned him away. He died on the steps of the hospital, while thousands of people in that same hospital had their lives saved because he gave them the technology of blood plasma preservation, which is used every day to save lives.

CHAPTER 3

Benjamin Banneker, Universal Genius

The intent, and not the deed, it is our
power, and therefore he who dares
greatly, does greatly.

Benjamin Banneker was a self-taught mathematician, outstanding astronomer, author of almanacs, a surveyor, humanitarian, and inventor. He was born near Baltimore, Maryland in 1731. He was the only child of a free mulatto woman and an African farmer, who purchased his own freedom from slavery.

Banneker lived all of his life on his parents' farm, on the Patapsco River in Baltimore County. Young Benjamin attended an integrated private school. He obtained an eighth grade education and by age fifteen he excelled in mathematics. He took over his parents' farm and became an excellent farmer.

Joseph Levy, a traveling salesman, showed Banneker a pocket watch, something he had never seen before. He became so fascinated with the watch, that Levy gave it to him. He took the watch home, and spent days taking it apart and putting it back together.

In 1753, using the watch as a model, Banneker produced the first wooden clock ever built in the United States. It was made entirely of wood and each gear was carved by hand. This clock kept perfect time, striking every hour for more than 40 years. News of the clock created such a sensation that people came from all over to see it and the genius who made it.

During the Revolutionary War, George Ellicott, a neighbor, introduced Banneker to the science of astronomy, which he rapidly mastered. His aptitude in mathematics and knowledge of astronomy enabled him to predict the solar eclipse that took place on April 14, 1789. In 1792, Banneker began publishing an almanac, which was widely read and became the main reference for farmers in the mid-Atlantic states. It offered weather data, recipes, medical remedies, poems, and antislavery essays. This almanac was the first scientific book written by a black American, and it was published annually for more than a decade.

Banneker's major reputation stems from his service as a surveyor on the six-man team which helped design the blueprints for Washington, D.C. President Washington had appointed Banneker, making him the first black presidential appointee in the United States. Banneker helped in selecting the site for the U.S. Capitol Building, the U.S. Treasury Building, the White House, and other federal buildings. When the chairman of the civil engineering team abruptly resigned and returned to France with the plans, Banneker's photographic memory enabled him to reproduce them in their entirety.

Washington, D.C., with its grand avenues and buildings, was completed and stands today as a monument to Banneker's genius.

Banneker's preoccupation with scientific matters in no way diminished his concern for the plight of blacks. In a twelve-page letter to Thomas Jefferson, he refuted Jefferson's famous statement that blacks were inferior to whites. Jefferson changed his position and, as a testimonial, sent a copy of Banneker's almanac to the French Academy of Sciences in Paris. Another was used in Britain's House of Commons to support an argument for the education of blacks. Banneker was living proof that the strength of mind is in no way connected to the color of a man's skin.

Banneker's predictions were consistently accurate, except for his prediction of his own death. Living four years longer than he had predicted, Banneker died on October 25, 1806, wrapped in a blanket, absorbing the stars through his telescope.

CHAPTER 4

The Black Man at the North Pole

*We should act with as much energy
as those who expect everything from
themselves, and we should pray with as
much earnestness as those who expect
everything from God.*

We were taught in school that Robert E. Peary, a civil engineer in the U.S. Navy, was the first to reach the North Pole. The version that I have read from an old history book is that he brought with him five other people: Matthew Alexander Henson, a black man, and four Eskimo Indians. The further up toward the North Pole they went, the colder it became. On April 6, 1909, as the traditional history tells it, two Americans planted the American flag. But two Americans did not plant the flag. Only one planted it, because only one got to the very top, where the flag was planted—Alexander Henson.

Henson was born of free parents in Charles County, Maryland in 1866. His mother and father died when Henson was very young, and he was reared by his uncle in Washington, D.C. He attended grammar school there, and at the age of thirteen, he took the position of cabin boy on the merchant vessel *Katy Hines*. He worked there for six years and became an able-bodied seaman. He read avidly and traveled the world over, crossing the Pacific Ocean to the China Sea, crossing the Atlantic and sailing into the Baltic Sea, and stopping in China, Japan, North Africa, Spain, France, and Russia. In 1888, Henson met Commander Robert E. Peary,

then a civil engineer in the U.S. Navy, and was more than
ready to join Peary's historical expeditions.

Henson was recommended to Peary as a valet, but Peary
soon realized that Henson's ability to chart a path and
handle a ship made him invaluable as a colleague. During
a congressional inquiry, Peary admitted that the expedition
was greatly aided by Henson's expertise. "I can't get along
without him. His adaptability and fitness for the work and
his loyalty made him a better man than any of my companions. He is a better dog-driver and handles a sled better
than any man living except the best Eskimo hunter."

Peary took Henson on all his expeditions, from 1891
through 1909. During this period, Henson became a jack of
all trades, including navigation, trading with the Eskimos
(who had a great respect for Henson), walrus hunting, and
building sleds and igloos in subzero temperatures.

On April 6, 1909, accompanied by four Eskimos, the
white man Peary and the black man Henson were the first
Americans to reach the North Pole. The conditions these
men faced were dreadful. For the final 68 days of the expedition, it became so cold that their hoods froze to their growing beards, and they had to stop to break away ice, which
had formed from their breath and their perspiration. Snow
could not be used for drinking, because it would have
reduced the body temperature and caused immediate
death.

In the face of these horrors, Henson drew upon reciting
the 23rd Psalm and the first chapter of the book of Matthew.
Henson possessed the unique ability to merge into and
even master his environment, to the extent that he could
enjoy the good and endure the bad.

When Peary became tired and weary, a few miles from
the North Pole top, he asked Henson to take the flag and
place it at the uttermost top of the Pole. Henson traveled
the final six miles and placed the flag at the North Pole.

Because of his race, Henson was initially denied his well-
deserved recognition. He was employed as a clerk in the
New York Customs House, from 1913 to 1936. By the order

of President Taft in 1937, he was made a member of the Explorers Club and was awarded a masters degree from Howard University in 1939. In 1944, congressional medals were awarded to him and the five white men who started but did not complete the 1908 expedition. In 1948, Henson was awarded a gold medal from the Geographical Society of Chicago.

Marian Anderson:
'The Voice of the Century'

The renown which riches or beauty confer is
fleeting and frail; mental excellence is a
splendid and lasting possession. —Sallust

Black women have also made a wonderful contribution to our nation's history and culture. In the forefront, there are many singers, among them Leontyne Price, Dorothy Maynard, and Jessye Norman. Probably the best known is Marian Anderson.

Marian Anderson possibly had a greater influence in opening doors for other black singers than anyone else. She fought for years for the right to sing opera and German lieder in the concert halls of our nation. She struggled from poverty to learn the French, Italian, and German languages, to be able to sing all the classical repertoire.

In 1936, Anderson was asked by Eleanor Roosevelt to give a performance at the White House. She confessed that this occasion was the first time she had ever really been frightened on stage. She and Eleanor Roosevelt became close friends, and that friendship became evident later during the famous incident with the Daughters of the American Revolution.

Despite Anderson's tremendous success, the Daughters of the American Revolution refused to let her perform in Constitution Hall in 1939. The public outcry was so great over this issue, that Mrs. Roosevelt withdrew her membership from the organization. Further, the White House made arrangements for Marian Anderson to sing on the steps of the Lincoln Memorial in Washington, D.C. Some 100,000 Amerians heard Marian Anderson sing at that concert on April 10, 1939.

I first heard Marian Anderson before she became famous. In 1932, she came to Selma, Alabama to give a concert at Brown Chapel AME Church as a benefit for one of the church's auxiliaries. As we entered the church, we found it filled to capacity. It was not long before this lovely, petite, well-composed young lady appeared.

The songs she sang that night fit everybody's musical taste, from Bach to Negro spirituals, and from lyric soprano to alto. It was most thrilling to hear her. This, of course, was at the beginning of her career, before she became known as "the voice of the century."

CHAPTER 6

Patriots and
Freedom Fighters

*There never was a good war or a bad
peace.*   —Benjamin Franklin

Numerous people during the Civil War became involved in the fight to free the black slaves. Not only did it mean freedom for the black man, but freedom also for the white man.

Two of the most important movements to help black slaves to get North were led by women. Sojourner Truth was an abolitionist, who moved about the country and encouraged poor blacks to leave the farm where they were getting nothing. She was able to take these people to Philadelphia, where they became free from slavery.

Harriet Ross Tubman, a black woman, became the greatest conductor of the underground railway, a network of way stations that helped blacks escape from the South to free states and to Canada. She was a leader in bitter cold or hot sun; it didn't matter at all. Being a clever and strong woman, she was able to lead thousands of people from the South to the North. But she was very watchful and she carried a gun with her. She was a sharpshooter. There were many times that she passed by whites, who would not bother her, because they knew she was a very good shot. She died with honors.

Mary Church Terrell was the daughter of a white man.

She was born with more opportunities than others. She inherited great wealth at birth, but instead of keeping it for herself, she freely shared it with those less fortunate than she. She spoke far and wide against slavery and encouraged people to leave the farm and become independent. She served the people wherever she could with all her might and died a very wealthy woman, wealthy because she shared what she had with others—she was wealthy internally.

In history, we all learn about this country's separation from Great Britain. We speak about the Boston Tea Party, but we rarely speak about the first man who lost his life to free America from Great Britain. That man was Crispus Attucks, who was born in 1723, and who loved his country. He was over six feet tall, and possessed remarkable qualities of leadership.

On the evening of March 5, 1770, the bells of Boston began to toll, informing the citizens of impending bloodshed and war. Freedom and independence were the topic of discussion in every household and on every street corner.

The townspeople ran, crying out in agony over past injustices. British soldiers stood with bayonets fixed. Attucks and his followers appeared with clubs and Attucks shouted, "The way to get rid of these soldiers is to attack the main guard. Strike at their roots." The first shot fired by a British soldier killed Crispus Attucks instantly. The second shot killed a comrade stepping forward to assist Attucks. In all, five Americans were killed. Seven British soldiers, along with their chief commander, were tried for murder and, as Daniel Webster said in later years, "from that moment, we may date the severance of the British Empire." The first blood shed in this country for freedom was that of a black man, Crispus Attucks.

CHAPTER 7

Inventors

Pain is short and joy is eternal.
—Friedrich Schiller

In history class, the children are always told about Thomas Edison, Benjamin Franklin, and a number of other people, who were inventors in the world of science. But they rarely hear what African-Americans contributed. It is something that is kept from black people and they don't know that they have made just as much contribution as anyone else.

Percy Lavon Julian was an organic chemist. He was born in Montgomery, Alabama in 1899. His father was a railway clerk and his mother was a school teacher. He attended the school teachers college there for blacks, a private high school in Montgomery.

After graduation he entered DePaul University in Green Castle, Indiana. He graduated as class valedictorian and was a member of two honor societies. Julian taught at this university before entering Harvard University, where he received a masters degree in chemistry. After accepting a teaching position at West Virginia College for blacks, he later transferred to Howard University in Washington, D.C., serving as associate professor of chemistry for two years.

Julian accepted employment at Gideon Company, a manufacturer of paint and varnish. In 1936, he was appointed chief chemist and director of research for soybean products.

His appointment was viewed as a turning point in the acceptance of black scientists. In 1929, with financial backing from the General Education Board, Julian went abroad to Vienna to study for his Ph.D. While there, he became interested in research on soybeans. In 1931, he received his Ph.D. in organic chemistry.

Upon returning to DePaul, he and his assistant were the first to synthesize physostigmine, a drug used in the treatment of glaucoma. The dean of the university wanted to appoint Julian as head of the chemistry department, but was advised against it because Julian was black.

Another black inventor was Lewis Howard Lattimer, who was born in 1848 and died in 1928. Lattimer was a pioneer in the development of electricity and invented the electric lightbulb. He was the only black member of the Edison Pioneers, a group of distinguished scientists and inventors, who worked with Thomas Edison.

Lattimer's father was a former slave and Lewis was born in Massachusetts. At the age of sixteen, Lattimer enlisted in the Navy and served as a cabin boy.

Around 1876, Alexander Graham Bell had recognized his need for a highly skilled draftsman to prepare blueprints for his new invention, the telephone. Bell went to Crosby and Gould, Draftsmen, for whom Lattimer worked, to prepare blueprints for his new invention. Later, Lattimer was given the assignment to draw up the plans for Bell's telephone, taking all the bugs out of it before it could be patented.

In 1879, Lattimer left Crosby and Gould to work as a draftsman for Howard Maxim, who invented the machine gun and also headed the U.S. Electric Lighting Company in Bridgeport, Connecticut. Although electricity was in its infancy, Lattimer perceived it to be the wave of the future. In 1882 he received a patent for what was probably his most important invention, an improved process for manufacturing carbon filaments. This process proved far superior to any other, due to longer-lasting properties, because the carbon filaments, made from the cellulose of cotton or bamboo, were excellent conductors of electricity.

He assigned this patent and others to the U.S. Electric Lighting Company. Lattimer later did more than just help to bring electric light to the streets of New York and its office buildings, homes, and subway stations. Through his many activities, he brought light to the lives of those around him. He worked for civil rights organizations and taught recent immigrants mechanical drawing and the English language in New York City centers.

Lewis Lattimer's death in 1928 was widely mourned; the world lost a great scientist.

Lattimer was not the only one. We have also Granville T. Wood, who was born in 1856 and died in 1910. Wood was known as the black Edison.

Wood was a brilliant inventor of electromechanical devices. His inventions produced broader and more efficient applications of electricity. Wood's early genius for modifying and improving electrical apparatuses was unsurpassed during the Industrial Revolution. He was a native of Columbus, Ohio. He attended school until the age of ten. He travelled to Missouri at age sixteen, and worked as a fireman-engineer on the railroad. Afterward, he traveled East, to study electrical and mechanical engineering, and was able to obtain a job on the British steamer *Ironsides*, where he remained for two years.

In 1881, Wood opened a factory in Cincinnati, Ohio, and manufactured telephones, telegraphs, and electric equipment. He filed his first application for a patent in 1884, for an improved steam-boiler furnace. Later that same year, he invented a telephone transmitter. His transmitter could carry the voice over long distances with greater clarity and more distinct sound.

Wood was awarded more than 35 patents for his electric innovations. In 1880 he introduced an electrically heated egg incubator, which made it possible to hatch 50,000 eggs at one time. He also invented a relay instrument, an electromechanical brake, a galvanic battery, an automatic safety cutout for electrical circuits, and many other devices. At the time of his death in 1910, more than 150 patents had been awarded to Granville Wood.

His achievements attracted universal praise from the scientific world community.

James Forten was born 1766 and died in 1842. He invented and perfected a sail designed to make the guiding of ships easier. In addition to becoming a prosperous businessman in the sail-making industry, he was an abolitionist, a champion of blacks' rights, and a leader of reform movements long before the emergence of Frederick Douglass.

Forten spent over half of his $300,000 fortune, which was a large sum at that time, to finance different crusades for abolitionists' activities. Along with black leaders, in particular Richard Allen and Absalom Jones, he enlisted the help of 2,500 blacks to help guard Philadelphia against the British during the War of 1812. He also used Garrison's newspaper, The Liberator, and donated money to help cover the paper's first 27 subscriptions. His Lombard Street home served as the underground railway and a way station for escaped slaves.

These are only a few examples of the many activities that Forten was involved in, for he maintained a strong stance against colonialization and slavery. This inventor-businessman used his resources to improve life for his people. He was a forerunner of civil rights activism and a true humanitarian.

Lewis Temple was the inventor of the whaling harpoon. This was known as Temple's Iron, and became the standard harpoon of the whaling industry in the middle of the nineteenth century. Lewis Temple was a skilled blacksmith. He was not a whaler. He had never gone to sea.

Temple was born a slave in Richmond, Virginia in 1800, and arrived in New Bedford, Massachusetts in 1829. By 1836, Temple was one of the 315,000 free black people in the U.S.A., and a successful businessman, who operated a whale craft shop on the New Bedford waterfront.

Temple accidently fell one night, while walking near his

new shop's construction site. He never fully recovered from his injuries. He was unable to return to work, and money became scarce for his family. He died destitute in 1854, at the age of 54. When his estate was settled, practically everything he owned was used to pay off his bills.

Joseph Lee was a master cook. He knew the superiority of anything that was cooked. Based on this, he invented and perfected a machine which, by a tearing and grinding process, reduced bread to crumbs. In his hotel kitchen, these breadcrumbs were used in making croquettes, scalloped oysters, dressings for poultry, batter for cakes, puddings, and in frying chops, cutlets, fish, clams, and oysters.

On June 4, 1895, the U.S. Patent Office in Washington, D.C. awarded him a patent for his bread crumbing machine. He sold his patent to a New Hampshire manufacturer and, in a short time, it became an essential piece of equipment in every first-class hotel's kitchen and restaurant. The Royal Worcester Breadcrumb Company in Boston became a lucrative business.

I think we all have heard the saying "this is the real McCoy." The original "real McCoy" was a man by the name of Elijah J. McCoy. Elijah was a mechanical engineer and the inventor of a revolutionary device, which made it possible to lubricate the moving parts of a machine while it was operating.

McCoy was born in Colchester, Canada in 1843. His parents, George and Mildred McCoy, had escaped as slaves from Kentucky, and fled to Canada by way of the underground railway. McCoy's father labored endlessly to send his son abroad to obtain a good education.

At age fifteen, young McCoy went to Edinburgh, Scotland to study. Upon completion of his studies in Scotland, he returned to the United States, well trained and eager to begin his career in engineering. Although his credentials were extraordinary, he was repeatedly denied a position in engineering, because of his race.

McCoy finally accepted a job as a fireman for the Michigan Central Railway, for which he had the menial task of shoveling coal into the engine and oiling all of the train's moving parts. Bored with this procedure, he asked himself, Why can't this train lubricate itself? This question prompted McCoy to begin experimenting with a mechanical self-lubricating device.

In 1870, McCoy gained instant fame in the field of mechanical engineering. He had started the Elijah McCoy Manufacturing Company in Detroit, Michigan. In the shop, he invented the oiling cup, which kept the trains and steamboats oiled even while they were moving. The use of the oiling cup became known as the McCoy System. When people say "it's the real McCoy," they mean it has what it takes to make it work perfectly.

My Collaboration With Amelia Robinson

I include this appendix in order to demonstrate to what lengths the racist "blue bloods" in America are willing to go to stop the political movement associated with Lyndon LaRouche. Lewis du Pont Smith and his wife Andrea are good friends of mine and work with the Schiller Institute in Philadelphia.

I first met Amelia Boynton Robinson in November 1985 in Rome, Italy. My girlfriend, Andrea Diano (now my wife), and I were attending the Schiller Institute's international conference on St. Augustine, the father of Western and African civilization, whose 1,500th anniversary of conversion from paganism to Christianity the Schiller Institute was celebrating. In that context, leaders from all over the world met to discuss the most urgent problems facing mankind: the economic and social misery that the majority of this planet, especially the so-called Third World, has been plunged into under a usurious, inhuman, and now thoroughly bankrupt international monetary system; the crisis of AIDS (HIV); the moral and cultural collapse throughout the world; and other relevant issues.

More important than merely documenting the apocalyptic nature of the crises facing mankind, the Schiller Institute conference on St. Augustine addressed concrete solutions to these urgent problems, solutions grounded in the Augustinian notion of natural law, God's law.

Amelia was one of the guest speakers. She gave a personal account of the history of the American civil rights movement: her struggles to get equal voting rights for blacks in Selma, Alabama, and the pain, violence, and hatred which she and her collaborators were subjected to. Her speech moved me to tears. I thought to myself: This lady's faith could move mountains; there is no vengeful bitterness in her voice, only hope and joy; she truly loves mankind.

What impressed me the most was that Amelia was still fighting; she had not given up. She documented in her speech the continuity of the civil rights movement led by Dr. Martin Luther King, and the international political movement of the Schiller Institute led by Lyndon LaRouche and Helga Zepp-LaRouche. I knew personally, that anyone who could stand up alongside of Lyndon and Helga Zepp-LaRouche and survive the subtle and outright attacks, slanders, and police-state brutality to which LaRouche and many of his associates and political and financial supporters have been subjected, had to have integrity and courage.

On November 12, 1985, one week after the conference in Rome, I was declared mentally incompetent by Judge Lawrence E. Wood in the Chester County, Pennsylvania Court of Common Pleas, Orphans Court Division. This outrageous decision was the result of a petition brought by my own family in April 1985, after I had made political loans ($212,000) to a publishing venture associated with the political movement of Lyndon LaRouche, to publish a 500-page history of the dope trade, and the financial institutions and leading families involved in the annual $500-billion, illegal narcotics business, which, on an international level, is killing our youth, destroying the social and cultural fabric of societies, and rendering nations' economies dysfunctional. The name of the book is *Dope, Inc.: Boston Brahmins and Soviet Commissars.*

As a consequence of Judge Wood's political ruling, I lost my right to contract (sign legal documents); I lost my right to control and manage my financial fortune; and I lost my right to marry. In effect, I had become a political dissident or prisoner in the United States of America.

It started back in 1983. I was teaching history, English, and geography at a private school. I ran into some LaRouche associates at a political table in the Philadelphia airport. I bought some books, magazines, and newspapers, and started reading. I was intrigued with LaRouche's political, economic, and historical analysis, as well as the insights into science and culture contained in this literature. I was equally impressed with the research and published works of many of LaRouche's colleagues. I decided to check out sources at various libraries and archives. The moral underpinnings and reasoned arguments of LaRouche's intellectual works and his active political organizing impressed me as quite sound, so it did not surprise me when I discovered independent historical evidence corroborating what I was reading.

By January 1985, I had decided to act. First, I decided to introduce historical materials into my tenth-grade classroom at the private Quaker school where I had been teaching in Philadelphia, Friends' Central School on City Line Avenue. These materials were not only not in the school's textbooks, but they contradicted, on many points, the conclusions of the textbooks. But I felt the truth was the truth, no matter whom it offended, and my students had the right to search for the truth and come to their own conclusions, approximating more closely, hopefully, the historical truth. In this way, my students would learn to be their own investigators, instead of regurgitating some putative authority's secondary source opinion.

In my discussions with the Schiller Institute in Philadelphia, I said that I did not want LaRouche to become the issue by bringing materials published by the Schiller Institute into the classroom. Instead, I wanted to use original (primary) documents: letters, diaries, manuscripts, official documents from leading historical figures, etc., and allow my students to analyze them and compare them to the secondary opinions expressed in their textbook. I did not realize the dangerous waters I was about to get into. It was brought to my attention that even if I were never to mention the "L" word—LaRouche—and just stuck to the method of searching for the truth by rigorously questioning assumptions of popular or respected opinion, using original source evidence, I would become controversial enough.

I had a hard time believing that advice. I thought that if I only stuck to the original source evidence, everything would be fine; no controversy, just a more stimulating class. Well, I was proven wrong. Some of the documents which I brought into my tenth-grade American history class proved that there were certain "respectable" bankers on the North Shore of Boston, Massachusetts, in the eighteenth and nineteenth centuries, who were involved in the opium and slave trade with the British East India Company, who made vast fortunes in what was known as the "Clipper Trade." These same Boston Brahmins ("blue bloods") who made their fortunes illegally selling drugs, supported the slave trade in the South, led by the South Carolina plantation owners, whose cotton they transported to England on their ships. This "economic system" of slaveocracy was referred to as "Free Trade" by the British East India Company's chief propagandist, Adam Smith, in his eighteenth-century tract, *The Wealth of Nations.* The East India Company's junior partners in New England and South Carolina were part of the old Tories, who remained in America, and did everything to oppose the American War of Independence, and made certain that Benjamin Franklin's efforts to make slavery illegal in the Constitution failed, so that a fatal "compromise" had to be reached in order to get the needed signatures to ratify the Constitution. It is also a curious fact, that certain abolitionists in the North in the mid-nineteenth century, such as Transcendentalist Ralph Waldo Emerson (based on sermons he gave at the Old North Church in Boston), were advocating "free trade" policies which justified the opium and slave trade, and were supported by the Palmerston-Marlborough faction of British secret intelligence, which was aiding and abetting the secessionist movement, in order to destroy the Union from within.

Within a short period of time, the headmaster of Friends' Central School, Tom Wood, threatened to fire me if I did not stick strictly to the textbook. In a very un-Quakerly way, he slammed his fists on his desk and shouted, "I'm responsible for getting your students to the next grade and finally to graduate them without creating waves. All you want to do is to create waves!" My students were being cheated of the truth.

As this man was accusing me of being brainwashed by "Nazis" (LaRouche, et al.), one of the heirs of the Boston opium and slave syndicate, William Weld, was abusing his office of U.S. Attorney in Boston by running a corrupt, illegal witchhunt against America's leading anti-drug fighter, Lyndon LaRouche. This same Weld was also protecting the drug money-laundering operation of the Bank of Boston, which had been found guilty of laundering $1.2 billion in drug money to Credit Suisse in Switzerland, for which Weld maneuvered a penalty equal to a slap on the wrist, a $500,000 fine and no prison sentences for any bank officers.

At that point, approximately March 1985, I decided to put my money where my mouth was. I saw the necessity of publishing the second edition of *Dope, Inc.* and other well-documented political literature. Where else would my students and others get the truth? Not from the textbook; not from their teachers; not from their parents; and certainly not from television, radio, or newspapers.

I really respected LaRouche and his political movement. This man had incredible courage and a brilliant mind, and he knew how to fight, like St. Augustine, the most evil forces in the world. LaRouche was right, and I knew it.

After I had loaned $212,000 to get *Dope, Inc.* out into the streets, my family and their lawyer, David Foulke, another "gentlemanly Quaker," went to see Judge Lawrence E. Wood on April 9 in a secret, ex parte hearing to discuss ways to stop me from financing the political movement of Lyndon LaRouche. (Judge Wood finally admitted five years later in court, while I was on the witness stand, that he is, in fact, a first cousin of Tom Wood, Friends' School headmaster. An honest judge would have recused himself.) On that date, Judge Wood, at my family's urging, signed a temporary restraining order, which froze all my money and bank accounts. It was illegal for me to even write a check. The judge also scheduled hearings on a petition to declare me mentally incompetent, submitted by my family.

There were about eight hearings, from April to September 1985. My family—mother, father, two brothers and sister all included—paid a New York psychiatrist, a real head-shrinker, Dr. David Halperin, to testify that I was suffering from a schizo-affective disorder, with paranoid and delusional features, as well as organic brain damage. This was real Nazi-style psychiatry, the kind we hear about in the Soviet Union. Dr. Halperin is affiliated with the American Family Foundation and the Cult Awareness Network.

Leading members of these organizations, like Maurice Davis, Dr. John Clark, Dr. Louis Jolyn West, and others worked with the CIA's MK-Ultra project in the 1960s, along with counterculture gurus such as Aldous Huxley, Timothy Leary, Alan Watts, and others. Their aim was to establish cults and experiment with mind-altering drugs on their victims. The London Tavistock Institute and the CIA were directly involved in this hideous project. They wanted to see what the effect of certain drugs, such as LSD, would have on controlling people, to see if assassins could be created who would take orders on command; the movie *The Manchurian Candidate* was an exposé of the project. In addition, the intelligence community found ways to shift America's family values away from the current emphasis on scientific progress, by setting up the counterculture with a proliferation of cults. One of these cults was the Jim Jones Cult, set up by Maurice Davis and Paul Moore, before he became bishop of the New York Anglican Cathedral of St. John the Divine.

After the mass suicide of the Jim Jones Cult in Guyana in 1978, the same people who set up this cult, as well as others, established an "anticult" organization, the American Family Foundation. This thought police now decides who are the cults and who aren't. This gang of mind-destroyers have brainwashed my family and are dedicated to destroying Lyndon LaRouche and his political movement.

My own psychiatrist, Dr. Robert Sadoff, testified that I was perfectly sane and competent to manage my financial affairs, but that I had a mixed personality disorder, which meant that I was not behaving up to the standards and expectations of my social mileu. In other words, I wasn't acting like a du Pont. Well, knowing just how my family has been behaving over the recent years, I had to laugh; that's one personality disorder I'm glad to have! It only proves that I'm competent. Also, I have to confess, that in the last five years, during which time I've been forced out of necessity or in some cases against my will, to see about ten psychiatrists and psychologists, I have yet to meet one shrink who was not crazy! But I never thought our legal system would use psychiatry in the way it was used in Nazi Germany or the Soviet Empire today.

I was declared mentally incompetent on November 12, 1985. In Judge Wood's two decisions, the final one made in July 1986, he states that he "would not equate the importunings of the LaRoach (sic) Organization with the Christian message." This comes from a devout Freemason. Then he states: "Lewis keeps complaining that I have denied him his First Amendment rights. It is not that kind of case. I have only limited his ability to use his money. He may go on and exercise his First Amendment rights as foolishly as he wishes."

In January of 1986, I informed my mother that I was going to get married to Andrea Diano. Andrea and I first met at the Irish Pub in Philadelphia in January 1985. She was a college student and had never heard of LaRouche. My family opposed the marriage because she is Roman Catholic and of Italian descent, and my family's cult-controllers convinced them that Andrea was a "seductress for LaRouche," who was sent to trap me at the Irish Pub, and seduce me for my money for LaRouche's coffers.

Soon after I told my mother of my engagement, the family filed a second petition, before even the first petition had been fully settled. In their new petition, they asked Judge Wood to appoint a guardian over my physical person. Such a guardian could place me into a mental institution and put me on lithium treatments for over a year, which were the exact recommendations of my brother Stockton, who was then under psychiatric treatment by Navy psychiatrists, according to his own admission. My father, at the same time, was under treatment for alcoholism, and my mother was on lithium treatments for a manic-depressive illness. Under these conditions, it was easy for politically motivated psychiatrists to prey on my family's weaknesses and manipulate them to go against their own son and future daughter-in-law.

In June of 1986, after headlines in the *Philadelphia Inquirer*, *Washington Post*, and *New York Times*, the judge dismissed the case in a nonsuit after the family presented their "evidence." He stated from the bench, "I can't go this far, but I think the family can achieve its original objectives in their first petition," on which the judge had not yet made a final ruling.

A month later, in July, his second and final ruling declared me mentally incompetent. I appealed the decision to the Superior Court of Pennsylvania and lost; then I appealed to the Pennsylvania State Supreme Court. They refused to hear the appeal. Then I appealed to the U.S. Supreme Court. In June 1988, they refused to hear the appeal.

In the meantime, the Virginia authorities (Andrea and I were living in Leesburg, Virginia) informed us that I couldn't get a license to marry because of my legal status as an incompetent, and that I also could not register to vote.

Andrea and I, at the suggestion of Helga Zepp-LaRouche, who was utterly outraged at this injustice, wrote Pope John Paul II a letter asking for his protection and help in order to get married. On October 10, 1985, Andrea and I flew to Rome and talked with many Catholic prelates, including cardinals, bishops, and Vatican officials. After the extensive meetings and interviews, our marriage was approved by the Vatican Council. We were married on December 14, 1986, at the Basilica of Santa Maria del Popolo, by Don Dario Composta. The ceremony was witnessed by Lyndon H.

LaRouche and Helga Zepp-LaRouche, our best man and matron of honor, as well as Cristina Fiocchi and Fiorella Operto, two Italian friends of ours from Rome. There were three other church officials present and about 50 friends, including Andrea's mother, father, and sister. This was certainly the happiest moment of my life.

It was discovered later through documents, maps, bills, and letters, that my family had hired a private investigator associated with the Atlantic City, New Jersey casino Resorts International, who employed a notorious cult deprogrammer and kidnapper, Galen Kelly, in an unsuccessful attempt to kidnap me before the wedding. These documents were presented to Judge Wood, who found sufficient evidence to sign a restraining order, warning my family not to attempt anything that would restrict my movements or First Amendment activities, an order which essentially said, "Don't kidnap your son." The physical evidence showed that every time the kidnappers had set up a stake-out in Paris, we were in Rome; when we were in Rome, they were staked-out in Paris. That's what I call incompetent kidnappers!

In June 1987, Andrea filed a petition before Judge Wood to validate our marriage under Pennsylvania law, not that the marriage was not already valid, but merely to protect Andrea's spousal rights and the rights of our prospective children, in the event that I should die and the marriage be challenged. We figured the family might challenge the validity of our marriage under some phony pretext. Sure enough, the family filed a countersuit to Andrea's petition in which they stated that the marriage is invalid for the following reasons: 1) the wedding never took place; 2) even if it did, it is still invalid, because at the time of the wedding, I was mentally ill and therefore did not know what I was doing; 3) Andrea was a seductress for LaRouche, therefore a designing person from whom I need protection; 4) Andrea deceived the Vatican.

Then the family set up a series of depositions of Andrea. This was another inquisition, in which Judge Wood ruled that Andrea's political beliefs were relevant. The judge, however, ruled that the family could not have access to political documents belonging to Andrea, that the family had requested.

During the second deposition of Andrea, conducted in West Chester, Pennsylvania, my father was in Leesburg, Virginia, breaking into and burglarizing our home, stealing many documents. He was caught by the Leesburg police and later an arrest warrant was issued. Later at one of the hearings, he lied on the witness stand that he had never been to my house. After a police report was presented to the court, Judge Wood gave my father the option of withdrawing his petition to have me examined by Dr. David Halperin again, or accept his lumps. My father withdrew his petition and to this day he has not been prosecuted for perjury, which is a crime in Pennsylvania, and he is still a fugitive from justice in Virginia. Finally, on November 10, 1988, Judge Wood "validated" our marriage.

My family has worked and continues to work directly with what the Department of Justice admits to be a federal, state, and private multi-jurisdictional "Get LaRouche Task Force."

This corrupt task force singled out my wife for prosecution and imprisonment in 1986 and 1987. Andrea was a volunteer petitioner in California for three months, getting signatures for a referendum known as Proposition 64, a referendum calling for AIDS (HIV) and related diseases to be treated as public health threats, and that standard public health measures be applied to these diseases. It was alleged by the state that she had illegally caused herself to register to vote and become a resident in California. After almost one year, when it was demonstrated that my father had provided a knowingly falsified deposition to the California attorney general's office, the case was finally dropped.

In the spring of 1987, Andrea and I met up again with Amelia Robinson at public hearings of the Commission to Investigate Human Rights Violations. Andrea and I both testified before the commission. Amelia delivered a major address to the assembled audience of about 500. Again she chronicled her struggles in the American civil rights movement.

At the end of her moving speech, we all stood up and together sang "We Shall Overcome." Again, many people in the audience were moved to tears of hope, including Andrea and me.

In September, Andrea and I participated again in a conference of the Commission to Investigate Human Rights Violations in Paris, France, and had the privilege to hear and speak with Amelia. After the conference, I led a tour of Americans around Paris. Andrea and I spent most of the time walking alongside of Amelia to the statue of Joan of Arc, the statue of Benjamin Franklin, and to the Eiffel Tower. Later that night we all went out to dinner. Amelia had an incredible source of energy, and was a constant source of old stories and anecdotes. She was a living, "primary source" of history.

Amelia really became a great source of strength and encouragement for Andrea and me. Here was a lady who had personally been through great struggles and had met great adversity, and she was still fighting like a warriorangel, and she did it with such grace and compassion and honesty.

In January 1988, Andrea and I moved to New Hampshire to volunteer for Lyndon LaRouche's Democratic presidential campaign. After the New Hampshire primary in February, we decided to stay there and help create a local political base of organizing.

In May, I announced my candidacy for Congress in the Democratic Party. In the September primary, I received close to 10 percent of the vote. Not bad for my first run at elected office. We had also organized local citizens to run for state legislature; one candidate won his race.

In January of 1989, Andrea and I were invited to the Martin Luther King Memorial Tribunal on Crimes Against Humanity, held in Rome, Italy. This was the last time we met with Lyndon LaRouche before he was framed up and

railroaded to jail. It was at this conference that Amelia gave
the greatest speech I ever heard her give. She told the story
of how a young black man from the South had been falsely
accused of raping a white woman. The evidence over-
whelmingly proved his innocence. The white woman even
confessed that he had not raped her, but the judge convicted
him and he was sentenced to a long prison term. Amelia's
husband tried to assist the black man, by bringing the first
black attorneys ever into Alabama to defend him. They won
his appeal and he was released after thirteen years in prison.

Amelia told us how she had so much hatred and bitterness in her heart after the initial trial that she could have
killed someone. Her husband told her that if you have so
much hatred and bitterness in your heart, you will stoop so
low that pretty soon you will become like your oppressors.
This changed her life, she said. Amelia taught me, by her
living example, the power of love, the power of faith, and
the power of hope. It then really became clear to me how
Amelia could be so strong and courageous. She is the
embodiment of St. Paul's concept of *charity* in Corinthians
I:13.

I submitted my own petition before Judge Wood in August
1989, asking him to remove the Wilmington Trust Company
as my financial guardian and declare me mentally competent. Back in the summer and fall of 1987, I warned the
Wilmington Trust Company, the du Pont family bank, which
had been appointed by Judge Wood to be the conservator
of all of my money, to sell off all my stocks before the
stockmarket crashed in mid-October. This forecast was
based on the analysis and forecast of Lyndon LaRouche,
the leading American System economist in the world today.
LaRouche's forecast checked out with certain European
financial sources, so I decided to act. The bank ignored my
warnings and pleas. On October 19, 1987, "Black Monday"
occurred, the biggest stockmarket crash in history. I lost
about $3 million.

So the conservatorship, or guardianship as it is called in
Pennsylvania, hasn't really worked out. One wonders who's

really incompetent, and who should be managing whose affairs. The family filed a countersuit, denying that I was competent. Then, within several days, they filed a lawsuit against Andrea and me, called a Petition to Appoint a guardian *ad litum*. They wanted a guardian appointed to our unborn and unconceived children.

In five years I've been forced to spend over $500,000 on legal and psychiatric expenses in efforts to defend my competence, our marriage, and attacks against my wife.

If it were just the money I wanted back, I could have gotten it back much more easily. All I had to do was give up my beliefs and come crawling back to my family and agree not to have anything to do with LaRouche. In fact, on one occasion, my father offered to buy me a ski resort in Colorado, where I could go and have fun for the rest of my life, if I would leave the LaRouche movement. I wonder how many times the FBI tried to buy off or blackmail Dr. Martin Luther King, before they killed him. The Bible gives me strength in such passages as found in Luke: "For what shall it profit a man, if he shall gain the whole world and lose his soul."

During the recent, ongoing hearings before Judge Wood, Amelia was one of my strongest witnesses. In addition to our travels together, fighting for human rights, economic and social justice, and freedom for political prisoner Lyndon LaRouche and his six codefendents, Amelia is now serving on my congressional campaign committee in Pennsylvania, along with O.G. Christian, a civil rights activist from Philadelphia, and former president of the West Philadelphia Chapter of the NAACP; Max Dean, president of the Constitutional Defense Fund, and former president of the Michigan Trial Lawyers Association; Rabbi Gerald Kaplan, who has fought together with the Schiller Institute on exposing the dangers of the drug trade; and finally, my wife, Andrea.

Andrea and I moved back to Philadelphia in December 1989 to prepare for my new legal case. I decided in April 1990 to run for Congress in the 5th Congressional District, which includes Chester County where the court case is taking place. The battle cry of my campaign is "Rebellion Against Tyranny is Obedience to God"—Thomas Jefferson. The most important issues of my campaign are defending the Constitution and the rule of law—which includes freedom for LaRouche and my being declared legally competent—and reversing 25 years of economic collapse, in which increasing numbers of poor and homeless have no voice in society.

The Constitution is under attack as never before. If a powerful, rich family such as mine, working with a corrupt, secret-police task force inside the Department of Justice, can abuse the justice system for their own perverted ends, then none of us is safe from such tyranny.

The world needs more heroines like Amelia Boynton Robinson, who will always be an inspiration to Andrea and me.

Lewis du Pont Smith
October 1990
Philadelphia, Pennsylvania